Forced to Flee

Program in Migration and Refugee Studies
Program Advisors:
Elzbieta M. Gozdziak and Susan F. Martin, Institute for the Study of International
Migration

Homecomings: Unsettling Paths of Return,
    edited by Fran Markowitz and Anders Stefansson
The Cape Verdean Diaspora in Portugal: Colonial Subjects in a Postcolonial World,
    by Luis Batalha
Refugee Women, 2nd ed.,
    by Susan Forbes Martin
The Refugee Convention at Fifty: A View from Forced Migration Studies,
    edited by Joanne Van Selm, Khoti Kamanga, et al.
Migration and the Externalities of European Integration,
    edited by Sandra Lavenex and Emek M. Uçarer
After Involuntary Migration: The Political Economy of Refugee Encampments,
    by Milica Z. Bookman
*Premigration Legacies and Immigrant Social Mobility: The Afro-Surinamese and
    Indo-Surinamese in the Netherlands,*
    by Mies van Niekerk
*Communication and Identity in the Diaspora: Turkish Migrants in Amsterdam and
    Their Use of Media,*
    by Christine Ogan
The Uprooted: Improving Humanitarian Responses to Forced Migration,
    by Susan F. Martin, Patricia Weiss Fagen, et al.
Crossing Over: Comparing Recent Migration in the United States and Europe,
    edited by Holger Henke
Catching Fire: Containing Complex Displacement in a Volatile World,
    edited by Nicholas van Hear and Christopher McDowell
Forced Migration and Global Processes: A View from Forced Migration Studies,
    edited by François Crépeau, Delphine Nakache, Michael Collyer,
    Nathaniel H. Goetz, Art Hansen, Renu Modi, Aninia Nadig, Sanja Špoljar-
    Vržina, and Loes H. M. van Willigen
Trafficking and the Global Sex Industry,
    edited by Karen Beeks and Delila Amir
Dialogues on Migration Policy,
    edited by Marco Giugni and Florence Passy
Forced to Flee: Human Rights and Human Wrongs in Refugee Homelands,
    by Peter W. Van Arsdale

Forthcoming:
New Immigrant Communities: Facilitating Immigrant Integration,
    edited by Elzbieta M. Gozdziak and Micah Bump
Transnational Migration to Israel in Global Comparative Context,
    edited by Sarah S. Willen

Forced to Flee

Human Rights and Human Wrongs in Refugee Homelands

Peter W. Van Arsdale

LEXINGTON BOOKS

A division of
ROWMAN & LITTLEFIELD PUBLISHERS, INC.
Lanham • Boulder • New York • Toronto • Oxford

LEXINGTON BOOKS

A division of Rowman & Littlefield Publishers, Inc.
A wholly owned subsidiary of The Rowman & Littlefield Publishing Group, Inc.
4501 Forbes Boulevard, Suite 200
Lanham, Maryland 20706

PO Box 317
Oxford
OX2 9RU, UK

British Library Cataloguing in Publication Information Available

Library of Congress Cataloging-in-Publication Data

Van Arsdale, Peter W.
    Forced to flee : human rights and human wrongs in refugee homelands / Peter W. Van
Arsdale.
        p. cm. — (Program in migration and refugee studies)
    Includes bibliograpical references and index.
    ISBN-13: 978-0-7391-1233-5 (cloth: alk. paper)
    ISBN-10: 0-7391-1233-3 (cloth : alk. paper)
    ISBN-13: 978-0-7391-1234-2 (pbk. : alk. paper)
    ISBN-10: 0-7391-1234-1 (pbk. : alk. paper)
    1. Refugees. 2. Migration, Internal. 3. Human rights. I. Title. II. Series.
HV640.V36 2006
362.87—dc22   2006007714

Printed in the United States of America

⊗™ The paper used in this publication meets the minimum requirements of American
National Standard for Information Sciences—Permanence of Paper for Printed Library
Materials, ANSI/NISO Z39.48-1992.

Dedicated to Arnold Ap, Equaar Desta, Aregash Adane, Patsy Spier,
and other colleagues who must remain anonymous.
They spoke out boldly on behalf of human rights at great risk
to their own lives. Not all survived.

Contents

Preface

In the spring of 1975 the United States and its allies withdrew from Vietnam. A seemingly endless and undeclared war was over. Television broadcasts from the southern Vietnamese city of Saigon captured images of American administrative personnel evacuating their compounds, military transport aircraft fleeing the airport, and citizens scrambling to find a way out. Hundreds of thousands of Vietnamese had worked or fought alongside Americans in what many analysts declared a losing effort, and therefore were given preference when they sought to enter the United States as refugees in the months that followed. The "modern refugee era" had begun.

My involvement with refugees began that autumn. In the summer of 1975 I had completed my Ph.D. in cultural and applied anthropology, following fieldwork in Southeast Asia, and shortly thereafter had accepted a teaching position at the University of Denver. The very first field project my graduate students and I initiated involved Vietnamese refugees. We conducted an assessment of their adjustment processes and adaptation strategies as several hundred moved into Denver's Sun Valley housing area, a site which until then primarily had been home to Latinos (Van Arsdale and Pisarowicz 1980). This proved to be the first study of its type ever conducted in Colorado. By early 1976 I had become convinced of the importance of refugee research to my career, as well as the importance of facilitating opportunities for students in such work.

In subsequent years my wife Kathy and I had the opportunity to serve as co-sponsors for Vietnamese, Hmong, and Ethiopian refugees. From assisting with visits to doctors, to painting apartments, to witnessing marriages, we were privileged to participate in a bit of what they were doing as their new lives were being constructed. Community-based *applied*, not just academic, perspectives became increasingly key for me. I focused on applied anthropology during the late 1980s when I co-founded the American

Anthropological Association's Committee on Refugees and Immigrants (CORI). I also focused on applied anthropology during the late 1990s when I co-founded the Rocky Mountain Survivors Center. This nonprofit agency assists refugee and immigrant survivors of war trauma and torture. As my work has emphasized, "ideals" must be balanced by "pragmatics." Time spent in academic settings must be balanced by time spent in field settings. Tom Farer, dean of the Graduate School of International Studies at the University of Denver (where I teach), recently stressed that one goal of education should be the production of students who are "practical idealists." As I have taught my graduate seminar, "Human Rights and the International Refugee System," I hopefully have contributed to the realization of this goal.

Through my work in this course, it has become clear that prospective "practical idealists" are extraordinarily interested in human rights and all that this term implies. It also has become clear that they prefer a perspective in which rights are presented as *experiential*. They prefer pedagogical approaches in which rights are analyzed in cultural context (i.e., using case-based ethnographic accounts). The provision of historical, ecological, political, and socio-economic details "surrounding rights and wrongs" appropriately follows suit.

*   *   *   *   *

This book was conceived to accommodate the above approaches. The six central chapters are based upon fieldwork I conducted on-site in six nations. Each of these chapters addresses four questions: What is the environmental background and recent historical context? What are the human rights issues? What causes people to flee? What are their experiences?

For practitioners and students alike, human rights indeed should be understood as experiential. By this, I mean that understandings of human rights—and the very rights themselves—have evolved from human experience. Our definitions and interpretations of human rights (and human wrongs) are continually being refined by the events that shape our lives. While it appropriately can be said that all people have rights, it cannot be said that rights are somehow primordial or preexisting. Cultural and individual achievement, shaped by aspiration and insight, provide much of the context from which rights emerge. Ominous events, abuses, and tragedies provide the remainder.

This book takes the stance that it is a mistake to become too legalistic about human rights. Taken to the extreme, rights can become technical abstractions, mere lists and analyses. They can become reified, taking on a monolithic life of their own. While human rights should indeed be seen as case based, reflecting both behaviors and attitudes, they should not be seen as legal cases per se. Concomitantly, overly detailed categorizations of rights are to be avoided. For example, viewed from the standpoint of the students who have studied with me, when considering the Universal Declaration of Human Rights it does not work well to dwell on "rights typologies" as applied to refugees. To understand refugee human rights issues and the humanitarian activities many individuals and organizations have engaged in to help, it is better to stress context, process, and outcome. It is better not to deconstruct human rights problems, category by category, into the laws, regulations, and covenants aimed at "preventing" or "correcting" the abuses, but rather, to present detailed ethnographic portrayals of the people impacted in concert with applicable laws and useful interventions.

In considering the evolution of human rights, as seen through the lens of human displacement, it would be tempting to categorize rights according to the numerous dichotomies that have been proposed by various analysts since World War II: Western vs. non-Western, universal vs. relative, liberal vs. conservative, individual vs. communal, right vs. obligation. This simple dialectical approach is neither useful nor entirely accurate. It is better to speak of processes, of systems, of interventions. What are the problems encountered, deliberations engaged, choices made, and decisions rendered?

However, two types of categorization have worked well. In the first instance, my students have found it useful to consider "refugee as process" (or "refugeeness") in terms of three categories: Preflight, flight, and postflight. Whether passing through a refugee camp, or fleeing bullets on foot, or traveling exclusively by airplane with little danger, all refugees—by definition—are involved in what can usefully be termed "preflight," "flight," and "postflight" experiences. Even for those whose short-term flight and long-term postflight experiences have converged at the very same locations, such as the camps in Palestine, it can be said that they have had these three definable and distinctive experiences.

In the second instance, my students have found it useful to consider the category of "persons of concern," as recently defined by the United Nations High Commissioner for Refugees. These include refugees per se, internally displaced persons (IDPs), returned IDPs, asylum seekers, and stateless persons. As of early 2005 there were approximately 19 million persons of concern in the world, some 9 million of whom were refugees (UNHCR 2005: 2). This aggregate has decreased slightly in recent years, a cautiously hopeful sign.

Much has been written, including by my fellow anthropologists, about the flight and postflight experiences of refugees. By comparison, less has been written and systematically analyzed about the preflight situations that produce refugees and other types of forcibly displaced people. A primary thrust of this text is explication of the preflight setting and preflight experience, with special attention being paid to critical environmental/land use, socio-economic and socio-political factors in refugee homelands. Psycho-social factors are introduced as appropriate. Explicit human rights abuses do not always occur in these settings, but they happen often enough that a multicase, multinational analysis of the type presented here is important. In researching this book, I have consulted the writings and speeches of an array of authorities. I also have interviewed a broad spectrum of specialists. They represent such diverse disciplines as anthropology, law, ecology, psychology, and theology. The perspectives of people of science, complemented by those of people of faith, provide the book's foundation (cf. Dean 2005). Each of the great religions contains essential humanistic elements that anticipated, and contributed to, the evolution of modern conceptions of rights (Ishay 2004: 5). Of course, most important are the perspectives of the "persons of concern" and those who assist them in the field, whom I have been privileged to meet and work with in each of the six nations represented.

REFERENCES

Dean, Cornelia. "Do God and Science Mix? More Now Saying Yes." *New York Times*, August 23 (pp. A1, A12), 2005.

Ishay, Micheline R. *The History of Human Rights: From Ancient Times to the Globalization Era*. Berkeley: University of California Press, 2004.

UNHCR. "2004 Global Refugee Trends: Overview of Refugee Populations, New Arrivals, Durable Solutions, Asylum-Seekers, Stateless and Other Persons of Concern to UNHCR." Population and Geographical Data Section Report, Division of Operational Support, United Nations High Commissioner for Refugees, Geneva, June 17, 2005 at www.unhcr.ch/statistics (accessed June 29, 2005).

Van Arsdale, Peter W., and James A. Pisarowicz, eds. *Processes of Transition: Vietnamese in Colorado*. Austin, Tex.: High Street Press, 1980.

Acknowledgments

Dozens of people have assisted and inspired me over the past thirty years. It is not possible to list them all.

The insights of the following colleagues, based primarily in the United States but with extensive cross-cultural and international experience, have been extremely helpful: George Shepherd, Ved Nanda, Tom Farer, Steve Werner, Ahmed Ali, Sarah Combs, Elzbieta Gozdziak, Gottfried Lang, Robert Hackenberg, Richard Butler, David Gallus, Ralph "Skip" Kerr, Paul Stein, Dennis Kennedy, Laurie Bagan, Anita Sanborn, John Prendergast, David Forsythe, Khalid Mansour, Harvey Martz, Charles Page II, Tsegaye Hailu, Abebe Takele, Wray Witten, Jack Donnelly, Micheline Ishay, Derrin Smith, Susan Erikson, Bill Canny, Todd Waller, Melissa Schaap, Bruce Finley, Georg Gadow, Jack Wackwitz, Mark Levy, and Doug Henry.

The insights of the following colleagues, based primarily outside the United States, have been equally as helpful: Nelson Gonzalez (El Salvador), George Bârlea (Romania), Ismail Mohammed (Sudan), Babiker Ali Khalifa (Sudan), Equaar Desta (Ethiopia), Barbara Harrell-Bond (England), Sir Nigel Rodley (England), Nashat Abdullah (Iraq), Arnold Ap (Indonesia), Abraham Kuruwaip (Indonesia), Omar Mansour (Palestine), Hannah Kessler (Israel), Otoniel de la Roca Mendoza (Guatemala), Fehro Mehinović (Bosnia), and Enver Alagić (Bosnia).

Significant ideas have been gained from the students with whom I have been privileged to work at the University of Denver and elsewhere. These include Susan Weinstein, Bayisa Wak-woya, Tsegay Wolde-Georgis, Debra Kreisberg, Perin Arkun, Bassem Hassan, Eitan Halevy, Lisa Schechtman, Hadidja Nyiransekuye, Andrew Paquin, Holly Porter, Michelle Lasnier, Keith Cole, Anna Schowengerdt, Leslie Olson, Martin Widzer, Kevin Lucas, Lance Finkbeiner,

Sandra Murcia, Craig Murphy, Patsy Spier, Ian Sethre, and Regina Nockerts. The documents from media sources Ian Sethre has forwarded me over the past five years regarding developments in the Balkans have proven extremely useful. The research on obligation and humanitarianism Regina Nockerts has been conducting, in concert with me, is both innovative and comprehensive. Her work proved essential as I finalized chapter 8.

Major portions of the manuscript were reviewed by several people, and their detailed comments proved very useful as I moved toward final publication: Doug Henry, Mark Levy, Patsy Spier, Elzbieta Gozdziak, Regina Nockerts, Sarah Van Arsdale Berry, Molly Ahearn of Lexington Books. My toughest critic, and most helpful editor, has been my wife Kathleen Van Arsdale. The tough love she showed my manuscript as it was evolving improved it dramatically. My entire extended family—Van Arsdales, O'Neals, Powells, Berrys, Almdales—have provided enthusiastic support throughout my career.

The important people noted above hopefully will recognize their contributions, even where their names are not always mentioned explicitly within the text.

Peter W. Van Arsdale
Denver, Colorado

Chapter One

Ideas that Work

What ails us is human injustice.

—Marcus Borg

THE QUEEN OF SARAJEVO

In one sense, Asija is the queen of all she surveys. From the porch of her two-story home on the flanks of Trebević Mountain, she can see the sprawling city below. Modest skyscrapers dot the skyline, some built within the last five years, others dating to the 1960s. Scattered in between are the red-tiled roofs of smaller businesses, apartment buildings, and single-family homes. Cutting diagonally through the town below is a river. No more than 100 feet wide and 2 feet deep, the Miljaka nonetheless provides a hint of the reason 600 years before that this settlement first gained an illustrative name—"palace in the fields."

Asija is but a captive Muslim queen, and the city she surveys was until recently a captive city: Sarajevo. Asija is missing three of her four limbs, lost in a land mine explosion. The city, while increasingly vibrant since the Bosnian civil war *cum* international war ended in late 1995, is the capitol of a state devised, deconstructed, reconstructed, and supervised more by outsiders than by its own citizens.

Just a few hundred yards down the mountain from Asija's home, one can see a slightly different panorama of Sarajevo. From here, patches of white and brown specks dot the landscape. These are grave markers, mostly new, reminders that nearly 13,000 people died in this city from 1992 through 1995. Older markers, representing older cemeteries, also can be seen. Some two

miles away, on a hill on the opposite side of the valley, a small Jewish cemetery is visible among the oak. To hike to Asija's house, my students and I had
to navigate a route among markers and mine fields.

Asija's story is one of horror, rehabilitation, and hope. She and her husband
Ekrem had been forced to abandon their residence during the war. Occupying
literally the last house up the road on the mountain's flank, they were in the
unenviable position of being on a key Serbian military route. Tanks and other
armaments were brought over Trebević Mountain, from the Bosnian Serb
"capital" at Pale, and one feeder route went right in front of their house.
Strategically overlooking Sarajevo, with a broad embankment perfectly
suited to artillery emplacement, Asija and Ekrem's three-acre plot became a
prime encampment. During the three-year siege, the city below was repeatedly shelled from places like this. Serb forces also planted mines everywhere,
to deter would-be Muslim snipers and paramilitary intruders.

On May 5, 1996, six months after the war had ended and shortly after they
had returned to reclaim their property, Asija stepped on an anti-tank mine while
working to clear her garden. Ekrem was nearby. As he described it, she was
blown thirty feet straight up. Mud, smoke, and blood filled the air. When he had
regained his bearings, Ekrem rushed to her aid. He bundled Asija in a blanket
and placed her in the back of his Volkswagen "bug." Speeding down the moun-
tainside toward the city center, he estimates he was at the main hospital's
doorsteps within fifteen minutes. A strange and unexpected vision awaited them
there—doctors and nurses already prepared for surgery. They had heard the
blast three miles away and knew that someone would be coming soon.

With her electric wheelchair and electric smile, Asija has rehabilitated herself to the point where she is highly functional physiologically and fully functional psychologically. The great irony in Asija's life is that Britain's Princess
Diana, a strong anti-mine advocate, had heard of her and planned to visit. Diana was killed in an automobile accident just a month before the trip to
Bosnia. "Diana was my hero," says Asija. If Diana had lived to meet Asija,
Asija would have been Diana's quiet hero.

It is this type of event that occurs all too often in refugee homelands. It is
the kind of incident that creates refugees, which forces people to flee. The remarkable responses of people like Asija are what inspire us to pursue issues
involving refugee human rights.

HUMAN RIGHTS AND REFUGEES

Human rights pertain to individuals, as they live out their lives within culturally defined groups. They are the rights of individuals in society. Human

rights are not abstractions or aspirations; they derive from moral precepts and are represented in particular claims listed in conventions and other international legal instruments such as the Universal Declaration of Human Rights. They afford "benefits deemed essential for individual well-being, dignity, and fulfillment, and that reflect a common sense of justice, fairness, and decency" (Henkin 1999: 3). They deal with both protections ("negative," immunity claims) against abuse of power by others, and resources ("positive," requirement claims) as to what society must do for its members. Human rights include liberties, expressed as "freedom *from*" (torture, unreasonable detention) and "freedom *to*" (speak, assemble). Such rights are inalienable; they cannot be "lost."

Issues associated with the enhancement, preservation, erosion, and destruction of human rights are especially well illustrated in the refugee field. As people make decisions (often forced) as to remain or flee, they deliberate as to how best to assure their own survival. Risk and vulnerability are weighed. Persecution, political unrest, and abuse emerge as undesirable pressures; autonomy, security, and personal or familial well-being emerge as desired outcomes. Memory emerges as a key adaptive device. Refugee human rights therefore best can be understood interactively, processually, and systemically. Specific cases are key to their analysis.

> Memories are not history. They are the raw material
> out of which history may grow.
>
> —Max Hastings

This is a book about conditions and processes. It is a book of cases, intended to illustrate the principles being discussed. Stated differently, it is a book about the complex situations that create refugees and force them to flee. Focusing on a number of nations where I have the opportunity to work onsite, it builds upon my observations and interpretations. Yet it is not a book about me or my career. Rather, its intent is to demonstrate the importance of first-hand field research in constructing pictures of "human rights and human wrongs" in some of the homelands that produce displaced persons. Several theoretic orientations are introduced, each complementary of the others. Therefore, the book is both inductive/empirical and deductive/theoretic.

My own fieldwork always has taken the perspective that first one must get to know "the lay of the land." A well-rounded investigation initially must establish the ecological parameters and resource-related underpinnings that influence human action and, ultimately, societal ideology. Stated differently, to understand political activity—and therefore human rights—it is essential to "work up" inductively from an examination of ecological and environmental resource factors. Deductive work comes a bit later. As a doctoral student in cultural anthropology at the University of Colorado during the 1970s, I was influenced in this regard by two of my professors, Gottfried Lang and Robert Hackenberg. Both had studied American Indians, among other populations, and both had been influenced by colleagues of their own at Cornell University, among other institutions. While not a cultural materialist or agricultural ecologist, I also am indebted to the insights offered by the late Marvin Harris (see, e.g., Harris 1977) and John Bennett (see, e.g., Bennett 1976).

Lang, Hackenberg, Harris, and Bennett all advocated paying careful attention to processes of short-term adjustment and long-term adaptation. All advocated careful empiricism. Each in his own way asked: How is population X adjusting to changes in its environment? How is it adapting through time, as viewed socio-culturally, socio-economically, and socio-politically? What are the demographic correlates of change? These questions also are asked, implicitly, throughout the present volume. Although I am a cultural and medical anthropologist, much of the material herein is not derived from anthropological research per se.

Paradigm

A paradigm, if properly employed, is an idea that works. If the writings of a single person could be said to have been more influential than others in shaping the human rights orientation used herein, it would be that of Michael Ignatieff. His essays have helped shape the overall paradigm I employ. As edited by Amy Gutmann (2001), some of his most important recent writings have been synthesized, with accompanying commentaries by other leading scholars. More than a theory, Ignatieff offers a unifying "umbrella" under which a sensible, humanistic, and nondeterministic view of contemporary human rights emerges.

Ignatieff believes that the notion of human rights, while extraordinarily important, is an emergent one. While recognizing the preeminent role that the West has played in shaping the contemporary human rights regime worldwide, he would chastise those who claim that the West's insights are superior, more profound, or based upon firmer belief structures. While also recognizing that human rights are (or are capable of becoming) political, Ignatieff believes that it is imperative to place their understanding in contexts that are humanistic, culturally attuned, and secular. He is by no means against religion. He is against foundational perspectives that ascribe human rights to belief systems—religious or otherwise—in ways that make such rights seem to be invariant, unerring, God-given, and/or "natural." From his perspective it is more accurate that rights be seen as emerging through human action and discourse, evolving through history as various actors wrestle with their implications. It is more accurate that they be seen as malleable and open to interpretation. In particular, it is more accurate that they be seen as affording venues for genuine deliberation and debate. Multiple viewpoints therefore can be considered.

We must avoid reifying human rights. As Ignatieff indicates, they are not a monolith or singularly unified set of principles. They are not a "secular religion," that is, something to be revered. The Universal Declaration of Human Rights, finalized in 1948 (and noted again in chapter 8), is to be viewed as an extremely useful set of propositions, not as a "sacred creed." There is a danger that, in the minds of some proponents, human rights are being idolized. That is, in the attempt to promote a rights regime that helps to eliminate such practices as torture, some advocates are placing rights on a metaphorical pedestal. Human rights idolatry is to be avoided at all costs. It is my opinion that Jimmy Carter came close to implicitly "practicing" this type of idolatry in the late 1970s as he advocated to other nations a human rights perspective that, while well intended, was relatively unidimensional and nonpluralistic in its conceptualization. In recent years, to his credit, through the Carter Center he has advocated a much more pluralistic and nonconfrontational form of rights, one steeped in cross-cultural understandings of such diverse topics as voter participation and mental health.

Ignatieff does not believe in innate rights, innate human dignity, or innate cultural characteristics. No particular appeal needs be made to "human nature" to understand either human depravity or human compassion. What must be recognized is the value of human agency, of the human decision-making process, of human deliberation, of human tolerance. Prudent deliberation can lead to decisions that, when translated pragmatically, protect people from actions that harm them. Such deliberation should include thoughtful consideration of relevant historical circumstances, events, and personalities. It should include analysis of the system in which "rights actions" are being contemplated, as framed by the system's institutions and political culture.

The "umbrella" advocated by Ignatieff is at once broadly philosophical and pragmatic. The universality in his approach is much less about rights per se, and much more about the need for universal acceptance of the significance of history, the value of multiple perspectives, the agency of individuals, and the role of deliberation. As Laqueur (2001: 131) notes, one of Ignatieff's central points is that "it is an error to rely for the protection of human rights on the conversion of the world's people and governments to a set of universal principles." Ultimately, Ignatieff stresses "human rights . . . are necessary to protect individuals from violence and abuse" (2001: 83). He draws upon a variety of fields and disciplines. The present book does the same. It should be stressed that I draw more inspiration than does Ignatieff from religious and theological materials.

Theory

A theory, if properly employed, is another kind of idea that works. If the writings of a single person could be said to have been more influential than others in shaping the theoretic approach used herein, it would be that of Paul Farmer. This increasingly famous yet still-humble physician-anthropologist has propounded a theory of structural violence, a theory that cannot readily be understood outside the context of human rights and social justice. Although he focuses on the intersection of human rights and health, his orientation is more widely applicable.

As I would identify them, Farmer's work delineates five central premises. His first premise is that differential power relations within society create structural inequalities. His second premise is that these inequalities become institutionalized by elites and create the oppressive conditions that produce human-rights violations. His third premise is that structural inequalities and structural violence are linked. His fourth premise is that structural violence is not always manifest in harshly aggressive physical terms (i.e., "guns and death"), but in the everyday situations confronting persons who are at risk in oppressive environments. This is as odious as any form of violent abuse. When a poor person in El Salvador is excluded from desperately needed (and otherwise available) access to a psychiatric clinic, this type of violence is at play. His fifth premise is that disproportionate access to needed resources is linked to disproportionate risk, a kind of risk that is manifested in suffering and death among those often least able to advocate for systemic change.

A cursory review of some of Farmer's essays on problems in Haiti and Russia (2003) might lead the casual reader to conclude that he represents but one more of the so-called blame-the-system liberals. However, this is not the case. His writings and thus his theory—owing much to firmly grounded experts such as Johan Galtung and Amartya Sen—demonstrate a thorough understanding of the socio-political and socio-economic order, this in turn tied to a thorough understanding of contemporary states and what makes them tick. He does not advocate disregard for state systems, nor does he simplistically demean them. He does advocate policy-based reform of such systems such that the voices (and thus the opinions) of the poor, of religious minorities, of women are better represented. While recognizing that structural inequalities, and thus structural violence, are extraordinarily difficult to eradicate, he believes gradual change is possible. Change can occur because the conditions that produce structural violence, and thus human rights abuse, are not accidental.

Farmer's work goes a long way toward relinking theory with concrete political engagement, as Maskovsky (2005) suggests. Farmer boldly acts in a "no-more-business-as-usual kind of way," through his "fusing of a broadly defined human rights perspective with an emphasis on the viewpoints of the poor" (2005: 283). Further demonstrating his pragmatic side, Farmer provides examples of how "outsiders" and "insiders" can work together to enhance local capacity and ultimately minimize dependency relationships. His work, as Doug Henry (2005) indicates, also goes a long way toward elucidating the interplay of (and differences between) "symbolic/everyday violence" and "spectacular violence." The latter is manifested in systematically and openly violent actions such as rape, forcible disappearance, and torture. Their ramifications percolate through systems; they are long lasting and insidious.

The theory of structural violence is particularly appropriate for the case studies included in chapters 2 through 7 herein. Just as the information on Papua, Ethiopia, Bosnia, El Salvador, Sudan, and Palestine emphasizes the conditions and processes that produce refugees, Farmer's theory targets the institutional conditions and processes that create suffering, oppression, and abuse.

Refugees

If the work of a single person could be said to have been more influential than others in shaping the approach to on-site, field-based refugee work referenced herein, it would be that of Barbara Harrell-Bond. In a career spanning well over thirty years, she has researched—and then written and lectured about—the refugee condition in ways that both stimulate and provoke others. Working in Africa, she was among the first to critically write about the notions of aid and relief, and to do so in ways that transcended the work of government, academic-, and NGO-based professionals. Featured was her critique of the so-called dependency syndrome associated with the refugee assistance provided in camps (Harrell-Bond 1986). One set of recent writings has addressed the factors associated with successful refugee resettlement and repatriation, as well as ways to effect the transferability of knowledge to practice (Voutira and Harrell-Bond 2000). Another set has addressed the essence of humanitarianism and what it means to be humane as assistance is offered (Harrell-Bond 2002). Meeting a decade ago in her office at Queen Elizabeth's House, on the Oxford University campus, she and I discussed the challenges of incorporating the work of aspiring students into the corpus of refugee-related literature. Of particular interest at that time was the work being done on traumatization and torture by students in the United States and United Kingdom, in conjunction with the rapidly evolving "torture treatment center movement." She reiterated that process, not just product, were of great concern to her. I had the privilege of becoming actively involved in this movement, as did a number of my students, shortly thereafter—through an assistance program that later came to be incorporated as the nonprofit Rocky Mountain Survivors Center.

The links between Harrell-Bond's earlier pragmatic work and that of John Prendergast (much of it more recent) are clear. His work has been of almost as great an influence on me. Also focusing on Africa, he has advocated for systemic changes that will reshape the aid process (1996), and most recently has worked on-site as a tireless advocate for refugees and internally displaced persons (IDPs) in Darfur, Sudan. In 2004 he told me how critical it is for him to spend significant amounts of time in the field, investigating human rights issues firsthand. Information presented in chapter 8 details his influence on what I term "pragmatic humanitarianism."

COMPASSION AND SUFFERING

Compassion involves emotion; you can feel it in your gut.

—Harvey Martz

Compassion and suffering are terms that are inexorably linked as obverse mirror images. Compassion is among the most important terms with which human rights specialists have to deal. Yet it also is extraordinarily nebulous and difficult to define. As Sir Nigel Rodley recently told me, only partially tongue-in-cheek, since compassion is difficult to grasp, it is the kind of term that human-rights lawyers tend to avoid when they are addressing cases brought before them.

While clearly a human trait, compassion is thought by some to have evolved as prehuman and human societies have evolved. The most far-reaching statement of this premise is the one recently made by David Lordkipanidze, director of the Georgia State Museum. In investigating the remains of an elderly *Homo erectus* male uncovered at the Dmanisi site and dated to 1.77 million years B.P., he speculates that he may have survived through the compassion of others. He had no teeth. They all rotted away long before his death. Others therefore may have chosen to feed him to keep him alive (Fischman 2005: 18–19).

Other paleoanthropologists also have speculated about the evolution of compassion. One of the first was Ralph Solecki. In 1960 he reported on a remarkable discovery at Shanidar Cave in northern Iraq. The remains of a Paleolithic *Homo sapiens* hunter, purposefully buried in a grave some 60,000 years ago, were found to be surrounded by flower pollen. Bunches of brightly colored flowers had been placed next to the corpse: hollyhocks, hyacinths, and daisies. Palynological investigations also revealed that herbs had been used. Perhaps a death rite had been enacted (Moore et al. 1980: 67). Since 1960, several other similarly adorned graves of early *Homo sapiens* have been discovered elsewhere in the Old World. Many graves indicative of extensive funerary rites, spanning the last few thousand years, have been uncovered by archaeologists working in the New World.

The evolution of understandings of compassion in major cultural and religious contexts has been traced by Karen Armstrong (2005). From Islam to Confucianism to Judaism, she finds evidence of a widespread belief in the value of "feeling with others," of empathy, and of not doing to others what you would not want done to you. When carried out in practice, not merely proclaimed through words, a "sense of the sacred" can contribute to the valuing of human life through acts of compassion.

Contemporary understandings of compassion are informed by a wide variety of disciplines. These include anthropology, sociology, psychology, philosophy, and theology. Cultural context clearly is important. The field of human rights also builds upon, and integrates, these perspectives. Viewed broadly in this way, compassion entails the ability to genuinely assist others, but is far more than simply being helpful. As my late colleague Carolyn Jaffe noted (1997), compassion centers on offering care more than help. It focuses on the provision of psychosocial support to a suffering person. It also can involve the provision of physical support and medical intervention in the case of illness. Spiritual assistance can be a key. Most importantly a compassionate person is one who actively listens to the other person, without treating him or her as "the Other." In listening, choices are considered. In listening, one's story truly can be told. Compassion does not entail telling someone what to do, but rather, assisting them in clarifying the options available to reduce their suffering.

Jaffe's work as a nurse with the hospice movement gave her ample opportunity to witness acts of compassion. In case after case, she found that it involves minimizing preconceptions of what the suffering person feels, as well as of what the person has experienced. Diverse experiences with diverse clients strengthen the abilities of those caregivers who (in her experience) prove to be most compassionate. The ability to be empathetic also proves to be essential. To Jaffe, this included sensing what the other person is experiencing from cognitive, emotive, behavioral, and moral perspectives (1997: 24). Compassion is not manipulative. It implies the development of relationships and through them, the reflexive development of trust on the part of all parties.

Suffering clearly involves pain, which can be psychosocial or physical. Just as compassion must be considered from a cultural perspective, so too must suffering. In addition to those working with hospice and health care, other perspectives on suffering come from those who have witnessed it first-hand during war. Writing now about what he and others saw during World War II, Freeman Dyson (2005) states that European civilians whose towns were subjected to massive bombing raids sometimes could be seen wandering about the ruins like disembodied spirits. Their own suffering, compounded by what they saw others experiencing, wore many out. It also transformed people; their detachment became a coping mechanism. Nobel laureate Elie Wiesel (1999) deftly describes the suffering of Jewish victims in point/counterpoint fashion with the sadism of their German SS torturers and executioners. A remarkable number of victims seemed to accept their fate passively. In fact, their faith helped them deal with their suffering.

To understand the purposeful infliction of suffering, Wiesel also relies upon the notion of "the Other." By distancing himself from those being abused, "the Other" is created. The torturer or executioner can more readily and dispassionately inflict cruelty. He has "the meaning," he inhabits an inductive universe of his own making, he becomes a fanatic following his own dictates. Hate creates such fanaticism. Fanaticism creates fear (1999: 369–72 *passim*).

Many people in refugee homelands suffer. It often is suffering, or fear of suffering, that causes someone to flee, thus becoming a refugee, an IDP, or an asylee. As reported in this book, people in refugee homelands suffer through physical mistreatment, torture, incarceration in concentration camps, forced migration and forcible disappearance, separation from family, and psychological abuse (which can include witnessing the suffering of others). The operational definitions developed over the past half century that are central to the understanding of the term "refugee" refer to "fear of persecution." In the minds of many, fear of persecution can be equated with fear of suffering. When purposefully inflicted by others, it can be even worse.

Philosopher and theologian Marcus Borg builds on emotive and moral perspectives. To him, compassion means feeling another's suffering. "To be compassionate is to feel for people as a mother feels for the children of her womb" (2005).

> Suffering is like a gas; it fills the available space.
>
> —Keith Smith

COMPASSION AND JUSTICE

Justice requires that we carefully weigh rights and privileges and assume that each member of a community receives his due share.

—Reinhold Niebuhr

Justice is the social form of compassion. Compassion is the personal form of justice. Compassion is a virtue. It shapes our relationships with each other (Borg 2003: 200). As it plays out systemically, in socio-political contexts, compassion is reflected in the quest for justice. Viewed interactively, the two terms then ask not only, "How do you suffer?" but "Why are there so many victims?" and "What factors caused the victimization?" To even begin considering these critical questions, one must be attuned to the cultural factors underpinning these socio-political contexts. One must be able to analyze the system's operative ethos. Whereas an archaeological perspective was useful in understanding the evolution of compassion, a historical perspective is useful in understanding the evolution of justice. Given the fact that I am a product of the West, a Western perspective is utilized here.

The principle of justice, loosely defined, is about "doing what's right" in the service of humanity. Interpretations and applications have varied tremendously. Retribution, revenge, and retaliation all have been promoted as just measures over the centuries by Westerners. Each of these might be viewed as reactive, and when carried out, also harmful. Unfettered assistance, rehabilitation, and restoration also have been promoted as just measures by Westerners. Each of these might be viewed as proactive, and when implemented, helpful. The contributions of politicians, warriors, medics, philanthropists, teachers, and myriad others variously have been promoted as useful in the pursuit of justice.

Debates about the principle of justice have spanned the past three millennia in the West. Most have been couched within the grand themes of peace, war, and human service. The notion of "just war" is singled out briefly here, due to the approach I take to historical benchmarking and humanitarianism, detailed in chapter 8. Traceable within early Roman times to the writings of Cicero, whose intellectual roots in this regard can be traced to the Greeks, it was stressed that wars are unjust when undeclared or undertaken without provocation. Those undertaken for defense and protection might be considered just. While offensive and defensive postures were considered, defense was given greater credence, hence greater justification. These stances were framed by postulations about universal or natural laws of justice, being clearly distinguishable from the laws of men and nations (Ishay 2004: 25, 44). Arguments about what properly constitute offensive and defensive postures continue to play out today as, for example, Palestinians and Israelis battle over domain and ideological prerogative in the Middle East. In this case, natural law (and inherent right) still is intoned by some of those I have interviewed.

My opinion is that compassion and justice must be viewed in tandem. Justice is about social transformation, about active understanding and active intervention in oppressive situations. Compassion is about active understanding of the personal, about active assistance to alleviate an individual's suffering. Hadidja Nyiransekuye takes a behavioral approach. She believes compassion is shown in the acts performed by others. One of my students at the University of Denver, she escaped the genocide in Rwanda in 1994 as a refugee, to re-create a life for herself and her children in the United States. Now a doctoral candidate in social work, she demonstrates compassion by assisting others in pragmatic fashion. A popular guest lecturer, Hadidja believes that education offers a powerful venue for constructive engagement and social change. (She was a school principal in her homeland.) Her talks to audiences in the United States are inspired by emotive as well as intellectual insights. Her own story of escape serves as a vehicle of expression, catharsis, and compassionate assistance.

The view I offer in this book is both progressive and liberal. Simply stated, my perspective on refugee human rights is "progressive" in that I believe such rights must be viewed as evolutionary and malleable. My perspective is "liberal" in that I believe individual agents of change, through grassroots activities and small-scale organizations, can make a difference. In the broadest sense, these also are ideas that work. This view complements the perspective of Paul Farmer (2003, cited above), who believes that individuals concerned with issues of social justice can make a great deal of difference, step-by-step, one person at a time.

THE NATURE OF EVIL

Evil moves fast.

—Countess Aurelia, in "The Madwoman of Chaillot"

What is evil? Whatever springs from weakness.

—Friedrich Nietzsche

To me, evil is the purposeful infliction of harm or fear upon the innocent. Is there a place for a discussion of evil in a book about refugee human rights? I have my graduate students at the University of Denver to thank for providing me with a resounding yes when I brought this question to them. Indeed, the present brief section builds upon ideas they offered in class discussions during 2003, 2004, and 2005.

Earlier Western perspectives saw evil as resident in individuals, as an irrationally destructive force exemplified in certain types of people like witches (Dillinger 2004). To paraphrase UN Secretary General Kofi Annan, *people themselves* cannot be evil. Rather, it is their *actions* that can be. Refugees, IDPs, and other forcibly displaced persons (such as those in Ethiopia subjected to "villagization," as discussed in chapter 3 herein) often suffer because of such actions. Michael Ignatieff, William Schulz, Elie Wiesel, and Marcus Borg are among the contemporary experts who have tackled the nature (and notion) of evil. Each believes it exists. Each offers a perspective that complements that of Annan. Their views are powerful, and allow me to bring this introductory chapter to a close.

The pragmatic humanism of Ignatieff (2001: 84–9) is clear as he examines evil in the context of both religious and secular convictions. He does so in balanced fashion. Examples are offered of Catholic priests who hid Jews during World War II; their religious beliefs translated into moral stances that effectively combated tyranny. Other examples are offered of those such as Primo Levi whose secular reason, expounded in speeches or written documents during the same era, demonstrated great courage in the face of evil. Failures also abound. "Before radical evil, both secular humanism and ancient belief [at times] have been either utterly helpless victims or enthusiastic accomplices" (2001: 86).

For Ignatieff (2001), evil is reflected in action. It is one result of freedom of choice. We all (at least theoretically) possess a conscience. We all (at least theoretically) can empathize with the condition of others. Yet, in choosing among alternatives, evil—the purposeful infliction of harm upon the innocent—sets one apart from conscience and empathy. Such choice is illustrated in this volume in chapter 3, as the issue of terror and torture within Ethiopia is discussed.

For Schulz (2003), evil is seen in purposeful, one-on-one actions. He cites the story of the soldier who makes sport by killing pregnant women and tossing their fetuses into the air in an attempt to impale them on his bayonet. It is eerily similar to the story shared with me by a man from Darfur (see chapter 6 herein). Schulz also believes the suicidal actions of terrorists are evil; innocent people die. Evil is not "floating around somewhere out there in the ether. . . .it is tethered to a select group of very real people committing very real deeds" (2003: 21). Human rights work should target such evil, he declares.

For Wiesel (1999), evil is exemplified in the deeds of the German SS during World War II. The torture, imprisonment, and execution of Jews, Roma, gays, and others demonstrated this. He also stresses the notion of complicity. The so-called good soldiers of the Wehrmacht were complicit in the deaths of others, through their support of the so-called bad soldiers of the SS. The *Einsatzkommandos* could not have carried out their horrific deeds at Babi-Yar and elsewhere if they had not had the support of the Wehrmacht. Chapter 4 presents an example of this type of evil, as concentration camps in Bosnia are discussed.

For Borg (2003), evil is embodied in the greed associated with political domination systems. Empires are to blame. Greedy representatives of the "core" exploiting the resources of representatives of the "periphery" are engaged in evil actions. Because of the insidious nature of such systems, he believes that economic justice is the hardest form of justice to achieve. Chapter 2 herein presents an example of such a system, as the case of Papua within Indonesia is considered.

For me, evil is reflected in negative actions that purposefully target the dispossessed, the marginalized, the vulnerable. Creating "the Other," then distancing oneself from him or her, and thus from responsibility, is part of this equation. Rape, torture, forcible disappearance, negotiated separation of mother and child—these are evil actions. While contemporary experts disagree on how to deal with it (see, e.g., Tiel 2004), it must be openly addressed. Refugees are disproportionately subjected to evil actions. Interventions can help empower refugee victims to become refugee survivors.

Ignatieff, Schulz, Wiesel, and Borg likely would appreciate the words of one of my colleagues, who is both a psychologist and a poet:

> We were progress
> demanding obeisance to God, to Caesar, to war lords,
>   to a new world order, to a Mc universe
> We were progress
>   marching the conquered
>   along a trail of tears
>   herding the conquered
>   into boxcars and open pits
>   profiling the others
>   into internment camps, into slavery, into gas ovens,
>   into open graves, into hangman's nooses
> We were righteousness
>   rooting out evil dead or alive
> We were righteousness
>   driven to be the answer
>   driven to convert through conquest, through persuasion,
>   through emersion, through perversion
>
> —Jack Wackwitz, The Lanell Group, from
> "Stained by Blood and Imperfection," 2001

Note: The italicized quotations in this chapter were obtained first-hand by the author (Borg, Martz in public lectures), as well as from published materials referenced in the bibliography (Hastings from Dyson; Smith; Niebuhr and Nietzsche from Williams; Countess Aurelia from Giraudoux). The "Queen of Sarajevo" is adapted from my article first published in the *Intermountain Jewish News* (September 8, 2000, pp. 4–5).

REFERENCES

Armstrong, Karen. "Compassion's Fruit." *AARP Magazine* (February 2005): 62–4.

Bennett, John W. *The Ecological Transition: Cultural Anthropology and Human Adaptation.* New York: Pergamon, 1976.

Borg, Marcus J. *The Heart of Christianity: Rediscovering a Life of Faith.* San Francisco: Harper Collins, 2003.

——. "The Heart of Christianity." Lecture series presented at St. Andrew United Methodist Church, Highlands Ranch, Col., March 2005.

Dillinger, Johannes. "Terrorists and Witches: Popular Ideas of Evil in the Early Modern Period." *History of European Ideas* 30, no. 2 (June 2004): 167–82.

Dyson, Freeman. "The Bitter End." *New York Review of Books* 52, no. 7 (April 28, 2005): 4–6.

Farmer, Paul. *Pathologies of Power: Health, Human Rights, and the New War on the Poor.* Berkeley: University of California Press, 2003.

Fischman, Josh. "Family Ties." *National Geographic* 207, no. 4 (April 2005): 16–27.

Giraudoux, Jean. "Notes on 'The Madwoman of Chaillot.'" *Inside Out*, Denver Center Theatre Company, Denver, Colo., March 2005.

Gutmann, Amy, ed. *Michael Ignatieff: Human Rights as Politics and Idolatry.* Princeton, N.J.: Princeton University Press, 2001.

Harrell-Bond, Barbara. "Can Humanitarian Work with Refugees be Humane?" *Human Rights Quarterly* 24, no. 1 (February 2002): 51–85.

——. *Imposing Aid: Emergency Assistance to Refugees.* Oxford: Oxford University Press, 1986.

Harris, Marvin. *Cannibals and Kings: The Origins of Cultures.* New York: Random House, 1977.

Henkin, Louis. "The Human Rights Idea." In *Human Rights*, by Louis Henkin, Gerald L. Neuman, Diane F. Orentlicher, and David W. Leebron. New York: Foundation Press, 1999.

Henry, Doug. Interview with Assistant Professor of Anthropology, University of North Texas, Denton. December 3, 2005.

Ignatieff, Michael. "Human Rights as Idolatry." In *Michael Ignatieff: Human Rights as Politics and Idolatry*, edited by Amy Gutmann. Princeton, N.J.: Princeton University Press, 2001.

Ishay, Micheline R. *The History of Human Rights: From Ancient Times to the Globalization Era.* Berkeley: University of California Press, 2004.

Jaffe, Carolyn, and Carol H. Ehrlich. *All Kinds of Love: Experiencing Hospice*. Amityville, N.Y.: Baywood, 1997.

Laqueur, Thomas W. "The Moral Imagination and Human Rights." In *Michael Ignatieff: Human Rights as Politics and Idolatry*, edited by Amy Gutmann. Princeton, N.J.: Princeton University Press, 2001.

Maskovsky, Jeff. "Book Review of 'Pathologies of Power,' by Paul Farmer." *American Anthropologist* 107, no. 2 (June 2005): 283–84.

Moore, Lorna G., Peter W. Van Arsdale, JoAnn E. Glittenberg, and Robert A. Aldrich. *The Biocultural Basis of Health: Expanding Views of Medical Anthropology.* Prospect Heights, Ill.: Waveland, 1987 (orig. 1980).

Prendergast, John. *Frontline Diplomacy: Humanitarian Aid and Conflict in Africa.* Boulder, Colo.: Lynne Rienner, 1996.

Schulz, William. *Tainted Legacy: 9/11 and the Ruin of Human Rights*. New York: Thunder's Mouth, 2003.

Smith, Keith. "Among the Peoples of the Agreste of Pernambuco: Thinking She was the Mother of the Murderer." *American Anthropologist* 99, no. 3 (September 1997): 513.

Tiel, Jeffrey. "Rights Argument Invalid When It Comes to Matters of Evil Conduct." *Science & Theology News* 4, no. 11 (July/August 2004): 1–2.

Voutira, Eftihia, and Barbara Harrell-Bond. "'Successful' Refugee Settlement: Are Past Experiences Relevant?" In *Risks and Reconstruction: Experiences of Resettlers and Refugees*, edited by Michael M. Cernea and Christopher McDowell. Washington, D.C.: World Bank, 2000.

Wiesel, Elie. *And the Sea is Never Full: Memoirs, 1969– *. Translated by Marion Wiesel. New York: Schocken, 1999.

Williams, Robert L. *Savoring Life: Wisdom that Inspires, Challenges, Comforts and Provokes*. Golden, Colo.: Great Undertakings, 2004.

Chapter Two

Papua and the Issue of Enclave Development

Beat them with a stick!

My wife Kathy and I heard the *bupati* yelling at his subordinates as he lined up over forty indigenous men on the deserted grass-and-mud airstrip in the Papuan village of Ewer. Hiding at the insistence of our mission colleague, Fr. Dave Gallus, with our cameras ready, we took advantage of an ominous situation to document the government's abuse of Asmat tribesmen firsthand. With the blessing—literally and figuratively—of the priest, we secretly shot about ten minutes of 8mm movie film and a dozen 35mm photos of admonitions, beatings, and other types of abuse as a local Indonesian official berated the men at gunpoint for a presumed lackadaisical work ethic. Outside lumber interests needed *kayu besi* hardwoods, and villagers were not responding fast enough in their logging activities. One by one, the men stepped forward, were beaten on the backs of their legs, and staggered off. A short time later, they were lined up again and, while squatting, forced to "duck walk" about half a mile.

This chapter develops the theme that external pressures have caused internal disruptions in Papua, Indonesia's eastern-most province. In attempting to develop a modern nation, first the Dutch and then especially the Indonesians have marginalized Papuan peoples while extracting their resources. Both colonial and neocolonial powers have taken advantage of the colony. The "core" has taken advantage of the "periphery." The colonizers have taken advantage of the indigenous population. "The elite" has taken advantage of "the savage." Dutch and Javanese administrative structures have been superimposed upon tribal socio-political structures. Enclave development therefore has occurred, and in concert, structural inequalities have emerged. Missionaries and miners have played key roles, both negatively and positively. As

17

Figure 2.1. Brutal tactics are used as punishment against villagers whom Indonesian government officials claimed were not working hard enough on lumber operations. Armed men monitor beatings inflicted sequentially on each of the workers. This photograph was taken in hiding with a telephoto lens.

correlates to this array of processes, significant human rights violations have taken place, killings have occurred, and refugees have been created.

GETTING THE LAY OF THE LAND

The landscape of Indonesia is as diverse as that of any country in the world. From the active volcanoes in Java (along the Pacific's "Ring of Fire"), to the beaches of Komodo, to the rainforests of New Guinea, the range of land forms and vegetation types is tremendous. In the province of Papua, in the span of only 150 miles, heading north from the Arafura Sea's mud flats, one could pass through mangrove swamps, tropical forests, deciduous forests, and temperate forests, past subalpine groves and alpine scrub, and top out near glaciers at over 16,000 feet elevation on Puncak Jaya, the highest mountain in the Pacific region. Papua's Central Highlands also contain the loftiest mountain chain in this region. Encompassing the Grand Valley, home to dense populations of Dani, Yale, and other Papuan peoples, the chain only began to be explored extensively by outsiders in the 1930s.

Indonesia consists of an archipelago spanning some 3,000 miles east to west. It includes several thousand islands, several hundred of which are densely populated. Demographically, it is the world's fifth-largest nation. With a population of about 225 million, nearly 200 million of whom are Muslims, it represents the world's largest Islamic nexus. Papua has about 2 million inhabitants, speaking over 200 distinct languages and dialects. Most also speak Bahasa Indonesia, the country's *lingua franca*.

As with the other chapters in this book, in understanding refugee homelands it is essential to understand ecological circumstances. This approach guided the pioneering work of Clifford Geertz, one of the world's leading experts on Indonesia, and it guides the approach taken here (cf. Geertz 2005).

COLONIALISM AND THE QUEST FOR INDONESIAN INDEPENDENCE

On a broad scale, this analysis addresses change in the province of Papua (also known as Irian Jaya, Irian Barat, or West Irian) in the context of economic and political change in Indonesia. On a smaller scale, it addresses change among the tribal Asmat and Muyu peoples in the context of economic and political change in Papua. Enclave development, as will be demonstrated, can only be understood in this way. The creation of refugees in this improbable environment also can only be understood in this way. Stated differently, the changes impacting the tribal peoples with whom I had direct contact—the Asmat and more briefly the Muyu—serve as exemplars of the problems confronting all indigenous residents of the province.

To understand the often tumultuous situation in Papua one must first understand the array of events that have occurred in Indonesia, especially over the past half century. Emerging from over 300 years of Dutch colonial rule, World War II battles that scarred the landscape (both environmentally and socio-politically), and a bold move toward independence that rocked Southeast Asia, Indonesia entered a period of increased population growth and economic development. Independence leader Sukarno's power and reach were strengthened when he became president, and—while challenged—were not appreciably diminished in the following two decades as the country moved into an autocracy supported by a strong-armed military.

While the Dutch presence in the archipelago dates to 1596, it was not until about 1910 that virtually all the islands that now comprise the Republic of Indonesia had been consolidated under their control. Indeed, the "idea of Indonesia" also emerged at about this time (Ricklefs 2001: 206–26 *passim*). Papua, comprising about half of the huge island of New Guinea and thus also comprising the eastern-most of the so-called Indonesian outer islands, has found itself at the archipelago's geopolitical margins ever since Europeans made first contact on its southwest coast in 1623 (Van Arsdale 1993: 5). As the colonial Dutch and their Javanese collaborators continued to combine forces to exert control over Indonesia's vast resources, the potential of Papua became increasingly obvious. During the twentieth century mineral deposits (including gold) and timber stands (including valuable *kayu besi* hardwoods) were systematically identified. Later, a broad-ranging search for oil also was initiated.

Indonesian independence was proclaimed in 1945. After deadly battles and contentious negotiations, the Netherlands formally transferred sovereignty, excluding Papua, in 1949. As Ricklefs (2001) stresses, the revolutionary nature of the nation was clearly manifested during this transitional period. Some claimed the years from 1950 to 1957 constituted a liberal period as economic and political vistas were expanded, and indeed it was in comparison to what transpired later (Van Arsdale 1975: 132). Paradoxically, Indonesia became more unified yet more diverse, more politically uniform "at the top" yet more politically fragmented "at the bottom," and in subsequent decades, more of an economic player internationally yet more of a trouble spot politically. Islam became more entrenched at the nation's ideological core despite claims that Indonesia was a secular state. The guerrilla-like strategies, which had helped Sukarno and his allies consolidate power, also came to be played out, increasingly to their consternation, in the Darul Islam movement. This included Acehnese of northern Sumatra, as well as residents of western Java and southern Sulawesi. By the 1960s a rudimentary yet distinctive guerrilla movement was underway in Papua as well.

The maelstrom of activity that created modern Indonesia, and that set the stage for ominous developments in Papua, has been described by Clifford Geertz (2004: 622) as "a cacophony of youth gangs, military irregulars, religious insurgents, leftist guerrillas, and regional separatists [fighting] wars within wars. . . . [Sukarno and then Suharto exerted power through decades] of economic growth, pervasive corruption, and military severity." But, as Ricklefs (2001: 311) notes, "as the nation fell apart, it also became one." The national motto, loosely translated, became "unity in diversity."

"THE SAVAGE" AND THE COLONIST

The indigenous Papuan peoples were variously perceived by early European explorers (including Captain James Cook) and later Indonesian traders as "primitives" or "savages." In subsequent centuries their headhunting and cannibalism were used to support this view. The seemingly benign (but in fact demeaning) term *orang hutan*, meaning "jungle people," came to be widely applied to Papuans by Javanese. Such perverse stereotypes served to further widen the gap between the more economically developed western and less economically developed eastern portions of the nation.

Along with the residents of East Timor, Papua's "savages" became Indonesia's "problem children" through much of the latter half of the twentieth century. Driven from the rest of the archipelago as unwanted colonialists, the Dutch sought to retain a toehold in Papua. Its resource potential was only matched by its potential to serve as a symbol. Its remoteness and cultural distinctiveness ironically played into both Dutch and Indonesian hands. A wrestling match unfolded. By August 1960 Indonesia had broken off diplomatic relations with the Netherlands over the Papua issue, while turning increasingly to the Soviet Union for overall governmental and military support (Ricklefs 2001: 325). This paralleled the increasingly important role of Indonesia's Communist party, the PKI. A settlement was not reached between Indonesia and the Netherlands until August 1962, after multiple rounds of negotiations (some of which included Robert F. Kennedy). Sukarno saw Papua as a symbolic galvanizer for a fracturing Indonesian state. Stated differently, it was being used as a pawn by both sides, with little regard for the long-term welfare of its indigenous peoples. The abortive Communist coup of 1965, which led to Sukarno's overthrow and the rapid ascendancy of Suharto, did not appreciably affect Papua.

Waves of Colonizers

Colonizers of various types have been settling in Papua for millenia. The original inhabitants likely reached New Guinea over 30,000 years ago (Howells 1977: 170). Peoples speaking languages of the so-called Austronesian (Melanesian) and Papuan families have extraordinary longevity on the island; archaeologically delineated lowland and highland cultures have been dated to over 7,000 years ago. There is even evidence of metal tool use over 2,000 years ago (Chowning 1977: 19). This evolving culture area came to be represented by very diverse peoples, with complex cultural heritages, a diversity not fully recognized nor respected as the premodern Indonesia continued its resource exploitation under the Dutch. As trade routes involving Europeans and Asians expanded during the colonial era, some traders and entrepreneurs established towns on the northern and southwestern New Guinea coasts. Non-Papuan Indonesians have gradually been settling in towns like Biak, Jayapura, and Merauke for more than a hundred years.

Missionaries, traders, and government officials contributed to what Knauft (1994: 396) terms "colonial constructions." Labor recruitment, and occasional enslavement, of the Melanesian inhabitants further east was accompanied by the spread of guns, liquor, and disease. Much later, as I witnessed firsthand, an epidemic of influenza still could decimate a village and undermine its social structure. Chinese traders established footholds in Papua early on. In several instances they were the first to set up shops and establish trade routes into the remote interior. Crocodile hides were a prime economic motivation.

World War II saw major battles between Australian and Japanese forces in Papua. At war's end towns such as Biak grew further as disengaged military personnel settled there. Thirty years after the war, indigenous Asmat residents of the southwest coast told me of the bombs that had been dropped and the disruptive incursions into villages that combatants had made. These same informants were hesitant to confirm the fact that several of their relatives had been recruited as mercenaries by both the Australians and the Japanese (cf. Petermeier 1986a).

During the first forty years of the twentieth century, the Dutch systematically conducted military expeditions, explorations, and government patrols. The lowland areas, although deemed impenetrable if traveling by land as opposed to river, received more attention than the highland areas. Some of the surprisingly dense populations of the Baliem Valley were not discovered until as recently as 1938. Punitive government expeditions along the southwestern coast became increasingly common. For example, some indigenous raiders in the Mimika and Asmat regions were captured and imprisoned in the town of FakFak in 1930 (Van Amelsvoort 1964: 62). As many as 300 Asmat raiders may have been killed by police in 1930 in the Mimika region, an event still mentioned with disgust to me by villagers forty-five years later.

Transmigration

The program of Indonesian transmigration, begun in 1904, contributed colonizers of a still different sort. A burgeoning population on Java had led Dutch administrators to conceive of a plan to "transmigrate" citizens from more densely populated to less densely populated areas on other islands. By coincidence, I visited the first transmigrant settlement, in southern Sumatra, during the course of a 1980 research assignment. Operating in fits and starts, over the course of a century the program has never reached its intended goals; but several million people (mostly Javanese) have been persuaded to participate. Over 200,000 have found new homes in Papua since 1980. With few exceptions, they have not been welcomed by the indigenous residents. Taking an extreme perspective, Monbiot (quoted by Howard 1995: 41) is among those who believe that Indonesian transmigration is designed to eliminate indigenous populations.

A Stereotype Revisited

Colonizations and incursions must be viewed in stark contrast to the remoteness—actual and perceived—of New Guinea, revered or reviled for centuries as one of the so-called last bastions of the savage. That ritualized violence was widespread, projected through headhunting and cannibalism, gave further credence to a stereotype of this nature (Knauft 1994: 395), and served to further distance villagers from the "civilized Dutch" and "aristocratic Javanese." Popular articles published in the West still exaggerate the exotic nature of those living in "the land of cannibals" (see, e.g., Raffaele 1996).

THE IMPACT OF MISSIONS

The penetration and presence of Christian missionaries in Melanesia, including Papua, is long-standing. Their history of proselytizing for religious purposes is well known. Less well known is their history of involvement in aiding local economic development, education, and health care. Least known is their involvement in promoting human rights.

Using local economic development as an example, early reports of missionary involvement are contained in the records of both Protestant and Catholic groups, the latter exemplified by the Catholic Order of the Sacred Heart in the late nineteenth century (Salisbury 1968: 486). Such activities included horticultural development, lumber operations, and even livestock raising. Missionaries assisted Papuans in establishing cooperatives and small businesses in a number of locations. By the 1950s small markets had been promoted, or codeveloped, in places like the Baliem Valley and Muyu region. Villagers were regularly hired to wage labor positions involving work on roads, airstrips, and schools.

From the perspective of religious conversion, a kind of behavioral modification was used early on by many missionaries. Known by its critics as "tobacco Christianity," it involved a straight forward, carrot-and-stick approach. If a man attended a church service, he might be given a fishing hook. If his wife attended, she might be given fishing line. Baptism would be rewarded with something extremely significant, such as a *lempeng* (large block) of tobacco. As this practice became entrenched, missionary Clarence Neuner—reflecting back twenty years—recalled people saying: "No tobacco, no alleluia!" (Fleischhacker 1988: 5).

Particularly in East Timor, and to a lesser extent in Papua and other "outer islands," by the 1980s the Catholic Church had become a powerful source of identity and transformation. Proselytizing and conversion had given way to socio-economic development and human rights activism. The spread of Islam over a 500-year span led to the diminution of Buddhist and Hindu influences in the archipelago, as well as the impacts of a variety of indigenous practices, but did not (until the last decade) diminish the influence of Christianity. Overall, Catholic activity became more progressive in terms of development and rights; Protestant activity (with a few notable exceptions, as documented by Finley 1996) did not.

Within the Asmat tribal region, where I worked on two separate occasions during the 1970s, the Catholic and Protestant mission presence is relatively long-standing and well established. Intermittent contacts between missionaries and the indigenous residents date to the pre-World War II era. A permanent Catholic outpost was established in 1953 and shortly thereafter, was taken over by members of the Crosier Order. In 1954 the Dutch government established regular headquarters. A permanent Protestant outpost was established in 1955. By contrast, the Muyu region, straddling the Papua/Papua New Guinea border, had been systematically penetrated and "missionized" earlier. The Order of the Sacred Heart had established a rudimentary church in 1933 and the government an outpost in 1935 (Schoorl 1976: 4). Members of scattered settlements were pressed to move into consolidated villages so that proselytizing and schooling could be facilitated. Colonial government administrators and mission supervisors often worked hand-in-hand as schools were established; the former recognized that the latter might be able to offer programs that were better funded and better organized than their own.

Among the last areas of Papua to be penetrated by missionaries, not far west of the territory occupied by the Muyu, was that of the Korowai people. A Dutch representative of the Mission of the Reformed Churches (ZGK) established an outpost in 1979, five years after an expedition which I co-led with Robert Mitton and Mark Grundhoefer had established first contact with other Korowai (van Enk and de Vries 1997: 5; Mitton 1983: 136–57 *passim*).

ENCLAVE DEVELOPMENT

The broadly theoretic—and highly pragmatic—concept of the political economy is appropriate in framing this analysis of developments in Papua. Simply put, a political economy is one wherein political expediencies and political pressures shape economic production targets and strategies of resource allocation. Potential free-market forces are manipulated. Centralizing tendencies predominate. Controlled by a core elite, those in the periphery have little say over what transpires as valued local resources are extracted. Residents of the periphery usually do the extracting, while being paid disproportionately low wages.

As it has played out in Indonesia, the political economy has evolved into a powerful force. In a classic neocolonial sense (cf. Arrighi 1973), the densely populated and elite-dominated core disproportionately extracts resources from the less densely populated and ethnically diverse periphery. Members of the periphery increasingly are pressured into seeking low-paying wage labor. From this perspective, only slightly oversimplified, the "inner islands" such as Java and Bali can be considered the core; the "outer islands" such as Timor and Papua can be considered the periphery. Oil, timber, spices, and minerals are key, and are tied to economic targets contained in each national Five Year Plan (the first of which was instituted in 1969). To the extent that resources can be extracted from outlying areas, despite negatively impacting the in-digenous residents, national gains are said to be realized. Transnational con-nections with countries such as the United States and Japan strengthen the process.

Enclave development drove early underdevelopment in Papua (Van Arsdale 1975). During the past three decades, processes of marginalization of indige-nous residents have increased as structural inequalities tied to centralizing governmental policies have become further entrenched. Extreme fluctuations in the once-robust oil market have contributed. Although offset to some extent by infusions of government developmental capital, influxes of tourist capital, and the creation of cooperatives, which have enabled some Papuans to gain modest economic toeholds in the regional economy, these marginalizing processes continue. Mining has created the biggest single problem.

Mining

The mineral potential of Papua was recognized by the Dutch as early as the 1930s. Gold was the original focus (Van Amelsvoort 1964: 64). Later, the po-tential of nickel, copper, and silver mining was recognized. The now Denver-based Newmont Mining Company was one of the first to expand mineral ex-plorations in Papua in the late 1960s, although no mines were opened. My 1974 partner-in-exploration, Robert Mitton, had previously worked for them. New Orleans–based Freeport McMoRan entered the picture in 1960, based on the promise of a rediscovered 1936 survey report, and came to develop the huge Grasberg mine through its Freeport Indonesia concession. It is estimated to contain the world's largest single gold reserve. It also contains substantial quantities of copper and silver.

Accusations have been leveled at both Newmont and Freeport McMoRan during the past decade. In July 2005, Indonesian prosecutors charged Newmont with dumping heavy metals into a fishing bay in Sulawesi in conjunction with one its gold mining operations (Griffin 2005). Papuan tribal leaders earlier charged Freeport McMoRan with operating in ways that caused mine tailings to flood neighboring lands, and for hiring too few indigenous people on its mostly transmigrant workforce of 17,000 (O'Neill 1996). The company has been accused of having inappropriate relationships with state security forces who guard the operations. Global Witness (2005) reports that from 2001 to 2003 nearly $250,000 may have been paid by Freeport to an Indonesian general named Mahidin Simbolon, now the Indonesian Army's inspector general and a former commander in East Timor. Attempting to supplement their meager wages, security forces have been accused of involvement in a diverse array of lucrative outside activities (Nakashima and Sipress 2002).

On August 31, 2002, three people—two Americans and an Indonesian— were killed and eleven wounded in an unprovoked ambush near the Grasberg mine's company town, Tembagapura. After extensive investigations by both Indonesian and American investigators (including FBI agents), in January 2006, 12 suspects were arrested. All were described as Papuan separatists, including Anthonius Wamang, who was indicted by a U.S. grand jury in 2004 on the murders of the two Americans. While overall responsibility has yet to be established, it is possible that the attack was perpetrated by members of the Indonesian National Army. Attack survivor Patsy Spier, whose husband was killed, has provided details to me (2005) of the ambush and the efforts she has engaged in to assure that justice eventually ensues. These include her useful meeting with Indonesian president Susilo Bambang Yudhoyono in May 2005 as well as repeated trips she made to Indonesia with investigators. U.S.-Indonesian relations continue to be strained by the ramifications of the attack.

British Petroleum (BP Indonesia) currently is exploring for natural gas in the so-called Bird's Head region of Papua. This corporation is attempting to learn from the earlier mistakes made by Freeport McMoRan. Among other initiatives, BP Indonesia is training and hiring Papuans as security guards, while also using local police (as opposed to Indonesian military personnel).

One of the boldest indigenous religious leaders to speak out about these issues in recent months has been the Rev. Socratez Sofyan Yoman, president of the Union of Baptist Churches of Papua. In his July 30, 2005, message to representatives of BP Indonesia, he asked: "When you first wanted to take our natural resources why didn't you first ask us Papuans, the owners of the land? . . . [The area near Tembagapura] is swarming with Indonesian intelligence agents, with armed soldiers [everywhere] and where Papuans, the owners of the land, are lucky to get a job clearing up rubbish. . . . What makes you so sure you can avoid Freeport's mistakes?" (Yoman 2005).

Logging

Like those for oil and minerals, timber surveys were conducted with increasing frequency during the twentieth century. Mapping began as early as the 1930s, with specific reserves throughout the province having been identified and charted by 1972 (Van Amelsvoort 1964: 64; Bari Ts. 1974). Japanese companies, operating concessions derived from the Indonesian government, came to dominate the hardwood market. The abuse reported at the beginning of this chapter stemmed from tensions involving one of those concessions. In 1972, a local Asmat leader presented his concerns about the negative, exploitative impacts of logging at a seminar (Omberep 1973), perhaps the first indigenous Papuan to make such remarks at a professional forum.

Michael Stevens is a river morphologist with extensive experience in Indonesia (1983). He is among the scientists (see also Geertz 2005) who strongly believe that environmental degradation, most dramatically symbolized in that nation by deforestation and indiscriminant logging, is a key negative indicator of enclave development. One day in 1974, during my first fieldwork assignment among the Asmat, one of my most valued informants—known as the "Old Master of Stories"—took me for a ride upriver in his canoe. "I want to show you something special," Yewcemin said. Elderly by the time I met him, this former "Big Man" and headhunter had found himself increasingly marginalized by the influx of government officials, missionaries, and traders. We paddled to a remote spot about two miles from his village and suddenly stopped. We were looking at a magnificent *kayu besi*, a prized hardwood, standing in isolation. "See that big tree? It's mine! It's my lineage's! The Indonesian government has come to Asmat and said they own the land, that we now live on their land. But they don't own that tree." Yet it later was cut down by a lumberjack, sawed into sections, loaded on an Indonesian vessel, and shipped to Java. Enclave development can strike one person, and one tree, at a time.

Increased sensitivity to the problems of indiscriminate logging in Papua has been demonstrated by Indonesian government officials during the past decade. Two large national parks are being developed in the province, following principles established by a diverse and respected group of environmentalists—some of whom are Papuans.

Health Care

As anthropologist/physician Paul Farmer (2003) has stressed, health care, human rights, and development are intimately related. To some extent in Papua, the negative impacts of economic development have been offset by the positive developments within health care. Dutch-sponsored medical surveys and systems of health care were introduced to northern regions of the island during the nineteenth century. Similar provisions were not made for inhabitants of the highlands and southwestern lowlands until well into the twentieth century. However, by the 1960s progressive systems of integrated rural care, based more on prevention than cure, had been introduced by Dutch medical officers. In the Asmat region these included training programs that incorporated indigenous residents, both male and female, and sought to synthesize indigenous practices with Western practices (Van Amelsvoort 1964). After Dutch officers left for good, the health care system suffered setbacks (Van Arsdale 1975: 266–67). Nonetheless, despite—or perhaps because of—erratic investments in care by the Indonesian government, missionaries have contributed substantially to the establishment of clinics and to innovations in health education.

Malaria is the leading cause of disease-induced death in the province. Other significant diseases include yaws (frambesia), whooping cough, tuberculosis, filariasis (elephantiasis), influenza, cholera, and ringworm. Leprosy has been eliminated for the most part. The demand for tobacco remains high, and lung diseases are prevalent.

CARGO CULTS, SEPARATIST MOVEMENTS, AND INDIVIDUAL REACTIONS

While considered extremely remote by Indonesia's neocolonial administrators, as well as their Dutch predecessors, Papua nonetheless has experienced police predations and forceful government interventions since the 1920s. Whereas a separatist movement can be viewed as primarily proactive, a so-called cargo cult can be viewed as primarily reactive. It is one form of reactionary response to the pressures indigenous people feel in response to the incursions of outsiders. Such cults are but one manifestation of a broader variety of nativistic reactivity, itself a kind of millenarian movement. Best typified by activities of Melanesian (including Papuan) peoples, cargo cults have been widespread, and serve as social indicators of cross-cultural stressors.

Cargo Cults

Research conducted among the Muyu indicate that some of Papua's earliest documented cargo cults occurred in an area adjacent to the Indonesian/Papua New Guinea border. This is important to the understanding of refugee displacements that took place in the same area much later. In 1953 a movement began under the leadership of a local prophet. Tying spiritual entreaties to real-world material aspirations, a so-called ghost school of devotees developed. As the word spread, so did the outspoken animosity toward foreigners. As Schoorl (1976: 74) stressed, it was a "wide-spread Muyu belief that foreigners control unlimited supplies of merchandise and money . . . [some even believing in a] 'money-factory.' [They perceived that there must be] endless hoards of goods. . . ."

The cult that Fr. David Gallus and I studied (1974) among the Asmat evolved in similar fashion, and was met with similar types of acceptance as villagers struggled to confront neocolonial pressures. A prophet arose, disciples were recruited, and bold messages were spread. It was prophesized that Jesus Christ would enter the village and that the rule of outsiders would be ended. A "Lord of the Earth" would take command. Specifics were offered as to how an Asmat government would be instituted and how *merdeka* (freedom) would be attained. "Take the best of the outsiders' goods, some of their beliefs, and none of their administrative rules" became the mantra (cf. Schoorl 1978). Like the movements in Muyu, the Asmat cult's impact was felt for several years.

A "New Order" and the Free Papua Movement

In 1974 pilot Tom Benoit, flying for the Associated Mission Aviation service in Papua, at my request took out a pencil and, on the back of a piece of cardboard, sketched the places where guerrilla insurgents were actively fighting. His flights sometimes took him near the action. His sketch indicated that the west-central New Guinea highlands and lake districts were especially active. Residents of lowland and swamp areas, such as the Asmat, were less active, although the Muyu were showing interest.

It is difficult to determine when reactionary movements targeting Java-centric Indonesian control first began in Papua. Choosing what was likely deemed an extraordinarily remote and punishing locale, as early as 1927 the Dutch government had exiled individuals accused of involvement in the Communist uprisings in Java and Sumatra to the Muyu region (Mitchell 1996: 642). From termination of formal Dutch colonial control in 1962, through transitional United Nations supervision, to incorporation into Indonesia in 1969 as its 26th province, Irian Jaya/Papua was rigorously controlled from afar. Pepera, Papua's so-called Act of Free Choice took place in August 1969. While involving over a thousand Papuan representatives, they were essentially handpicked by the central government and did nothing more than rubber-stamp the non-separatist, inclusionary platform Suharto was advocating for the territory (Ricklefs 2001: 358). The vote resulted in no substantive changes for the better for the indigenous population. Many activists claimed that it was only a token vote meant to placate dissidents. This served to exacerbate Pan-Papuan, anti-Indonesian sentiments. Thus, the actions and reactions that created enclave development in Papua came to a head during the mid-years of the 1965–1998 reign of President Suharto, and similarly, the actions and reactions that created a forceful guerrilla movement in Papua came to a head during that period under the coercive military leadership of Prabowo Subianto, Suharto's son-in-law. His paracommando initiatives in Papua against leading separatists and their supporters became increasingly oppressive and brutal.

By 1976 Suharto had solidified a "new order" and concurrently solidified the Indonesian military, known by the acronym ABRI, in ways never envisioned by Sukarno. In 1977 there were student demonstrations in Jakarta against human-rights abuses. Although not put down with force, they were closely monitored. In 1978 the government began a campaign of nationwide indoctrination in the principles of Pancasila, the proclaimed "pillars of the republic." While ridiculed by some intellectuals, the simplistic pillars nonetheless were propounded as a unifying ideology. In 1979 the so-called Village Law was passed. It standardized Javanese terminology—and restructured political units—for districts, town, villages, and hamlets, much to the dismay of non-Javanese throughout the archipelago. During the early 1980s, ABRI began a program whereby it would systematically enter villages to assist with economic development and local infrastructure projects. This, too, was designed to strengthen the internal reach of the military and bring "wayward inhabitants" such as those in Papua under greater control (Ricklefs 2001: 372–374).

The Free Papua Movement, known in Indonesia by the acronym OPM (Organisasi Papua Merdeka), emerged through the efforts of a diverse and at first loosely organized group of indigenous Papuans. Some covert assistance was provided by outside change agents. Living in New Guinea on both sides of the Indonesian/Papuan New Guinea border, members sought to drive out the colonial and neocolonial powers. According to reports I received in the field, on at least three occasions Indonesian fighter jets strafed the villages from which the movement's guerrilla leaders were operating. Fighting peaked during the 1970s and 1980s, when as O'Neill noted (1996: 11), several thousand Papuans were killed.

OPM still operates near the Indonesian/Papua New Guinea border, as well as in other rural (and some urban) areas. Limited gains have been realized. For example, on December 1, 1999, the Papuan flag (originally designed in the 1960s) was allowed to be raised in the major governmental centers and towns. To prevent riots and other forms of destructive behavior, church and government leaders called for a day of celebration and prayer. Yet, two days later, nearly 200 people suffered beatings and gunshot wounds when they refused to take down the flag in the town of Timika, near the Grasberg mine (Petermeier 2000).

Individual Reactions

At the local level, reactions to outside pressures take many forms. Many traditionally important "Big Men" found their power attenuated, their prestige diminished, and their everyday roles altered. Played out in the actions of everyday people, I saw Asmat villagers who "went *amok*." One man whom I knew well showed up at my doorstep one morning, a dazed expression on his face. He demanded in an uncharacteristic tone that I give him tobacco. He then marched off, goose-stepping up and down the pathway that bisected his village, shouting military-like orders at bemused but deferential villagers. Still in a dazed state, he threatened children with his spear and shot arrows harmlessly in their direction. By nightfall he was exhausted. He collapsed in the arms of other men, who had kept a careful watch over him as he played out his reactionary theatre. I later learned that he had seen—and been threatened by—Indonesian troops acting in just the same way. Culture-bound syndromes of this type are now recognized as significant psychiatric manifestations of localized, pressure-laden situations. An appendix to the DSM-IV Diagnostic and Statistical Manual of Mental Disorders includes a detailed description of *amok*, among other syndromes (American Psychiatric Association 1994: 845).

Papuan coastal cities such as Jayapura (nee Port Numbay) are experiencing explosive population growth. Not unexpected problems are accompanying this. Leslie Butt (2005) reports that as the prevalence of HIV/AIDS and the number of sex workers—the so-called lipstick girls—both have increased in the province, some Papuans are postulating a broad government conspiracy to eliminate the indigenous population. While extremely unlikely, such a belief must be taken seriously as human-rights issues are considered.

There are some indications that homicide rates have increased owing to the pressures being felt by villagers. Demographic/statistical measures are not well developed in Papua in this regard, and in addition, it is not easy to ascertain which killings are primarily linked, for example, to accusations of sorcery and which to stresses associated, for example, with the incursions of transmigrants. It is also not easy to tally which have targeted members of one's own ethnic group as opposed to members of other groups, or targeted outside agents of change. In prior decades the murder of missionaries was not unheard of; one priest was killed execution-style in 1965 by a government official in the Asmat region. Although not answering these questions, the complexities of political violence in New Guinea have been tackled adroitly by Knauft (1987).

Conversely, Visser (1997: 208) is among those who suggest that headhunting may increase in response to the "very real expression of people's anxiety and vulnerability in coping with the Indonesian state order." While systematic documentation for this type of death is lacking for Papua, it is not inconceivable.

STRUCTURAL INEQUALITIES

It is my contention that the structural inequalities entrenched in Papua during the late colonial and early neocolonial eras led to the increasing marginalization of the province's indigenous peoples. These inequalities also led to the creation of refugees. As previously noted, outside traders, including Chinese, came to dominate certain markets, such as those for crocodile hides. The development of mining interests, including the Freeport McMoRan operation, offered employment for some Papuans, but economic marginalization for others. Over a twenty-five-year period it is likely that as many as 200,000 transmigrants from the so-called inner islands settled in Papua. While an oil boom never materialized, numerous exploration companies penetrated the interior (even cutting straight through and destroying local gardens so as not to alter the surveyors' geodesic survey lines). Mining and logging operations caused substantial environmental degradation. Through 1998, Indonesian policy under Suharto continued to prove repressive.

At the individual level, reactions have been exemplified by those who "go *amok*" and in accusations of government conspiracies. Homicides may be increasing. At the village level, reactions have been manifested in cargo cults. At the regional level, they have been manifested in guerrilla activity and separatist movements. The traditional role of the "Big Man" has been severely attenuated. Refugees have been created among people whose grandfathers were headhunters. The Papua/Papua New Guinea central border area, owing to the reactionary stances taken by the Muyu for nearly half a century, has proven conducive to assisting displaced people and nurturing their aspirations for a Pan-Papuan nation. Progressive missionaries, as well as several Indonesian intellectuals, have assisted many of these.

AFFECTIVE ACTION: THE ROLE OF MISSIONARIES

Nonstandard Collaboration

In academic circles, it generally is unpopular for social scientists to claim that certain of the activities of missionaries are beneficial. It also is unpopular for them to claim connections (and especially, amiable affiliations) with missionaries. Yet such alliances are not infrequent and from a human-rights perspective, often helpful to indigenous peoples. Long prior to the emergence of contemporary human-rights regimes, anthropologists and missionaries collaborated in New Guinea. Seen as liberal in their day—the late nineteenth and early twentieth centuries—they fought the presumed negative influences of traders, labor recruiters, and other outsiders (Knauft 1994: 398). Anthropologists and missionaries in Papua have continued to collaborate in several beneficial ways (Kaplan quoting Miedema 1991: 716; O'Neill 1996; Lang 1973). Exemplified by my own experiences, Fr. David Gallus and I researched the "Lord of the Earth" cult together. Certain of the findings about enclave development that I originally published were incorporated in training seminars conducted by members of the Crosier mission. Bishop Alphonse Sowada (representing the Diocese of Asmat) utilized knowledge of our photographs of gunpoint harassment and beatings (presented at the beginning of this chapter) in his successful quest to have abusive government officials removed from office.

Integrative vocational and leadership training programs targeting the residents of Papua have become increasingly common. Some of the most innovative have been developed by the Crosiers. These can be dated to 1972, when a dramatic series of seminars were held. Missionaries, anthropologists, development specialists, and local leaders were in attendance. One purpose was to debate long-standing missionizing practices and contemplate new ones that would be more integrative and participatory. "Tobacco Christianity" was to be abolished. As Gottfried Lang (1973: 41–42) stressed, "growth without development" needed to be replaced by integrative forms of socioeconomic development. "Outside development" needed to be replaced by facilitative development. This approach has been followed by Crosiers to the present day.

Missionaries indeed can play helpful roles. Rev. Fred Ingold and his wife Polly, whom I first met in 1976, spent twenty-four years as Methodist missionaries in Indonesia. Their efforts were generally well received by everyday citizens and government officials alike (Gorski 2005). Fr. Gerard Zegwaard, who established the first permanent Catholic mission post in the Asmat region, also contributed pioneering anthropological studies on the area. His balanced, nonjudgmental analysis of headhunting practices remains a frequently cited classic (1959). In the Asmat region, progressive missionaries like the Crosiers—many of whom have taken advanced courses in anthropology— have integrated traditional and externally derived practices in ways that have benefited the local residents (see, e.g., Needles 1993). More well-known for their dramatic headhunting rituals, the Asmat also had a number of traditional peace ceremonies that were studied by the Crosiers. Food exchanges, the breaking of arrows, the ritualized exchange of women, and even the exchanging of small children between formerly warring villages all were examined (Petermeier 1986b). Most members of the Crosier staff in Asmat now are indigenous Indonesians, including Papuans, this speaking further to favorable future prospects.

Indicators of Change

Humanitarian assistance recently was provided by members of the Catholic Diocese of Vanimo, in Papua New Guinea, to refugees from Papua who were about to become secondary migrants within that country. Because of the church's track record, members of another diocese were contracted by the office of the United Nations High Commissioner for Refugees to provide health and education services to other refugees within Papua New Guinea (UNHCR 2004).

That villagers have gained key leadership positions within many Catholic and Protestant churches, as well as within the educational system, offers hope. That some have become social workers who can utilize traditional and nontraditional modes of intervention offers hope. That some, such as my Muyu colleague Abraham Kuruwaip, have spoken out for a more inclusive political system and protection of indigenous rights—supported by church officials—offers hope.

Since the end of Suharto's rule in 1998, several persons have served as president in rapid succession. One was Sukarno's daughter, Megawati Sukarnoputri. None has been able to establish a real presence in office nor an effective mandate for the nation, and certainly not for Papua. Yet more openness to innovation and reform is being seen. In February 2000 a Papuan Conference was held near Jayapura; the establishment of a transitional Papuan government was discussed. Later that year a Papuan Congress was held; human-rights issues were openly debated. Missionaries were involved in many of these discussions.

It is possible that an ambitious World Bank program "to reform Indonesian society from the bottom up" will make a difference (Li 2005). The initiative focuses on village infrastructural planning decisions, intending to make them more accountable, transparent, and efficient. Villages compete for funds, with as many as a third nationwide hoping to become involved. Designed in large part by anthropologists, local wisdom is carefully being taken into account. Social capital is being maximized, top-down regulations and blueprints conversely being minimized.

POSTSCRIPT: THE MURDER OF INNOCENTS
AND THE CREATION OF REFUGEES

The murders of Americans Rick Spier and Edwin Burgon, along with that of Indonesian Bambang Riwanto, in August 2002 in Papua present an ominous specter. They serve as powerful reminders of the difficulties and dangers encountered by those who attempt to help others as teachers and aid workers, as well as those who speak out on behalf of human rights in chaotic political environments. Human-rights concerns were openly addressed by my outspoken colleague Arnold Ap, murdered in 1984 in Papua. An anthropologist, musician, and rights spokesman, Ap was affiliated with the University of Cenderawasih. More recently, a Papuan independence leader, Theys Eluay, was murdered by members of Kopassus, the Indonesian special forces. Concerns over such violence and abuse also have been openly addressed in Papua by leading religious figures, such as former Catholic Bishop Alphonse Sowada.

The flight of refugees from Papua to Papua New Guinea was first documented in the 1960s. While under Australian control, Papua New Guinea was generally permissive to the arrival of refugees, not all of whom were from Papua (van der Veur 1966). After Papua New Guinea gained its independence in 1975, its atmosphere of tolerance and assistance continued. Increasing numbers arrived from Papua, many being assisted by those living in the Muyu borderland. The refugees consisted of OPM members, their supporters (such as the wife of Arnold Ap), and everyday villagers who felt threatened. Knowledge of the ongoing murders of Papua's residents, which over a thirty-year period had reached several thousand (as estimated by Petermeier 2000: 10), continued to exacerbate their fears.

Indonesia is not a party to the 1951 UN Refugee Convention or the 1967 Protocol. By contrast, Papua New Guinea is. While Indonesia recently has assisted several thousand of those who were displaced in the fighting on the island of Timor (and earlier, many thousands of Indochinese refugees, in concert with the UNHCR), it has not systematically assisted those displaced by the tensions in Papua. By labeling those displaced as political dissidents, insurgents or guerrillas, the government likely perceives that it can "officially avoid" helping those in need.

The UNHCR opened refugee camps in Papua New Guinea over twenty years ago. During this period the numbers, living both in and out of camps, have been reported to have ranged from about 7,000 to 12,000 at any given time. The largest numbers of refugees entered the region in the mid-1980s at the height of the Indonesian paracommando assaults under Prabowo Subianto. Traditional networks of social support have played important roles as the dis-

Figure 2.2.   During the late 1970s and early 1980s, Arnold Ap became one of Papua's most eloquent spokesmen for human rights. A
talented musician and arts curator, he composed songs that told
stories of victimization and survival. He was murdered on April 26,
1984, by government soldiers.

placed adjust to life in the camps and neighboring forests, and it can be expected that those tribes whose members straddle the international border (such
as those on the Upper Fly/Digul plain) will continue to assist them. Yet those
living in the East Awin camp, just east of the international border, have been
buffeted by transnational logging interests and changes in the stance of Papua
New Guinea's own government (Namaliu 2005; Greenpeace 2003; Glazebrook 2001). "Permissive Residency" has been offered as a way of better in-

tegrating these Papuans into the national life of Papua New Guinea (UNHCR 2004). Members of the now-dispersed Muyu tribe—given their range of experiences—hopefully might be invited to play important roles as facilitators.

REFERENCES

American Psychiatric Association. *DSM-IV: Diagnostic and Statistical Manual of Mental Disorders*. 4th ed. Washington, D.C.: American Psychiatric Association, 1994.

Arrighi, Giovanni. "Labor Supplies in Historical Perspective: A Study of the Proletarianization of the African Peasantry in Rhodesia." In *Essays on the Political Economy of Africa*, by Giovanni Arrighi and John S. Saul. New York: Monthly Review Press, 1973.

Bari Ts., Abdul. "Potensi Hutan Irian Jaya dan Prospeknya." *Irian: Bulletin of Irian Jaya Development* 3, no. 3 (October 1974): 1–50.

Butt, Leslie. "'Lipstick Girls' and 'Fallen Women': AIDS and Conspiratorial Thinking in Papua, Indonesia." *Cultural Anthropology* 20, no. 3 (August 2005): 412–42.

Chowning, Ann. *An Introduction to the Peoples and Cultures of Melanesia*. 2nd ed. Menlo Park, Calif.: Cummings, 1977.

Cutts, Mark, ed. *The State of the World's Refugees 2000: Fifty Years of Humanitarian Action*. Geneva: UNHCR/Oxford University Press, 2000.

Farmer, Paul. *Pathologies of Power: Health, Human Rights, and the New War on the Poor*. Berkeley: University of California Press, 2003.

Finley, Bruce. "Mission for God." *Denver Post*, October 27 1996, pp. 1A, 10A–11A.

Fleischhacker, Marcus. "Reflections and Dreams Inspire." *Crosier Drums* 3, no. 4 (November 1988): 5.

Geertz, Clifford. "Very Bad News." *New York Review of Books* 52, no. 5 (March 24, 2005): 4–6.

———. Review of *Violence and Vengeance: Discontent and Conflict in New Order Indonesia*, edited by Frans Hüsken and Huub de Jonge. *American Anthropologist* 106, no. 3 (September 2004): 622–23.

Glazebrook, Diana. "Dwelling in Exile, Perceiving Return: West Papuan Refugees from Irian Jaya Living at East Awin in Western Province, Papua New Guinea." Unpublished Ph.D. dissertation abstract, Department of Anthropology, Australian National University, Canberra. www.papuaweb.org (accessed June 6, 2005).

Global Witness. *Paying for Protection: The Freeport Mine and the Indonesian Security Forces*. Washington, D.C.: Global Witness Publishing, 2005.

Gorski, Eric. "Proselytizing During Relief Efforts Divides Christian Groups." *The Denver Post*, January 17, 2005, pp. 1A, 12A.

Greenpeace. "East Awin Decision Could Spark a Humanitarian Crisis." *Greenpeace/Australia Pacific: Media Release* for November 17, 2003 at www.greenpeace.org.au/media/press (accessed June 28, 2005).

Griffin, Greg. "Indonesia Charges Newmont, Mine Boss." *Denver Post*, July 12, 2005, pp. 1C, 8C.

Howard, Bradley Reed. "Mind-Forged Manacles: Resistance, Rebellion, and the Twilight of the Idols (or How to Anthropologize with a Hammer)." *PoLAR: Political and Legal Anthropology Review* 18, no. 2 (November 1995): 35–44.

Howells, W. W. "The Sources of Human Variation in Melanesia and Australia." In *Sunda and Sahul: Prehistoric Studies in Southeast Asia, Melanesia and Australia,* edited by Jim Allen, Jack Golson, and Rhys Jones. London: Academic Press, 1977.

Kaplan, Martha. Review of *The Ambiguity of Rapproachement: Reflections of Anthropologists on Their Controversial Relationship with Missionaries. American Anthropologist* 93, no. 3 (September 1991): 716–17.

Knauft, Bruce M. "Foucault Meets South New Guinea: Knowledge, Power, Sexuality." *Ethos* 22, no. 4 (December 1994): 391–438.

——. "Reconsidering Violence in Simple Human Societies" (with commentaries and rebuttal). *Current Anthropology* 28, no. 4 (August–October 1987): 457–500.

Lang, Gottfried O. "Conditions for Development in Asmat." *Irian: Bulletin of Irian Jaya Development* 2, no. 1 (February 1973): 38–61.

Li, Tania Murray. "Beyond 'the State' and Failed Schemes." *American Anthropologist* 107, no. 3 (September 2005): 383–94.

Mitchell, William E. "The Ethnography of Change in New Guinea." *American Anthropologist* 98, no. 3 (September 1996): 641–44.

Mitton, Robert. *The Lost World of Irian Jaya.* Melbourne: Oxford University Press, 1983.

Nakashima, Ellen, and Alan Sipress. "Indonesian Police Chief Visits Site of Ambush." *Washington Post,* September 5 2005, p. A22, at www.washingtonpost.com/ac2/ wp-dyn?pagename=article&contentId=A38032-2002Sept4 (accessed October 4, 2005).

Namaliu, Amanda. "Refugees and PNG's Timber Industry." *PLN [Pacific Legal Network] News,* Summer 2005, p. 2. www.pln.com.au (accessed July 5, 2005).

Needles, Colleen, producer. "A World Away: Crosier Fathers and Brothers." VHS. WCCO-Television, Minneapolis, Minn., 1993.

Omberep, Joseph B. "Penindjavan Asmat Tahun 1963 dan Keadaan Sekarang Tahun 1972." *Irian: Bulletin of Irian Jaya Development* 2, no. 1 (February 1973): 19–23.

O'Neill, Thomas. "Irian Jaya: Indonesia's Wild Side." *National Geographic* 189, no. 2 (February 1996): 2–33.

Petermeier, Virgil. "Crosiers Embrace a Pastoral Plan for the Papuans." *Crossview* 11, no. 2 (Summer 2000): 10.

——. "Peace Comes to Asmat." *Crosier Drums* 1, no. 4 (November 1986a): 3.

——. "Exchanging Children Brings Peace." *Crosier Drums* 1, no. 4 (November 1986b): 1–2.

Raffaele, Paul. "The People that Time Forgot." *Reader's Digest* (August 1996): 100–107.

Ricklefs, M. C. *A History of Modern Indonesia since c. 1200.* 3rd ed. Stanford, Calif.: Stanford University Press, 2001.

Salisbury, Richard F. "Early Stages of Economic Development in New Guinea." In *Peoples and Cultures of the Pacific: An Anthropological Reader,* edited by Andrew P. Vayda. Garden City, N.Y.: Natural History Press, 1968.

Schoorl, J. W. "Salvation Movements among the Muyu of Irian Jaya." *Irian: Bulletin of Irian Jaya Develoment* 7, no. 1 (February 1978): 3–35.

———. "Shell Capitalism among the Muyu People." *Irian: Bulletin of Irian Jaya Development* 5, no. 3 (October 1976): 4–78.

Spier, Patsy. Interview with former teacher, International School Services, Princeton, N.J. September 16, 2005.

Stevens, Michael. Interview with river morphologist for PRC Engineering Consultants Inc. Semarang, Indonesia, July 16, 1983.

UNHCR. "In PNG, Refugees from Indonesia's Papua Province Start Complex Journey to New Home." *UNHCR News*, October 1, 2004. www.unhcr.ch/cgi-bin/texis/vtx/news (accessed July 20, 2005).

Van Amelsvoort, V.F.P.M. *Early Introduction of Integrated Rural Health into a Primitive Society: A New Guinea Case Study in Medical Anthropology.* Assen, the Netherlands: Van Gorcum, 1964.

Van Arsdale, Peter W. *The Asmat: An Ethnography and Film Guide.* Denver, Colo.: Center for Cultural Dynamics, 1993.

———. *Perspectives on Development in Asmat: An Asmat Sketch Book, No. 5.* Hastings, Neb.: Crosier Press, 1975.

Van Arsdale, Peter W., and David E. Gallus. "The 'Lord of the Earth' Cult among the Asmat: Prestige, Power, and Politics in a Transitional Society." *Irian: Bulletin of Irian Jaya Development* 3, no. 2 (June 1974): 1–31.

van der Veur, Paul. "West Irian's Refugees: What is 'Permissive Residence?'" *New Guinea and Australia, the Pacific and South-East Asia* 1, no. 4 (1966): 13–19.

van Enk, Gerrit J., and Lourens de Vries. *The Korowai of Irian Jaya: Their Language in Its Cultural Context.* New York: Oxford University Press, 1997.

Visser, Leontine E. "On the Meanings of Headhunting in Eastern Indonesia." *Anthropology and Humanism* 22, no. 2 (December 1997): 208–10.

Yoman, Socratez Sofyan. "If you love our natural resources. . . ." [Letter to Lord Browne, Group Chief Executive, BP Indonesia.]" Copy received November 2, 2005.

Zegwaard, Gerard A. "Headhunting Practices of the Asmat of Netherlands New Guinea." *American Anthropologist* 61, no. 6 (December 1959): 1020–41.

Chapter Three

Ethiopia and the Issue of Terror

They used Number Thirteen.

This statement was made to me in 1994 by an Ethiopian man named Equaar Desta. He had been tortured several years earlier, during the Red Terror. Taken to a jail in the northern Ethiopian city of Mekelle, he had been hung upside down by the knees, over a metal bar, like an acrobat. The soles of his bare feet had been beaten to a pulp. "Number Thirteen" was the code used by the man in charge as he selected the type of torture to be used. The person actually inflicting the abuse was likely a member of Equaar's own ethnic group, forcibly recruited for the purpose. The overall agony was thus amplified.

Under the reign of the so-called Dergue regime, Equaar and other Tigrayan people had been captured, tortured, and—in some instances—summarily executed. To his credit, this man has allowed me the use of his name so that his story can have the greatest possible impact. The beating of the soles of the feet, a widespread technique known as *falanga*, is said to be among the most painful of tortures. Equaar noted how the use of a number or code serves to psychologically distance the torturer from the person being tortured. It creates "the Other." It also adds an imperious, even official, aura to the proceedings. Torture of this type is always a state-based, state-sponsored process.

One purpose of this chapter is to demonstrate both the resiliency and fragility of Ethiopia's people in the face of terror. As with other cases presented in this book, a view toward environmental history—particularly that of the northern province of Tigray—is essential to set the stage. The ecological, socio-economic, and socio-political factors that led to the overthrow of the regime of Emperor Haile Selassie and the take-over by the dictator Mengistu Haile-Mariam in 1974 are featured. So are the processes leading to Mengistu's ouster and the take-over by the victorious guerrilla

41

leader Meles Zenawi in 1991. Subsequent problems have emerged under his nominally democratic regime as well. Throughout much of the past thirty years, in the face of terror and environmental tragedy, refugees and IDPs have been created.

Some 1.4 million people died under duress or were killed in Ethiopia from the 1960s through the 1990s. These deaths were not random. Another purpose of this chapter is to present ethnic politics, civil war, and forcible displacement as interactive, systemic forces. Their seemingly chaotic manifestations have in no way been unpredictable. A special focus is placed on forced relocation. Couched in the euphemistic terms of long-distance "villagization" and localized "regrouping," it sprang from the vicious Red Terror of the late 1970s. While environmental degradation and agricultural problems are covered briefly here, more emphasis is placed on the role that terror—and thus "spectacular violence"—has played in the lives of everyday people. Torture is covered within that context. Drought and famine figure as prominently in Ethiopia as they do in Sudan (see chapter 6), but are not treated in depth here.

GETTING THE LAY OF THE LAND

A banker in the northern Ethiopian town of Adwa, having completed our financial transaction, turned whimsical as he recounted the history of his town to me. "Our country was never conquered by colonial powers. The Italians invaded twice, but failed. See that mountain just outside the city limits? Our people climbed to the top and threw boulders down on the Italian soldiers. They had guns, we didn't. They retreated. We won." Indeed, the Battle of Adwa, fought in 1896 under the leadership of Menelik II, gained legendary status among Ethiopians. It still symbolizes the tension between European powers and African peoples, a tension exacerbated in 1937 when Italians under Mussolini carted off the famous Axum obelisk and placed it on display in Rome near the Circus Maximus. Only within the past year, after intense and protracted negotiations, was the 1,900-year-old obelisk at last returned to its northern Ethiopian home. This 180-ton granite object, not coincidentally, now rests within half a mile of the small chapel said to house the Ark of the Covenant.

Zazamanc, Cush, Punt, Habash, and Abyssinia all are names variously applied through history to Ethiopia or parts thereof. Although not as large geographically as its neighbor to the west, Sudan, it is home to many more people, some 60 million. The population is growing by about 2 million people annually (French 2005). Ethiopia is home to the Blue Nile River. It is home to the famous Australopithecine fossil nicknamed Lucy. And as many of its Christian residents would claim, home to the Ark of the Covenant, the proverbial box of acacia and gold said to have contained the original tablets of Moses.

History, legend, and myth come together in intriguing ways in this African country. Richard Pankhurst (2004: 57) notes that Homer, writing in his ninth century B.C.E. Odyssey, included references to Ethiopians (*eschatoi andron*), or the most remote of men. In the Iliad he has Zeus, the king of the gods, visit the "blameless Ethiopians." John Sorenson (1993) uses the phrase "imagining Ethiopia" as he reconstructs the histories and narratives that have shaped what outsiders, perhaps even more than insiders, have come to see and believe. Empires past and regimes present, in concert with remarkable human resources and challenging terrain, have created an image that synthesizes fact and fiction. The landscape itself is extraordinarily diverse. The west-central and northern regions are dominated by the Ethiopian Highlands. Caves pepper the landscape; these provided refuge for people displaced during the recent civil war. The peak known as Ras Dejen reaches nearly 15,000 feet, making it one of Africa's tallest mountains. Indeed, some 85 percent of Ethiopians live in relatively fertile highland areas, a strategy that also provides a refuge from malaria (French 2005). The province of Kaffa claims to be the ancestral home of coffee. Its relatively lush landscape serves to remind that Ethiopia is not simply the stereotypical dry and windswept country seen on television as famines are reported. Pulses, oilseeds, cereals (including *teff*), potatoes, sugar cane, and various fruits and vegetables all are grown in Ethiopia. The Danakil Desert, bordering on Eritrea to the northeast, continues to reveal hominid fossils dating back more than 3 million years. It contains traces of the ancient caravan routes that crossed west to the Sahel. The Oromo region in the south, bordering on Somalia, has both welcomed refugees and produced them.

All totaled, nearly 100 different ethnic groups are recognized. Some seventy languages and dialects are spoken. The major regions follow ethnic patterns, the largest being Oromo, Amhara (increasingly dispersed), Tigray, and Somali. Regions are subdivided into administrative units known as *woredas*. Christianity and Islam are followed by roughly equal numbers of adherents; the Ethiopian Orthodox Church predominates among the former. Approximately 2 percent of the population follow other beliefs (Munro-Hay 2002: 39).

ENVIRONMENTAL DEGRADATION, POLITICAL INSTABILITY, AND RESOURCE DEPLETION

The story of contemporary Ethiopia could be told by focusing on any one of several regions. Since my work was conducted in the northern province of Tigray, and since Tigray features so prominently in national events of the past twenty-five years, the emphasis is placed here. Long-evolving historical, socio-economic, and ecological forces set the stage for seemingly rapid political change. The purported lineage of 225 generations of Ethiopian kings and emperors, dating from the time of Solomon and Sheba's son Menelik I some

3,000 years past to Haile Selassie some thirty years past, serves as a symbolic overlay to the complex and at times confusing foundational political developments of recent decades.

Like a majority of the Ethiopian population, contemporary Tigrayans are predominantly subsistence cultivators and agriculturalists. Exceptions include the Afar nomads of the Danakil Desert and the Raya Oromo, who are mixed cultivators and pastoralists. Millet, barley, sorghum, and *teff* (used to make the ubiquitous pancake *injera*) are the principle crops. Despite recent televised images of desolate brown hillsides, good rains in concert with good farming practice bring remarkably green visions of terraced valleys and rolling hills. Yet the past 500 years have produced pretelevision images of both types.

A sixteenth century Portuguese missionary named Alvarez reported on dense populations and abundant crops in Tigray. However, over time this was only intermittently the situation. My collegues and I believe that environmental degradation, resource depletion, and increases in rural population over subsequent centuries caused a crisis that lasted into the twentieth century (Hailu et al. 1994). Population pressure led to agriculturally risky terracing of steep slopes, too many cattle for too little pasturage, and attenuated fallowing practices. In many northern areas, overall productivity declined. Internal migration rates fluctuated, but increased overall.

Civil wars and associated political instability exacerbated the agricultural and resource decline. During Ethiopia's so-called Age of Princes (1769–1855 A.D.) there was almost continuous warfare among the nobility. Without a regular standing army, militia exerted disproportionate power in the countryside. Communities were pillaged and resources extracted. Compensation was rare. The Christian emperor Tewodros II was able to reduce internecine conflict but not to restore the overall resource base.

During the late nineteenth and early twentieth centuries several external and internal conflicts battered the Tigray region. The British, Egyptians, Sudanese Mahdists, and Italians all invaded. Socio-economic activities were significantly impacted (McCann 1990). King Menelik II, named after the kingdom's putative first king three millenia earlier, attacked Tigray and Welo provinces in order to vanquish a royal contender. Over 50,000 troops were involved, again depleting regional supplies. Two subsequent internal campaigns further strained resources (Hailu et al. 1994: 25).

A 1916 coup d'état in Addis Ababa led to the accession of Tafari Makonnen (later known as Emperor Haile Selassie, the second "Lion of Judah"). Antigovernment resistance movements were organized from Tigray several times during the ensuing decades. The region was at one-and-the-same-time perceived by other Ethiopians as integral and anathema to the country's development. The Italian occupation under Benito Mussolini (from 1935 to 1941) never led to a full-blown colonial relationship, but did exacerbate the already erratic, internal political dynamic. The later Mengistu regime's policies, detailed below, only worsened the situation. The seeds were sown for the debilitating famine of 1984–1985 (when as many as 300,000 may have died) and for civil war.

The Woyane I and Woyane II are names given to major struggles initiated by Tigrayans. The first occurred during 1943. Unlike previous revolts, it involved cross-class collaboration. It was aimed against a new tax policy set by corrupt government officials appointed from the Shewa region. In challenging the authority of Haile Selassie's government, he could only suppress it with the aid of British ground and air forces. Many peasants lost their land and cattle as punishment; the leaders were exiled to remote parts of Ethiopia. The second began in 1975 under the leadership of the Tigrayan People's Liberation Front (TPLF). It targeted oppressive policies of the Dergue regime, while ironically initially also espousing a vision based on orthodox socialism and Marxist. As it evolved, it gained increasing grassroots support and its ideology mellowed. Using traditional guerrilla warfare and community-based mobilization strategies, over a fifteen-year period (after a number of set-backs) it eventually was able to drive the Mengistu administration's provincial government out of Tigray. Some of its leaders later assumed control of the national government.

Our work in Tigray during the 1990s took place after the civil war had ended. It focused on water resource development. Supplemental opportunities opened up so that human rights and refugee issues also could be explored. Multiple field visits by our Denver-based team made it clear that, as water was concerned, lack of technical support for peasant farming systems, resource mismanagement, and inadequate soil conservation measures had led to further environmental degradation. Successive regimes had not invested in natural resource management, as Dejene (1990) has noted. The flexibility afforded by traditional agricultural techniques was compromised by political exigency, and further compounded by climatic change, as Butler and D'Andrea (cited in Browman 2003) also have noted. Yet non-agricultural employment opportunities were severely limited as well. Some men and women alike reluctantly engaged in U.S.-affiliated Food for Work programs; road construction was one task near the village of Mai Misham where we were based briefly.

THE MENGISTU HAILE-MARIAM REGIME

Col. Mengistu Haile-Mariam currently lives in exile in Harare, Zimbabwe. One of the few people to have interviewed him in recent years is the journalist Riccardo Orizio (2003). Now a seemingly peaceful man living in a well-guarded but modest home, from 1977 to 1991 he ruled Ethiopia with absolute authority and brutality. Believing that Emperor Haile Selassie had grown out of touch with contemporary issues and grown apart from the Ethiopian people, as many others also had stated, he and a small cadre of military officers arrested the emperor in September 1974. Believing that a socialist state, modeled partially on that of the Soviet Union, would improve the country's economic malaise, he pursued a torturous path that ultimately failed.

Orizio is one of those who believe that the famine of 1972 opened the doors to the take-over by Mengistu. (Ethiopian custom dictates that the first name be used.) Our perspective also takes this into account, but seriously considers the longer-term degradation of the country's environment, agricultural, and political systems (Hailu et al. 1994). Agriculture is a form and reflection of environmental history (McCann 1990). Others believe that, having arrested Haile Selassie in 1974, Mengistu later personally killed him by smothering him beneath a pillow. Still others believe that, as his reign solidified, Mengistu became one of Africa's most tyrannical leaders. Whatever the beliefs regarding the early years of Mengistu's reign, it is clear that a Leninist/Marxist-style ideology was introduced, one that complemented the ideology of the Soviet Union. The USSR eventually provided nearly $12 billion worth of military aid (Orizio 2003: 142).

Mengistu had solidified his control over the country by 1977. As his identification with and supplication to the "Soviet Reds" became stronger, he came to be called the "Red Negus." As noted below, the first portion of his reign came to be known as the "Red Terror," borrowing a term used decades earlier in the emergent Soviet Union. Throughout, as his so-called Dergue government implemented a diverse array of land reform and militaristic policies, he claimed to have the welfare of the Ethiopian people uppermost in mind, and indeed the welfare of other Africans. He told Riccardo Orizio: "I helped and financed the ANC [African National Congress] when South Africa was still in the grip of apartheid. I was on their side when they needed me" (2003: 148). He claims to have turned to the Soviets only after the Americans and Chinese turned down his requests for assistance. He hoped that his overall strategy would make him a respected pan-African leader, while at the same time ridding Ethiopia of its "tribal and feudal past."

As Mekuria Bulcha (1988: 70) so poignantly stated: "In the hands of the [Dergue] the revolution was skillfully converted into an expression of aggressive but covert Amhara nationalism. Covert, because it [was] expressed in the broader terms of *Ethiopia tikdem* (Ethiopia first) and *ennat ager weym mot* (Motherland or Death)." The notion of "Greater Ethiopia" was continuously played up, while in fact ethnic politics and the marginalization of ethnic groups predominated.

Tigray was severely marginalized by the central government during this period. Resources were withheld. As administrative authority was centralized, the northern region experienced diminution of capacity. Several communities took the initiative to develop facilities on their own. For example, in order to cover a shortage of health facilities, residents of the town of Adigrat decided to build a hospital in the late 1970s. They raised over half a million dollars and completed a structure with 120 beds. However, a request to the Ministry of Health for medical personnel and medicine was refused. Only subsequent intervention, via personal contacts through the Ministry of Defense, enabled the resources to flow (Hailu et al. 1994: 27).

The famine of 1984–1985, exacerbated by policies of the regime, came to complicate the situation. The armed insurgencies of Tigrayans and Eritreans during this two-year period later proved pivotal to the toppling of the regime.

THE RED TERROR

The Red Terror spanned the years 1976 to 1978. Its repercussions extended long after. Estimates of the number killed by the government vary widely (cf. Hammond 2004: 34 and Orizio 2003: 151), but many thousands perished. Mass detentions, torture, and executions served as grisly hallmarks. Those people attempting to claim the bodies of their loved ones experienced a bizarre kind of extortion; they were required to pay a "ransom" equivalent to the cost of the bullets used in the family member's killing. In other nations in similar circumstances the phrase "culture of terror" has been used (see, e.g., Suarez-Orozco 1990). A "terror" indicates a move from arbitrarily oppressive and abusive tactics to systematically, institutionalized oppression and abuse; it is an ominous watermark (Applebaum 2003: 93). It exemplifies "spectacular violence," one type of structural violence (Nordstrom 2004). This aptly applies to what took place in Ethiopia.

The Red Terror was instituted as Mengistu tightened his grasp on the nation. Oppression was complemented by a "retooling" of key institutions. The forced conscription of thousands of men from Tigray, Wollo, and Gondar characterized one of its earliest and most ominous chapters, and has been thoroughly analyzed by Bulcha (1988). It began in May 1976. The conscription euphemistically was called the "Peasant March on Eritrea." Just recuperating from the drought and famine of 1973–1974, which claimed some 200,000 lives overall, a large proportion of the conscripted men previously had been displaced and were just then attempting to rebuild their homes. Many were mid-way through their first planting season in several years. Being forced to leave these activities uncompleted effectively prolonged the drought's effects, even though adequate rains did fall in 1976 and 1977.

The march itself was intended to complement the military's efforts to bring the province of Eritrea back into line. Yet it was poorly organized and the peasant marchers poorly equipped. Their trucks were attacked well before reaching the frontlines. Rather than face extinction, a massive and chaotic retreat ensued. Those who survived either made their way back home (begging food and shelter as they went), gave themselves up to guerrilla forces (thus being imprisoned for up to a year), or joined the ranks of internally displaced persons (IDPs) and refugees fleeing to Sudan (therefore abandoning their homes). Continuing a pattern of attempting to overwhelm its adversaries by sheer force of number, 1977 saw a similar massive conscriptive campaign by the Dergue among Oromo and other people of the south.

The loss of skilled manpower during the Red Terror, as militarization increased and nonmilitary industrial production decreased, created a vicious cycle. Conscriptive or corvée labor thus became another strategy of the Dergue. Although this practice had existed prior to their take-over, it worsened under their rule. State farms had been created in 1975 as a part of the nationalization of rural lands. Some operated on a "labor camp" model. Forced to leave family farms to work on these farms, with little or no recompense, peasants came to express avid resentment. The forced payment of "dues" further exacerbated the situation. This system extended well into the 1980s, with the farms running large losses owing to poor management and inadequate parts supplies. Rather than participate, many peasants fled as refugees (Bulcha 1988: 112–4).

The Red Terror was characterized by oppressive military tactics, unwarranted imprisonments and executions, and a forced restructuring of Ethiopian society. Funds were mismanaged and/or misdirected as the military was strengthened, in concert with Soviet assistance. Although taking place several years after the Red Terror ended, the self-congratulatory national celebrations of 1984 witnessed the same type of mismanagement and misdirection. These events recognized the regime's tenth year in power. The Dergue spent several million dollars on festivities, funds which could far better have been directed toward agricultural development at the height of the 1984–1985 famine (see Bulcha 1988: 238). The Tigrayan and Eritrean armed insurgencies, noted previously, served to heighten the Dergue's sensitivities at precisely this time.

Particularly terrifying for Ethiopia's residents was the fact that the Red Terror made individual vendettas possible. The newly elected *kebele* (urban residents' associations) guards, militia, and other security forces used their positions to justify and revenge old grudges. *Kebele* defense guards were primarily recruited from among the unemployed and uneducated. They targeted persons suspected of being "anti-revolutionary." Uncoordinated, aggressive home searches and nonjudicial detentions were common. A large number of children were among those killed during this unofficial yet implicitly sanctioned campaign (Bulcha 1988: 102–4).

Myth and Reality

The Red Terror spurred interest and concern in the outside world. A number of authors penned fictional and factual works referencing it, as well as the array of events involving Mengistu's reign (Pankhurst 2004). Much as with Cambodia under Pol Pot, the Red Terror drove intellectuals and other skilled professionals into rural regions, which in fact led to the bolstering of rebel forces who later overthrew Mengistu (Hammond 2004: 34). Also as with Cambodia, the emergent Dergue regime manipulated myth, tradition, and history to recast their strategies in a more favorable light. This was not the first time this had been done. The notion of an ancient empire arising from the leadership of Solomon and Sheba's son Menelik and his descendants, of an early Jewish "satellite home," of an early Christianity benefiting from the power of obelisk-raising angels, of a warrior queen withstanding the onslaught of infidels, of a medieval land of the mysterious outside ruler Prester John, of a noble trans-African people able to withstand the incursions of African and non-African enemies, all were presented and reinforced through recent centuries. The *Kebra Negast* ("Glory of Kings") document, likely compiled in the thirteenth century, brought much of this together. Haile Selassie, like Menelik II several decades before, used the phrase "Lion of Judah" to emphasize his unifying power and ability to bring ever-more valued forms of Christianity to the homeland. In the process, the Amharization of the country was reinforced (Bulcha 1988: 47–49).

In fact, Ethiopia only emerged as a polity approximating what is seen today within the past century. The push of Amharization, in counterpoint to the pull of Tigrayan and Oromic forces, with swells exerted by groups such as the Sidamo, have created a somewhat fragile and potentially fragmentary nation-state. A variant form of Amharization, influenced by Leninist-Marxist forces, evolved under Mengistu's leadership.

Torture

The most ominous and pervasive forms of torture are state-sponsored. Clinical analyses can yield substantive insights into the effects of terror and torture (Kreisberg-Voss et al. 1998). Ethiopian refugees interviewed in Denver, as well as in Tigray, provide similar accounts. Lingering, subliminal effects are among the most difficult to treat medicinally. Those involving the abuse of family members—often as the survivor is forced to watch—are among the most difficult to treat therapeutically.

To understand torture in Ethiopia, a broader analysis is required. Mine began with a tour of a "museum of torture" in southern Germany fifteen years ago. The evolution of methods of torture became apparent. I saw metal masks, racks, hacksaws, and iron weights. Prior to the eighteenth century certain horrific techniques remained legal. For example, in England the threat of "pressing to death" under weights was employed to force the accused to testify (Ishay 2004: 86). In a sense, it might be said that methods of torture have evolved from the use of intrusive devices (i.e., those that squeeze, extend, and pierce the body) to the use of intrusive techniques (i.e., those that probe, manipulate, and terrify the psyche). Pharmacological, psychological (including forcible disappearance), and technological methods are employed by various regimes ranging from Ethiopia to the United States. A recent report by Amnesty International lists sixty alleged incarceration and interrogation practices used by the United States at its detention centers (including Guantánamo, where enemy combatants thought to represent Al-Qaeda are held). These include electric shock, humiliation (e.g., being urinated on), sexual taunting, immersion in water to simulate drowning, and mock execution (Judt 2005: 17). As reported to investigators for Amnesty International and later, Human Rights Watch, the various kinds of torture reported in Iraq under the regime of Saddam Hussein included the more "traditional" beatings, hoodings, rapes, and mock executions. In addition, investigators learned of other techniques—boring a hole in the leg with a drill; castration; tying a string around the penis and tightening it; hammering nails into the hand; inserting bottle necks into the rectum; pumping air into the anus; extinguishing cigarettes into the eyeball; burning and blinding people with acid and other caustic materials; and subjecting prisoners to extremes of heat and cold (Langewiesche 2005: 72). Some of these practices also were described to me as being used by Ethiopians, on Ethiopians.

Since the eighteenth century, a majority of nations have come to condemn the use of torture. In the West various condemnatory statements were authored early on (e.g., by Voltaire), but it was not until the latter part of the twentieth century, with the 1975 Declaration on the Protection of All Persons from Being Subjected to Torture and Other Cruel, Inhuman or Degrading Treatment or Punishment ("the Declaration") and the 1984 Convention Against Torture and Other Cruel, Inhuman or Degrading Treatment or Punishment ("the Convention"), that the world had substantive documents at its disposal. The Convention was not ratified by Ethiopia until March 1994.

Representatives of the Mengistu regime inflicted _supplice_ (public torture and execution of purported criminals) on a number of occasions. In other instances it was carried out behind closed doors. It came to be justified as a necessary state response to insurgency and rebellion; from the perspective of human-rights analysis, it appears that Mengistu used the "collective rights" argument, that is, that the torture of individuals can be justified to enhance the greater good (cf. Orizio 2003). As Nagengast and Vélez-Ibáñez (2004: 11) note, once a state comes to justify torture, it is easy to imagine that family members of "suspects" and others in their extended social networks also will come to be tortured. As a process of intimidation, torture has few equals. The Convention does not work well in certain instances, as Tomaševski (1998) stresses. Whereas freedom from torture should be a universally agreed upon and enforced human right, not debatable even in the constructive manner suggested by Ignatieff (see chapter 1 herein), governmental obligations are territorially circumscribed. Intervening to stop torture is extremely difficult, and indeed, was not achieved by the West (as manifest by the United States) in the 1980s in the case of Ethiopia. Foreign policy is one means for potentially rectifying abuse if the external arbiter has a favorable power relationship with the state in question. The United States, increasingly imperfect in its own internal actions, lost this potential when Ethiopia shifted to the Soviet camp. A summary listing for the mid-1990s, contained within the first thematic report on state abuses of power compiled by the UN, listed Ethiopia as one of the problem states under the heading "torture, disappearances, and summary executions" (Tomaševski 1998: 188). That this continued to occur well after Mengistu was deposed was viewed as very problematic by Ethiopian rights activists I interviewed.

Villagization

One of the most ominous strategies triggered by the Red Terror, but that emerged later, was the 1980s government program of "villagization." It was conducted in concert with a resettlement program. While nominally intended to redistribute segments of the population so that resources could better be exploited, these two programs in fact were characterized by forcible displacements and large-scale societal disruptions. Human rights regarding property, privacy, and enslavement were disregarded. Refugee flows were created. My description relies extensively on the authoritative account of Mekuria Bulcha (1988), supplemented by our own earlier analysis (Hailu et al. 1994).

The Ethiopian government began villagization in the mid-1980s. It was ostensibly triggered by the 1984–1985 drought (also discussed in chapter 6). In fact, the program was in large part tied to governmental fears regarding the strengthening of the Tigrayan People's Liberation Front, discussed below. The government rationalized its plan as a needed response to the drought and desiccation of northern lands. It also reasoned that internal migration of one type or another had long been an adaptive strategy within the nation. By moving people to more fertile regions in the south and southwestern portions of the country, the landscape could be revitalized. Peasant self-sufficiency could be enhanced.

Input from those to be moved was minimal. Considerations for those in the south and southwest who would be impacted by the newcomers also were minimal. Existent infrastructure was inadequate. Financing was insufficient. Unlike the transmigration program operational for decades in Indonesia that is discussed in chapter 2, incentives such as new farming tools to motivate people to relocate were virtually absent. Coercion became the "motivation." Support structures were few, control structures many.

The ecological problems encountered by these internal migrants parallel those so ominously detailed for the Ik people of Uganda in a classic study by Colin Turnbull (1972), when they were forced to resettle in a strange, incompatible environment. Those from Tigray were transported several hundred miles into an unfamiliar landscape. "The distance [was] not only spatial but also socio-cultural and ecological" (Bulcha 1988: 116). Some who had been seminomadic were forced to become sedentary; others who had been urban residents were forced to become rural dwellers, with little advice or training as to how to survive in an agro-economic environment.

Between the resettlement and villagization programs it is estimated that over 1 million people were moved from the north to the south in the span of a decade. Operating unevenly, with a brief cessation during the early 1980s owing to complaints from relocatees and those in resettlement receiving areas, it was estimated that the process resulted in some 600,000 persons from Tigray and Wollo being relocated to southwestern Ethiopia during 1985 alone. Up to 7 million more were "regrouped" in the central and southern regions. Although the Dergue eventually fell well short of its overall goal, it had planned to resettle, villagize, or regroup up to 30 million people—at that time over half of the country's total population (Bulcha 1988: 116–7). Despite the Dergue's claims to the contrary, these massive population movements during times of deprivation were neither humane nor developmental, and indeed, violated the basic human rights of those involved (Clay and Holcomb 1986: 84–88).

Villagization often would lead to the displacement of a local majority group by a minority group, the latter then taking on functions of the former. This would include policing authority, a tactic that served to alienate the former majority still further.

Three conditions allowed the process to move forward at all. These provided a veil of justification for the international community as well. (1) Famine victims needed more stable, fertile environments, where they could re-establish themselves. (2) Having been weakened by the famine, potential internal migrants were more vulnerable to the tactics being employed by the Dergue. Small allocations of grain provided by the government's Relief and Rehabilitation Committee proved enticing. (3) Substantial quantities of international humanitarian aid were available. These resources were re-allocated by the government so as to benefit the relocation process.

The systemic effects of villagization were profound. Two cases indicate this clearly. In October 1985, the Ethiopian army entered the town of Korem, where approximately 600 Tigrayans—then receiving relief—were rounded up. An already fragile environment was fractured. This had a ripple effect, and eventually nearly 10,000 others (including hospital patients) were dispersed (U.S. Committee for Refugees 1986: 44). A few months earlier, some 60,000 people from highland regions were forcibly relocated to the Gambella region, bordering Sudan. The resettlement villages were located on lands claimed by the Anuak people. The increasing flow of Sudanese Nuer over the past century, exacerbated by recent refugees from the Sudanese civil war, already was creating hardships for the locals. With the highlanders arrival, Anuak effectively became a minority in their own land (Human Rights Watch 2005), a situation that had still later perverse ramifications as noted later in this chapter.

Aid Agencies, Rebels, and Cross-Border Operations

The oppressive tactics of the Mengistu regime led to the emergence of extensive rebel operations. While some could be traced to the era of Haile Selassie, others emerged in direct response to policies of the Dergue. While some operations were focused on countering internal problems, others were focused on cross-border operations. Like aid agencies, certain rebels were concerned with helping refugees, especially those going to Sudan. Innovative programs were developed where agencies and rebel groups worked together, outside governmental channels. They thereby tackled the interactive problems of political disruption and famine.

Cross-border relief operations between Sudan and Ethiopia became quite successful in the mid-1980s. As described by Cuny (1999: 145–46), a consortium of agencies with offices in Sudan and Europe recognized the need to use local logistics and local operatives (i.e., rebels) to effect rapid relief and staunch refugee outflows. Planning in concert but behind the scenes, so as not to alert Ethiopian authorities, the overall mission was to deliver food to people in their villages. Internal and external displacements would therefore be reduced. All transportation and deliveries of supplies were handled by agencies such as Relief Society of Tigray (REST) that had rebel ties. By 1988, the operation was handling approximately 5,000 metric tons of supplies per month; some 400,000 people eventually were assisted on an emergency basis. Cash assistance to families with vulnerable children and internal purchases also were used. Given the severity of the 1984–1985 famine, fewer Ethiopians fled their homeland than might otherwise have been expected. Far fewer were negatively impacted during the less-severe 1987 famine. People I interviewed in the Tigrayan villages of Mai Misham and Beleho made this same point.

Internal purchases were integral to the innovations accomplished in Tigray. Again as reported by Cuny (1999: 147–48), in theory the purchase and distribution of locally available food reserves can provide a viable alternative to the import of foodstuffs. Cereals, pulses, and livestock usually are targeted. In addition to being less costly than imports, such purchases can serve to stabilize local socio-economic structures and village markets. REST's 1984 identification of 25,000 metric tons of grain in western Tigray, which usually would have been sold to Eritrean merchants or held in reserve, triggered the process. After some donor hesitancy (which saw the available tonnage dwindle), churches in Europe provided the first block of capital, $200,000. Hard currency was sent to Sudan, drawn from the bank in cash, then exchanged into *birr* (the Ethiopian currency) at the border. As successes were realized, other donors got on board. Food reached needy people months earlier than it would have if imports had been the principle sources.

THE MELES ZENAWI REGIME

One hot afternoon in 1994 I visited a large cave cut by water into a cliff in a ridge of reddish hills in central Tigray, not far from the Tekezze River. A band of monkeys frolicked nearby. Sitting inside the cave were a dozen children. They told me they were revisiting an important place. As the civil war was drawing to a close four years earlier, the Dergue's MIG jets had repeatedly strafed their town. Refuge always was sought in this and other caves; few therefore had been killed. Tsegaye Hailu told me of an earlier time when he had visited another cave hidden in the Tigrayan highlands. There he had met a guerrilla leader who would later become president of Ethiopia. Meles Zenawi, from the northern town of Adwa, was at that time leading the Tigrayan People's Liberation Front (TPLF) in its battle against the regime of Mengistu Haile-Mariam.

The TPLF was able to build much of its successful grassroots movement on three unofficial but widely discussed platforms: (1) land reform, (2) local community empowerment, and (3) disdain for the Mengistu regime. That it had supported REST in its program of internal assistance provided further validation. From an incipient movement begun in 1975, through the armed insurgency of 1984–1985, through the rhetoric of both socialism and capitalism, through ongoing battles in the northern and central regions, through the substantive assistance of needy and displaced people, the TPLF had laid the groundwork for its eventual overthrow of Mengistu and installment of its own regime. As I traveled through the countryside in 1994, I would occasionally be introduced to a "hero or heroine of the people"—a member of the victorious TPLF.

Figure 3.1. The Tigrayan children pictured here had used this cave as shelter at the height of Ethiopia's civil war. Government jets regularly strafed this area, near the town of Abi Adi, attempting to root out TPLF militia. Future Ethiopian president Meles Zenawi (then a TPLF leader) had used a cave like this as temporary headquarters while planning counterattacks.

Upon the overthrow of Mengistu in 1991, the Transitional Government of Ethiopia came to power. Meles Zenawi assumed the presidency shortly thereafter. An eighty-seven seat Council of Representatives was instituted. The parties sharing the government were numerous. The largest were built upon structures established by revolutionary groups under the umbrella of the Ethiopian People's Revolutionary Democratic Front (EPRDF): the Tigray

People's Liberation Front, the Ethiopian People's Democratic Movement, the Oromo People's Democratic Organization, and the Ethiopian Democratic Officers' Revolutionary Movement. Smaller parties sprang from organizations such as the Ethiopian Democratic Coalition, with regional representatives from groups such as the Afar, Burji, Wolayta, and Somali (Munro-Hay 2002: 37).

The transitional structure was replaced by a federated one following the elections of August/September, 1995. The Federal Democratic Republic of Ethiopia was created. The country then, along ethnic lines, was divided into nine regions or states, one southern "nationalities zone," and a zone for the capitol of Addis Ababa. Meles became prime minister. A bicameral parliament was established. The idea was that each region would actively participate, with no single region dominating—an ancient cause of resentment.

When the Meles regime came to power, many of those who had been forcibly displaced and resettled under the Mengistu regime chose to return to their original homes. For example, in the Gojam region, over 60 percent returned. However, some returnees did meet with problems (including violence) as they attempted to reintegrate with host populations. Italy, previously a thorn in the side of Ethiopia, was among the nations to provide substantive assistance (Gebre 2003). Other programs of assistance and reconstruction were instituted by the central government; human services improved measurably. Useful political debates ensued as the new constitution gained traction.

Yet in recent years the Meles Zenawi regime has been accused of becoming increasingly autocratic, and of disproportionately favoring Tigrayan people. Land values have risen precipitously in Addis Ababa during the past five years. My colleagues report that members of the bureaucratic elite have taken advantage of inside connections and tax advantages to secure significant parcels for themselves. Lewis (2003: 443) states: "Politicized Amhara are bitterly opposed to the new [Tigrayan] rulers . . . both because of the loss of their leadership position in the state and because the new rulers have reorganized the Ethiopian state along ethnic lines. This decentralization of language, education, and regional administration denies the superiority of the 'Ethiopian way,' which, in reality, means the Amhara way."

The opposition has announced plans that would liberalize certain sectors of the economy, improve the interethnic balance of power, and enhance international relations. One of my colleagues believes their ties to academe, while intellectually stimulating, may have caused them to lose touch with on-the-ground realities. Furthermore, opposition protests over the results of the May 2005 parliamentary elections provoked rioting. Through the remainder of the year indicators of instability became more obvious. A crackdown by security forces in November 2005 resulted in nearly fifty deaths, a situation indirectly

Figure 3.2. Men and women have equal say in many of the council meetings run under Ethiopia's *baito* system. Here representatives in the village of Mai Misham discuss postwar rehabilitation of the community water system.

exacerbated by renewed tensions and troop buildups along the Ethiopian-Eritrean border (earlier border tensions are discussed below).

Ethnic Politics

Ethiopia is an amalgam of many cultures and ethnic groups. At various times within the past century Amharic and Tigrayan heritages have been used as unifying themes. Most of the nationalists trace their history to the ancient empire of Axum, which flourished in what is now the province of Tigray from the first through sixth centuries A.D. A meta-narrative of "Greater Ethiopia" has been developed that binds legendary and actual figures with legendary and actual events. It stretches from Menelik I through Haile Selassie, as noted earlier. As Donald Levine (cited in Sorenson 1993: 40–41) stresses, the *Kebra Negast* assured the Tigrayans and their Amhara successors of their superiority. It implicitly presented imperial expansion as a kind of "manifest destiny." Yet this narrative currently is not serving the nation well. Meles Zenawi has had to confront this fact, as he also has had to confront the fact that the "tie that binds" Amhara and Tigrayan peoples in a sweeping historical narrative is a "festering wound" in contemporary political affairs. Stated differently, historicity has been replaced by animosity, unity by division.

Dissident nationalism is the name given to the liberation movements that have swept regions of Ethiopia over the past century. In one sense most have been anti-Amhara in nature; in another sense most have been libertarian in nature. Those of the Eritrean People's Liberation Front (EPLF), the Tigrayan People's Liberation Front (TPLF), and the Oromo Liberation Front (OLF) have been the most prominent. More populous than any of Ethiopia's other ethnic groups, the Oromo have not held a central place in governmental affairs. They reside in the south. Oromo sometimes refer to the Amhara and Tigrayan people of the north by the ancient terms, Abyssinians or Habash, to distinguish them from other Ethiopians (Lewis 2003). While on the one hand interacting boldly and often negatively with Somali still further south themselves, the Oromo resent the long-standing northern hegemony. One indigenous author states: "Using the fear of famine, poverty, Oromo and Islam, the Meles regime has made these former [TPLF] freedom fighters state terrorists to assassinate or murder, intimidate and control Oromos and others, and loot their economic resources" (Jaleta 2002: 39).

Institutional instability and patronage politics have characterized the Somali region. Leaders loyal to Somalia's Siyaad Barre regime occupied positions of power in this southern Ethiopian region as recently as 2004. Removed and replaced by persons loyal to the EPRDF, residents of this region feel pressured by a centralized, distant, and ominous bureaucracy. Some central bureaucrats perceive the Somali region to be backward. A neo-patrimonial rule has evolved, which does not bode well for the future (Hagmann 2005).

The complexities of ethnic politics are further illustrated in the case of Ethiopian Jews (some of whom also known as *falasha* or *falash mura*). This small but vibrant population has a long history in the country, but within the last few decades many began immigrating to Israel. Beginning in 1984, Operation Moses and Operation Solomon brought nearly 75,000 out. Other Jews saw them as being "rescued" from Ethiopia, since Israel's Sephardi chief rabbi, Ovadia Yosef, had issued a ruling in 1973 recognizing the *falasha* as Jews who were descendants of the "lost tribe of Dan" (Nussbaum 1998). Policies of the Dergue contributed to their exodus. Despite the difficulties encountered in adapting to life in Israel, others have followed. Fewer than 20,000 remain in Ethiopia.

Other small populations also live in Ethiopia. They play minor roles in national politics and for the most part are marginalized. These are exemplified by the Armenians (Pankhurst 2004: 75). Human Rights Watch (2005) has reported that members of the small population of Anuak people, residing in the southwestern Gambella region, have been raped, tortured, and killed by Ethiopian troops. A massacre led by Ethiopian National Defense Force (ENDF) troops in December 2003 led to the deaths of nearly 500 Anuak. Claiming pursuit of *shifta* (bandits), the ENDF in fact has terrorized a number of communities and subsequently killed as many as 100 additional people. It is possible that the troops had become frustrated by their inability to assist the highlanders who had been resettled there two decades earlier. A governmental commission of inquiry absolved the military of any wrongdoing in the recent deaths.

Ethnic policies persist. They have been transfused and transformed by nationalistic policies. Returning from a visit to his natal home of Bahir Dar in September 2005 Abebe Takele reported to me his frustration with the increasingly restrictive policies of the Meles regime. This constriction is reminiscent of the pendulum-like policy swings that characterized much of the twentieth century, in broad brush best illustrated by relations between Ethiopia and Eritrea (which borders Tigray). As recapitulated by Bernal (2004), Italy had ruled Eritrea from 1886 to 1941. The following year, it passed to the British, who administered it as a trusteeship until 1952. It was then federated to Ethiopia, which subsequently violated provisions of the federation and annexed it. Shortly after the overthrow of the Mengistu regime, and with the nominal blessing of the new Meles regime, an independence referendum was promulgated. Passing by a wide margin, with voting allowed throughout the Eritrean diaspora, Eritrean nationhood was formally attained in 1993. The determination shown by the TPLF during the civil war of the late 1980s had been matched by that of the Eritrean People's Liberation Front (EPLF), which traced its origins to 1971. After independence this group's value to the new nation was reaffirmed.

In May 1998 war broke out between Ethiopia and Eritrea over a desolate yet sought-after border area within Tigray. Ancestral ethnic ties between Tigrayans and Eritreans were overridden by powerful nationalistic sentiments on the part of the latter, these exacerbated by a growing distrust by Eritreans of the Meles regime. In but one bloody example, citizens of Mekelle (Tigray's capitol) reported the carnage wrought by Eritrean jets as they bombed the city. Photos were angrily displayed of school children who had been killed. The border war was not formally resolved until December 2000, after some 70,000 lives had been lost. Millions of dollars were spent by both sides toward what outside observers deemed to be futile military actions. Newly created refugees from Eritrea suffered the same travails as those from Ethiopia. Eritrea continues today as a one-party state with few good words being expressed for its neighbor; as of late 2005 tensions again were rising between the two nations.

The Axum Obelisk

As noted previously, the famous Axum obelisk was returned by Italy to Ethiopia in 2005. Ethiopians I have spoken to, while not in total accord, see this as a symbolic victory for the country as a whole. "Greater Ethiopia" benefits. The Solomonic dynasty is no longer, having ended with Emperor Haile Selassie, and thus other unifying symbols are needed.

Over fifty obelisks were erected in Axum during the empire's run. King Ezana (ruling during the fourth century) was key to the effort. Few remain standing today. Most lie in ruin. Yet the culminating efforts to finalize the return of the grandest of these served as a different, cross-ethnic kind of unifying process for the country. The government, everyday Ethiopian citizens, and those in the diaspora have been praised for their persistence.

By contrast, opposition parties (recently campaigning against forgiving Ethiopia's foreign debt by the G8—Canada, France, Germany, Italy, Japan, United Kingdom, United States, and the Russian Federation), have lamented the money spent to return the monument. They claim the money should have been used to feed the poor instead.

EFFECTIVE ACTION: RE-ESTABLISHING HOMES

While this is not a book about flight and postflight experiences, it is important to make several points about emplacement, that is, about the re-creation of homes by refugees repatriating to Ethiopia and (noted more briefly) the creation of homes by those resettling in the United States. This is because these processes greatly influence the "Greater Ethiopia" of today, the Ethiopia of the diaspora. It is also because these actions have been effected by refugees themselves. They constitute durable solutions.

Several million refugees fled the country during the 1970s and 1980s. The Eritrean–Ethiopian border war of 1998–2000 led to the flight of several thousand more. In addition to those forcibly displaced through the resettlement and villagization programs of the Dergue, thousands more became IDPs in regions ranging from Oromia to Tigray. The United Nations estimates that at its peak, 1980, over 2.5 million Ethiopian refugees were in other countries of transience and asylum; twenty years later the number had been reduced to about 50,000 (UNHCR 2000: 314–15). Hundreds of thousands had not repatriated, but rather, remained in the diaspora as citizens of receiving countries.

All of Ethiopia's proximal neighbors—Eritrea, Djibouti, Somalia, Kenya, and Sudan—have received Ethiopian refugees at various times since 1970. Those traveling to Kenya, with some exceptions, have been received in relatively well-organized and well-funded camps. Those traveling to Sudan merit additional attention here, since so many eventually repatriated to Ethiopia and re-established homes.

Laura Hammond (2004) has written the definitive account of the emplacement of Tigrayan refugees returning to Ethiopia. By way of background, in addition to thousands of others at other times, some 200,000 had arrived at Sudan's border in 1984. Their trek was spurred by Dergue air raids and ground attacks. Lack of administrative clarity, compounded by Dergue reluctance to admit a major political problem, led them to be initially classified as "drought victims" rather than "refugees." Delays ensued in establishing adequate means of aid, in part because the Sudanese government did not want to be drawn into a quagmire and in part because so many refugees had ties to the officially nonrecognized TPLF. Nonetheless, by 1985 the United Nations, working in concert with NGOs and the government of Sudan, was able to institute a camp program for them. While initially only intended to be temporary, camps such as Wad Kowli instead became quasipermanent homes for a majority (a minority were able to return to Tigray almost immediately). Some of those encamped in eastern Sudan stayed for as long as eighteen years.

The camps were highly politicized, whether by contacts with the TPLF, REST, or the Ethiopian Democratic Union. The TPLF had helped many escape Tigray's upheaval in 1984–1985, and refugees still looked to the organization for signs of when best to return. The year 1993 later proved propitious for this.

During their long camp sojourn, these refugees lost access to their original lands. They lost other forms of property outright. Old social networks became attenuated. Original political ties were weakened. Dependency relationships were inadvertently created by aid agencies. Yet new coping strategies were developed, some of which included innovative kinds of entrepreneurial activity. After the overthrow of Mengistu, when the camp long-stayers finally returned, Hammond chose to ask the following important questions (as summarized in my 2005 review of her work): Which experiences of displacement can be "tapped" to facilitate community (re-)development? What are the central processes at work as a new home is created under conditions of uncertainly and resource constraint? In what ways can (or should) the new home re-create the life ways of the old home?

The people studied by Hammond were not resettling near their former residences in the Tigrayan highlands, but far away in the lowlands. They came to the western Ethiopian town of Ada Bai. Homes different from both their originals in Tigray and those in the camps were created in the months that followed. This had little to do with architecture and everything to do with emplacement. It was not "design of structure" but "design of life" that came to matter. For example, the weekly markets (which I also saw exemplified in the Tigrayan town of Edaga Arbi) were nonexistent; there were daily markets. Wage labor played a more important role in the local economy. Long-distance migratory labor was less prevalent. REST initially assisted the returnees, as did some of the local residents.

While in Sudan's camps, refugees had retained a desire to return. Indeed, the persistence of this theme helped them maintain a sense of identity and a semi-cohesive social network. Yet, due to the often chaotic nature of camp life, these Tigrayans learned how to deal with disorder. It is not accurate to say that disorder became the norm, but rather, that returnees learned how to cope with it. For example, the bargaining skills needed to secure scarce credit were honed. Yet its procurement once back in Ethiopia proved erratic. Banks and local associations gradually were able to assist some, but by no means all, who needed it. As new homes in the old homeland were established, it was not a re-creation of what had been, but a creation based on their preflight, flight, and emergent postflight "lived experiences." There were many ups and downs. The returnees did not so much utilize a social organization that had laid dormant while they were away, as utilize pieces of an ongoing social organization that was imperfect but useful. Geography became far less important than "the conceptual and affective space in which community, identity, and political and cultural membership intersect. . . . [Home] is a variable term" (Hammond 2004: 10). An "imagined homeland" may well reside in the mind's eye, just as an "imagined Ethiopia" resides in the collective lore.

Here as elsewhere, people attempted to cope in ways that minimized risk. Insurance policies were nonexistent; seed repositories became a form of insurance. Those Tigrayans returning to Ethiopia truly lived "at the margin" as they gradually re-established means of livelihood and established relationships with new neighbors. They faced dangers ranging from the loss of cattle to raiders, to the loss of loved ones to disease. Yet within a decade viable homes within a viable community had been established by most of them.

During recent decades many refugees have stated that they left Ethiopia owing to impoverishment, in concert with civil war and related violence (Hammond 2004; Hailu et al. 1994; Bulcha 1988). The 40,000 who have resettled in the United States since 1980, usually well educated, have worked so as to be able to leave the refugee label behind and—while striving to attain self-sufficiency—to avoid the stereotype of "burden," which they perceive to be associated with welfare recipients (cf. McSpadden 1993). A leading resettlement assistance agency was formed by Tsehaye Teferra and his Ethiopian colleagues. Their Ethiopian Community Development Council now has offices and affiliates throughout the United States, as exemplified by the African Community Center in Denver. Relying upon a combination of federal and state contracts, as well as private grants and donations, the agency is able to perform a variety of "emplacement functions." Recently these include the initial resettlement of Somali Bantu, one of the newest groups to enter the Unites States as refugees.

Relatively few Ethiopian refugees who have resettled in the United States have chosen to return to Ethiopia permanently. However, many lend substantive support to their homeland through remittances, aid agency outreach, and political activism. Through the diaspora they practice what might be termed "long-distance nationalism." Effective collective action requires a mix of services and service providers, home and abroad (Van Arsdale and Witten, 2006). Those Ethiopians in the United States that I know keep in close contact with their relatives back home. They also remain actively involved in activities that promote cultural awareness, such as the Sister Cities Program.

POSTSCRIPT: FROM VICTIMS TO SURVIVORS

Some of the Ethiopians who have been terrorized and tortured have been assisted by nonprofit agencies such as the Marjorie Kovler Center in Chicago and the Rocky Mountain Survivors Center in Denver. As a co-founder of the latter organization, I believe strongly in the need for treatment services that combine psychological, sociological, health, and human-rights elements into a single, cohesive framework (Van Arsdale and Kennedy 1999). Clinical distinctions must be made between those who have been tortured (i.e., intentionally traumatized and made to suffer), and those who have experienced war trauma (i.e., unintended traumatization from human rights violations and organized violence). Humane professional assistance can enable victims of either type to become survivors.

Innovative and indeed unique in U.S. history was the enactment by congress of the Torture Victims Relief Act of 1998. Refugee advocates played primary roles in the passage of this legislation, known as Public Law 105–320. Not only were funds appropriated to assist with treatment centers in the United States, but (building upon the Foreign Assistance Act of 1961) funds were appropriated to assist centers and programs overseas as well. Both concept and funding were reaffirmed through passage of the Torture Victims Relief Reauthorization Act of 1999. Adding significance is the fact that the work of both the Special Rapporteur on Torture and the Committee Against Torture (which serves to enforce the Convention, noted earlier) were strongly cross-referenced in the legislation.

As torture is addressed, the issue of what might be called "deep justice" must be considered (cf. Langewiesche 2005; Shepherd 2002). It is discussed in more detail in chapter 8. One component of deep justice is non-malevolence. As interpreted here, this suggests that those accused of the gravest of human-rights abuses must be given the most thoughtful, careful, and well-organized opportunities to defend themselves in courts of law and/or in front of international tribunals without fear of retribution. The perpetrators' own often rushed efforts to eliminate enemies, torture those who would become refugees, and skirt systems designed to protect the citizenry must be matched point by point with slow, deliberate, well-conceived proceedings designed to give them every opportunity to prove their innocence, while also providing every opportunity for prosecutors to bring forth detailed information about the alleged abuses. Torturers who come forward also must be afforded therapeutically beneficial mental health care.

Ethiopians within the diaspora continue to assist their brethren back home in significant ways. Their assistance in the return of the Axum obelisk exemplifies this. As a state party to the 1951 UN Convention Relating to the Status of Refugees, to the 1967 Protocol, and as a member of the UNHCR's Executive Committee, various governments of Ethiopia have demonstrated a nominal commitment to assist refugees in the broader context of the world system. This needs to be actualized still further.

REFERENCES

Applebaum, Anne. *Gulag: A History*. New York: Doubleday, 2003.

Bernal, Victoria. "Eritrea Goes Global: Reflections on Nationalism in a Transnational Era." *Cultural Anthropology* 19, no. 1 (February 2004): 3–25.

Browman, David L. Review of *The Archaeology of Drylands: Living at the Margin*, edited by Graeme Barker and David Gilbertson. *American Anthropologist* 105, no. 1 (March 2003): 179–80.

Bulcha, Mekuria. *Flight and Integration: Causes of Mass Exodus from Ethiopia and Problems of Integration in the Sudan*. Uppsala: Scandinavian Institute of African Studies, 1988.

Clay, Jason W., and Bonnie K. Holcomb. *Politics and the Ethiopian Famine, 1984–85.* Cambridge, Mass.: Cultural Survival, 1986.

Cuny, Frederick C. (with Richard B. Hill). *Famine, Conflict and Response: A Basic Guide.* West Hartford, Conn.: Kumarian, 1999.

Dejene, Alemneh. *Environment, Famine, and Politics in Ethiopia: A View from the Village.* Boulder, Colo.: Lynne Rienner, 1990.

French, Kristine L., researcher. "Africa: A Storied Landscape." *National Geographic* 208, no. 3 (September 2005): map supplement.

Gebre, Yntiso. "Resettlement and the Unnoticed Losers: Impoverishment Disasters among the Gumz in Ethiopia." *Human Organization* 62, no. 1 (Spring 2003): 50–61.

Hagmann, Tobias. "Beyond Clannishness and Colonialism: Understanding Political Disorder in Ethiopia's Somali Region, 1991–2004." *Journal of Modern African Studies* 43, no. 4 (December 2005): 509–36.

Hailu, Tsegaye, Tsegay Wolde-Georgis, and Peter W. Van Arsdale. "Resource Depletion, Famine and Refugees in Tigray." In *African Refugees: Development Aid and Repatriation*, edited by Howard Adelman and John Sorenson. Boulder, Colo.: Westview, 1994.

Hammond, Laura C. *This Place Will Become Home: Refugee Repatriation to Ethiopia.* Ithaca, N.Y.: Cornell University Press, 2004.

Human Rights Watch. "Targeting the Anuak: Human Rights Violations and Crimes Against Humanity in Ethiopia's Gambella Region." *HRW On-Line Report* 17, no. 3A (March 2005): 1–67. www.hrw.org/reports/2005/ethiopia0305 (accessed September 22, 2005).

Ishay, Micheline R. *The History of Human Rights: From Ancient Times to the Globalization Era.* Berkeley: University of California Press, 2004.

Jaleta, Assefa. "Oromo Nationalism and Ethiopian Ethnocratic Politics." *Horn of Africa* 20 (2002): 11–58.

Judt, Tony. "The New World Order." *New York Review of Books* 52, no. 12 (July 14, 2005): 14–18.

Kreisberg-Voss, Debra, Dennis Kennedy, Peter Van Arsdale, and Karl Ferguson. "Clinical Considerations Concerning Refugees in the Denver Region." *Torture* 8, no. 3 (Fall 1998): 90–97.

Langewiesche, William. "The Accuser." *Atlantic* 295, no. 2 (March 2005): 54–81.

Lewis, Herbert J. Review of *Ghosts and Shadows: Construction of Identity and Community in an African Diaspora*, by Atsuko Matsuoka and John Sorenson. *American Anthropologist* 105, no 2 (June 2003): 443–44.

Limbach, Ian. "Special Report: The Axum Obelisk Returns, but Some Still Grumble." *Archaeology* 58, no. 4 (July/August 2005). www.archaeology.org/0507/etc/special-report.html (accessed August 30, 2005).

McCann, James C. *People of the Plow: An Agricultural History of Ethiopia, 1800–1990.* Madison: University of Wisconsin Press, 1995.

———. "A Great Agrarian Cycle? Productivity in Highland Ethiopia 1900–1987." *Journal of Interdisciplinary History* 20, no. 3 (Winter 1990): 389–416.

McSpadden, Lucia Ann. "Resettlement for Status Quo or Status Mobility: Ethiopian and Eritrean Refugees in the Western United States." In *Refugee Empowerment and*

Organizational Change: A Systems Perspective, edited by Peter W. Van Arsdale. Arlington, Va.: American Anthropological Association, 1993.

Munro-Hay, Stuart. *Ethiopia, the Unknown Land: A Cultural and Historical Guide*. London: I. B. Tauris, 2002.

Nagengast, Carole, and Carlos G. Vélez-Ibáñez. "Introduction: The Scholar as Activist." In *Human Rights: The Scholar as Activist*, edited by Carole Nagengast and Carlos G. Vélez-Ibáñez. Oklahoma City: Society for Applied Anthropology, 2004.

Nordstrom, Carolyn. *Shadows of War: Violence, Power, and International Profiteering in the Twenty-First Century*. Berkeley: University of California Press, 2004.

Nussbaum, Debra. "Israel Ethiopia-Policy Debate: Hardship Cases? 40 Million More?" *Intermountain Jewish News*, July 3, 1998: 5.

Orizio, Riccardo. *Talk of the Devil: Encounters with Seven Dictators*. Translated by Avril Bardoni. New York: Walker, 2003.

Pankhurst, Richard. "Ethiopia as Depicted in Foreign Creative Literature: An Historical Analysis." *Africa Quarterly* 44, no. 3 (November 2004): 57–78.

Shepherd, George W., Jr. *They Are Us: Fifty Years of Human Rights Advocacy*. Philadelphia: Xlibris, 2002.

Sorenson, John. *Imagining Ethiopia: Struggles for History and Identity in the Horn of Africa*. New Brunswick, N.J.: Rutgers University Press, 1993.

Suarez-Orozco, Marcelo M. "Speaking of the Unspeakable: Toward a Psychosocial Understanding of Responses to Terror." *Ethos* 18, no. 3 (September 1990): 353–83.

Takele, Abebe. Interview with staff member, Colorado Mental Health Institute. Ft. Logan, Denver, Colo., October 4, 2005.

Tomaševski, Katarina. "Foreign Policy and Torture." In *An End to Torture: Strategies for Its Eradication*, edited by Bertil Dunér. London: Zed, 1998.

Turnbull, Colin M. *The Mountain People*. New York: Simon and Schuster, 1972.

UNHCR. *The State of the World's Refugees: Fifty Years of Humanitarian Action*. Oxford: Oxford University Press/United Nations High Commissioner for Refugees, 2000.

U.S. Committee for Refugees. "Country Reports: Africa." *World Refugee Survey: 1985 in Review*. New York: American Council for Nationalities Service, 1986.

Van Arsdale, Peter W. Note on *This Place Will Become Home: Refugee Repatriation to Ethiopia*, by Laura C. Hammond. *Human Rights & Human Welfare* 5 (July 2005): 1–2. www.du.edu/gsis/hrhw/booknotes/2005/vanarsdale-2005.htm (accessed September 20, 2005).

Van Arsdale, Peter W., and Dennis F. Kennedy. "Treating Refugee Victims of Torture: Creation of the Rocky Mountain Survivors Center." *Journal of Immigrant Health* 1, no. 3 (Fall 1999): 155–64.

Van Arsdale, Peter W., and M. Wray Witten. "Effective Collective Action: A Consultative Approach to Enhancing Ecologically Responsible Development in Tigray, Ethiopia." *The Applied Anthropologist* 26, no. 1 (Spring 2006): 65–80.

Chapter Four

Bosnia and the Issue of Concentration Camps

All sides were brutal.

A Bosnian Serb whispered these words to me in 1997, about a year and a half after the Bosnian civil war had ended. He had been captured by Bosnian Muslim forces, incarcerated in a makeshift prison near Sarajevo, and beaten on a regular basis. Escaping with his wife as refugees, they had made their way to the United States. Now working as a machinist, he quietly—and without fanfare—wanted to stress that it was not only Serbs and Croats who had mistreated others during the war of 1992–1995.

The purposes of this chapter are threefold. First is description of Bosnia's history, with special attention paid to issues of ethnic identity. The emergent Serb, Croat, and Bosniac/Muslim populations, all of Slavic origin, reflect a complex web of cooperative, competitive, and combative relationships that span over 1,300 years. Second and central is analysis of the concentration and rape camps that were developed during the recent war, most (but not all) under Serbian auspices. Atrocities occurring at the Omarska and Foča camps are featured, reflecting underlying structural violence and manifest in "spectacular violence." The aggressive disruptions of the social order, as fear was instilled and abuse inflicted, were intended to bend the will of one population to that of another. Fearing capture, reprisal, and/or torture, hundreds of thousands of people fled as internally displaced personal (IDPs) and refugees. Those crossing the border sought asylum in countries as near as Croatia and as far as the United States. Third is description of the important roles played by nonprofit organizations and nongovernmental organizations (NGOs). Also covered briefly are the ways in which local residents, like those living in and near the rural town of Vareš, attempt to assist one another despite few resources.

While detailed analysis of the recent civil war is not within the scope of this chapter, the events spanning 1992 to 1995 in Bosnia gripped the world's attention. A region long at Europe's margins gained center stage. As my analysis implies, hatred was not the cause of the strife that swept over the Balkan landscape. Neither were religious differences, in and of themselves. Political turmoil, extreme forms of ethno-nationalism, and socio-economic dysfunction better account for what erupted. Historical events were recalled and often reconstructed as "explanatory" by leaders of various factions. Despite these inaccuracies, the Bosnian bridge—itself of great historic significance and reinterpretation—usefully can serve as a symbol of both tragedy and triumph.

GETTING THE LAY OF THE LAND

Just a few blocks from the spot in Sarajevo where Gavrilo Princip assassinated Archduke Franz Ferdinand on June 28, 1914, an event that is said to have sparked World War I, a small plaque resides. Affixed to the railing of a bridge crossing the Miljacka River, it does not commemorate Ferdinand. Rather, it commemorates the life and death of Suada Dilberović, the first person killed in the more recent and equally deadly civil war (Van Arsdale 2004: 72).

As one walks through Sarajevo, and other Bosnian towns as well, it becomes apparent that bridges play extremely important logistical and symbolic roles. A number of twisting rivers span portions of the Balkans, and those in Bosnia—while not as famous as the Danube to the northeast—have historically both helped and hindered travel. The Drina River delineates most of Bosnia's eastern boundary. What is left of Yugoslavia proper lies immediately to the east. The Sava River frames much of the Bosnia's northern boundary, separating it from Croatia. The Bosna River, initially draining from the hills near Sarajevo, runs northward and meets the Sava at the border. Perhaps most important symbolically is the Neretva River, which does not form a national boundary but drains much of Herzegovina. Running southwest to the Adriatic Sea, it passes through the town of Mostar.

Bosnia is a mountainous country. The Dinaric Alps run in semicontiguous chains roughly from northwest to southeast. They rest on a geologic foundation of Kapela karst. The intermountain valleys afford moderately fertile farmland, although it is scattered and not nearly as productive as the vast plains of Hungary. The tracks of key roadways date to medieval times. The twists and turns reinforce the notion of slow travel and relatively limited long-distance commerce in comparison with other European nations.

Mostar lies in a somewhat drier portion of the country. As Herzegovina's premier town, it has featured in virtually every aspect of regional affairs: economic development, transportation, military logistics, politics (and political intrigue), and cultural affairs. Even ten years after the civil war, as one walks down the main boulevard, the devastation inflicted by Croatian and Muslim combatants still is striking. The skeletons of stone buildings, some four and five stories in height, remain unclaimed and unrestored. Rockets penetrated virtually every edifice. Bullet holes mark virtually every doorway and windowsill.

On a hot July afternoon not long after the war had ended, an elderly Muslim man invited me into his home just off this boulevard. His apartment was located on a side street directly overlooking what had been the frontline in Mostar. Once my colleague Patrick Welage and I had greeted his wife, daughter, and granddaughter, he said that he wanted to show me something important. "You'll have to come to the bedroom. This is sensitive." Leaving the others to chat in the small living room, we entered the bedroom, where he pushed open the windows. From the third floor we were able to look down on, and across, the main boulevard. There were few cars, even fewer pedestrians. "See that building across there? That's where the Croat soldiers were stationed. See this clothes cabinet in here? That's where the rocket grenade hit." He carefully opened his desk drawer and pulled out an artifact of war: The heel of a small rocket, fins intact, which had penetrated his window and cabinet. "I was a few feet away. We're lucky it didn't explode, aren't we?"

His granddaughter and other family members had already left, becoming refugees, before this 1993 attack had taken place. They had resettled in the United States. They were excited to learn that the famous, all-stone Mostar bridge—destroyed by a rocket during the civil war—had been reconstructed and formally dedicated during 2004. The Bosnian Croats living on one side of the bridge could symbolically be reunited with the Bosnian Muslims living on the other side. I thought about this simple truism as I sat on the banks of the Neretva River, gazing at this amazing structure, the day after the dedication ceremony.

IDENTITY UNDER FIRE

To many, the most positive elements of Bosnian identity are symbolized by stone bridges. One ethnic group bridges with another. One village bridges with another. One farmer bridges with another. While the issue of Bosnian concentration camps also must be framed by an understanding of Bosnian identity, such notions of bridging are shattered. Identity in Bosnia is multifaceted, representing a roller coaster ride through the centuries. Throughout its recorded history, a span of over one thousand years, the country has been both exerting its identity and having it suppressed by neighboring polities. Leaders have been both extolling the virtues of the citizenry and suppressing their opportunities. Peasants (and to some extent urbanites) have been both supported in their quests for freer expression and persecuted to the point of extermination.

It is thought that Slavic peoples first migrated to what 1,300 years later came to be called Yugoslavia during the sixth and seventh centuries A.D. They were descended from Iranian peoples. They encountered, and mingled with, peoples of Illyrian descent. While most of today's Bosnian Serbs, Bosnian Croats, and Bosnian Muslims certainly can (and should) trace their origins to these early Slavic migrants, it is important to note that debates have been ongoing for centuries as to their "true cultural and racial roots." Some claimed that their true ancestors were the Goths, who invaded this area of the Balkans in the third century A.D. Others claimed that the invading Avars, who arrived in sixth century A.D., deserved a genetic claim. Even hereditary ties to the Vlachs have been claimed by some (Malcolm 1996: 5ff).

The Ottoman Turk invasion, in concert with Turkish empire building, came to dominate the process of identity formation and identity reaction. The year 1463 can be used to mark the beginning of the incursion. Bosnia was under the thumb of the Ottoman Turks for some five centuries. Yet, as has been noted by a number of authors (e.g., Glenny 1999; Andrić 1977; Malcolm 1996), Turkish rule was by no means all-oppressive. A primary interest in administrative authority and enhancement of the tax base did not mean that more "traditional" (i.e., Christian) religious beliefs would be stamped out, nor, that more "traditional" (i.e., Slavic) ethnic ties would be suppressed. For those who chose to convert—or were forcibly converted—to Islam, long-standing Slavic cultural foundations were largely retained. Then and now, Bosnian Muslims primarily have seen themselves as *bošnjak* ("Bosniac"), not Turkish or Ottoman. As Glenny (1999: 78) notes, the term *bošnjak* had become firmly embedded in the local vocabulary by the mid-nineteenth century.

Civic movements and social activism were exemplified by Bosnian Muslims. The Muslims of Mostar were often at the forefront of these efforts. In the late nineteenth and early twentieth centuries the growth of Muslim activism, not only in Herzegovina but throughout much of the rest of the country, can be traced to Mula Mustafa Džabić and other like-minded religious leaders (Malcolm 1996: 147). Yet the movement had secular roots as well. By no means was it based upon a litany of *fatwa* or other proclamations. Youth groups were but one example of the pragmatic, community-based organizations that attempted to promote the notion of *bošnjak* and *mlada bosna* ("young Bosnia").

By 1908 Bosnia had moved from the status of an occupied Ottoman territory to a nation fully annexed by the Austro-Hungarian Empire (Malcolm 1996: 150). Serbs in Serbia saw this as yet another affront to their aspirations, to their desires not only for what at various times has been termed "Greater Serbia," but also to territorial expansion *qua* consolidation bridging lands from the Dinaric Alps to the Adriatic Coast. That Archduke Ferdinand was assassinated in Sarajevo on the anniversary of the Battle of Kosovo, the most important mythic holiday in the Serbian calendar, only served to reinforce these interethnic tensions.

During the period between world wars, Bosnia became part of "the first Yugoslavia." After World War II, it became part of "the second Yugoslavia." Sarajevo's hosting of the 1984 Winter Olympics drew favorable attention to Bosnia's beauty and aspirations for increased tourism. Its withdrawal from this second Yugoslavia on April 5, 1992, was the main precipitant to the civil war. As images of the war came to pepper viewers of CNN and other networks on a daily basis, "Bosnia" became a household word in the West.

In post–civil war Bosnia it is estimated that about 40 percent of the country's 3.5 million people are Serb, 38 percent Muslim (Bosniac), and 22 percent Croat. It also is estimated that as many as 1 million additional persons—representing all these ethnic groups—fled as refugees and/or remain internally displaced. Over 200,000 likely had been killed by the time the Dayton Peace Accords were signed on November 21, 1995. The role played by the United States was instrumental in negotiating this agreement (Holbrooke 1998), even if earlier American efforts had been spotty and disjointed.

What has transpired in Bosnia over recent centuries can be understood in ways that do not overly emphasize the religious affiliations of the ethnic groups involved. That most Serbs are Orthodox Christians, most Croats are Catholics, and most Bosniacs are Muslims necessitates both sensitivity to religious values and recognition that religion does not cause human rights abuse. A Serb may blame a Croat, noting the latter's Catholic ties, as Cohen (1998) stresses. Yet this does not yield substantive insights into the strains the two may be experiencing within their neighborhood.

Despite being buffeted by Ottoman, Serbian, Croatian, Hungarian, Austro-Hungarian, and Germanic forces for much of the past millennium, the externally recreated post–civil war para-state of Bosnia retains a definable and well-known identity in the twenty-first century. Today, as has been the case for nearly 1,400 years, the so-called Southern Slavs comprise almost all of the country's population. That Croats, Serbs, and Muslims all are Slavic peoples, is a claim that ironically came to be reinforced in the twisted work of Biljana

Plavsić, the recent Bosnian Serb president whose science saw Bosnian Muslims as degenerate and corrupted versions of the purer, non-Islamic Slavic people.

A HISTORY OF CAMPS

Camplike prisons can be traced to the Ottoman era. For example, the local ruler Omer Paša often placed ordinary Bosnian citizens in such settings. By the mid-1800s his temporary military headquarters in the town of Travnik had, in effect, become "one enormous prison" (Glenny 1999: 80). While it was said that he wanted to assist the Christian population, his mercurial policies offered little of substance to either Muslims or Christians. People representing various ethnic and religious groups were severely mistreated during these incarcerations.

The first thirty-five years of the twentieth century saw numerous aggressive campaigns against various peoples of the Balkans. Some of the campaigns were led by Balkan forces. Yet networks of concentration camps were not present. Evolving transnational fascist influences in mid-twentieth century Europe led to the establishment of true concentration camps throughout the region. From Romania to Yugoslavia, from Wallachia to Krajina, camps with the still-ominous names of Sremska Mitrovica and Jasenovac were created. Fascist Ustaše forces, in alignment with German Nazi forces, were responsible for many of the worst atrocities. The Ustaše was renown for its brutality. Croatian by nationality, the Ustaše followed Nazi patterns in brutalizing, intimidating, and killing their enemies. The Germans set the agenda in most of this region during World War II. Sarajevo, for all practical purposes, was under joint Ustaše-*Wehrmacht* control (Glenny 1999: 498). Some believe that the very term "ethnic cleansing" has its etymological and experiential roots in this era, in this part of the Balkans.

As mentioned above, concentration camps were established throughout the region. Jasenovac was the most notorious; a majority of Croatia's gypsy population is thought to have perished there. As Glenny (1999: 501) notes, what happened in the nearby village of Gradina was even more gruesome. It served as the Jasenovac slaughterhouse, with "hammers . . . used to beat victims to death in night-long orgies of mass murder." Other camps were almost as cruel in their treatment—and use—of prisoners. For example, hundreds of typhus-infected internees from the Stara Gradiška camp were forcibly transported to another camp near Djakovo so as to spread the infection. At various times and in various ways, Serbs, Muslims, Jews, and gypsies all were targeted. The resentment toward Croatian brutality was extreme, and still is recalled with great emotion today. (Some see Serbian paramilitary Chetnik activities of the 1992–1995 period as ongoing retribution for past Croatian transgressions.)

Ironically foreshadowing the 1995 slaughter of Muslim men near the eastern Bosnian town of Srebrenica, where women and children were spared by Serb forces, combined Croat-German forces gunned down some 10,000 Jewish men near Belgrade during the first part of World War II. Regional *Wehrmacht* officials refused to execute the women and children on the grounds that this would be "dishonorable" (Glenny 1999: 502).

The Omarska Camp

Today there are few visible signs that one of the world's most ominous post–World War II concentration camps once existed in the hills east of Prijedor. A mid-sized industrial town, Prijedor is located in the extreme northwestern portion of the country, within Republika Srpska. Martin Bell, a veteran of the Bosnian civil war, described Prijedor as "the hometown of ethnic cleansing" (1996: 58). As my University of Denver colleague, Todd Waller, learned at about that same time, a number of Serb-instigated atrocities occurred here.

According to ABC News, early one May morning in 1992, residents of Prijedor looked out their windows in shock. One said, through an interpreter: "A long line of Muslim people were passing under my kitchen window. They were being pushed along by Serbian soldiers. It reminded me of a bad dream. The soldiers were bearded and dirty. They were using guns and machine guns to force old men, women and children down the street. It was a horrible sight." Shortly thereafter, during the single day of May 30, it is estimated that more than 1,000 Muslims and Croats were killed by Serbs in this city. Also at about this time, in a scene eerily reminiscent of World War II, it was reported by Muslims and Croats in the area that they had seen members of their communities packed into railway and cattle cars. "They saw people's faces and hands reaching out from within the slats of the cattle cars. They weren't given water. They weren't given food. There was (sic) no toilets."

Roy Gutman of *Newsday* provided the above quote, and was the first to report on the emerging problem of the Omarska camp. This was on August 2, 1992. Britain's International Television News (ITN) broadcast the first pictures from the camp on August 6 Ed Vulliamy was the first journalist to be admitted to Omarska, that same week. Helsinki Watch's human rights investigators arrived at about the same time. As reported by Danner (1997: 55), Vulliamy and his colleagues saw men whose "bones of their elbows and wrists protrude like pieces of jagged stone from the pencil-thin stalks to which their arms have been reduced."

In Omarska as in Auschwitz the masters created these walking corpses from healthy men by employing simple methods: withhold all but the barest nourishment, forcing the prisoners' bodies to waste away; impose upon them a ceaseless terror by subjecting them to unremitting physical cruelty; immerse them in degradation and death and decay, destroying all hope and obliterating the will to live. 'We won't waste our bullets on them,' [said] a guard (p. 55).

As information began to leak out of Omarska, aided by the fearless reporting of newsmen like Gutman and Vulliamy, it became clear that a concentration camp—in every sense of the word—was fully operative. Following the lead of researchers at the U.S. Holocaust Memorial Museum (2000), the term "extermination camp" also could aptly be applied. Muslims and Croats from Prijedor and elsewhere in northern Bosnia were being forcibly transported by rail and bus, incarcerated in the harshest of conditions, tortured, raped, and executed. A large shed had been converted into a kind of "human hen coop," in which hundreds—and possibly thousands—of men (and some women) were jammed. One prisoner told Vulliamy that lying down was impossible owing to the incredibly tight conditions. He said he counted about 700 packed immediately around him: "when they went insane, shuddering and screaming, they were taken out and shot" (Danner 1997: 55).

A Bosnian Muslim journalist got a very different view of Omarska. Rezak Hukanović was taken there from his home in Prijedor as a prisoner, and after his release months later, wrote the gripping book *The Tenth Circle of Hell*. He witnessed firsthand that extermination was frequent. Virtually every prisoner was severely abused. One man had his genitals and part of his buttocks cut off; he died almost immediately. So many were brutally killed during the months that Hukanović was in the camp that he referred to the Serb guards as "killing machines" (1996: 109). Bosnian Croats were not exempted from the guards' wrath, as many also were tortured and murdered. He recounts one man, tortured and then run through with a sword, who was singled out because his mother was thought to have been associated with the Ustaše a half century earlier.

Hukanović also sheds light on the issue of identity. He believes that some Serbs were whipped to a frenzy by what he terms their "pipe dream of a state" (1996: 102). The fiery Yugoslavian leader Slobodan Milosević (whose first name roughly—and ironically—translates to "freedom") was calling for a massive Serbian resurgence. His proclamations propelled much of the violence as he exacerbated the Bosnian civil war. For the guards at Omarska, the perception of reunifying a discordant place like Bosnia within a larger Serb-dominated state was tantamount to reclaiming the homeland lost six centuries earlier to the Turks on the plains of Kosovo. The efforts of the International Red Cross, in concert with the United Nations and other organizations, led to the release of several hundred of the Omarska prisoners while the war still was relatively young. Hukanović was among them. Analyses, although initially timid, of the situation in Bosnia by members of President George Bush's administration led to consideration of the possibility that true genocide was occurring. Responding to international pressure, the camp was closed shortly thereafter. It is likely that a large number of those released in turn became refugees.

My colleague, psychologist Dennis Kennedy, commented on the unfolding psychiatric horrors of these camps—reflected in the Bosnian refugee clients first entering the Rocky Mountain Survivors Center he and I co-founded— shortly after the war ended (Martin 1996: 8). It was ironic, too, that some of the horrors were promulgated by Bosnian Serb leader Dr. Radovan Karadžić, himself trained as a psychiatrist. When in 1997 I interviewed one of his former colleagues at the hospital in Sarajevo where he once had practiced, she confirmed his idiosyncratic and malevolent disposition. "He mixed politics and psychiatry in the worst way," she said.

The Foča Camp

Located in the extreme southeastern portion of Bosnia, the town of Foča rests near the furthest extreme of any Bosnian town—measured "as the crow flies"—from the town of Prijedor in the northwest. Like Prijedor, Foča lies within Republika Srpska. The country of Bosnia spans some 250 kilometers southeast to northwest, and while diverse terrains and ecosystems separate the two, little separates them in terms of the atrocities committed in each. In a real sense, human–rights abuses of the civil war period were defined most clearly by what happened in the Prijedor and Foča areas.

Located directly south of the strategically more important border town of Višegrad, also on the Drina River, Foča nonetheless occupies a viable position geopolitically. It has long been a way station for goods and peoples flowing among Bosnia, Montenegro, and Macedonia. Jewish traders were among those dominating the route during the Ottoman Era. Slaves captured in this area during the medieval era were shipped to cities in what are now northern Italy, southern France, and northern Spain (Malcolm 1996: 25). Early in World War II it also became a way station for interethnic atrocity, a seeming precursor to what unfolded half a century later at the same location. In reprisal for severe Ustaše attacks against them, Bosnian Serbs organized themselves into Chetnik units and set upon the Muslims and Croats of Foča. As reported by Glenny (1999: 494–95), himself quoting the testimony of Derviš Bačića of December 1941:

> After they brought us [to the Foča railway bridge], they began the slaughter. They killed like this. One Chetnik fell to his knees, holding a huge knife in his hand. Every victim [mostly Muslims] had to lie down under the knife and if he refused to do so, he was hit with the butt of a gun until he collapsed on the ground. Another Chetnik would then drag him until he was in position under the knife. After each killing, they would search the victim and take anything of even the slightest value. They would then disembowel the body and throw it into the river. . . . But just before I was due to die, my Chetnik guard turned away and I was able to escape [to the Drina River].

Thus, while it would be accurate to say that Bosnia—in the context of the greater Balkans—has a legacy of violence, widespread killing, and political disruption, it would be inaccurate to say that this is due to some kind of inherent genetic flaw or cultural dysfunction. Similarly, while it would be accurate to state that interethnic tensions have contributed to geopolitical instability, it would be inaccurate to state that these are rooted in the Balkans. That Ustaše fascists were able to exert inordinate pressure on the region during World War II has much more to do with their well-oiled political machinery and ties to the German Nazi movement's interests in resource exploitation than to any historically entrenched hatred of Bosnians. As with the Nazi policy, Jews, gypsies, and homosexuals were targeted as well.

During the Bosnian civil war, rape came to be used by Serb military and paramilitary forces (and to a much more limited extent by non-Serbs) as a tool of war. Roy Gutman of *Newsday* again was among the first to systematically document this abuse (1992, 1993). Interviewing Muslim IDPs in Bosnia and Muslim refugees in Turkey, he uncovered stark accounts of the truly brutal tactics being used. Near the towns of Caparde, Brcko, and elsewhere, rape was being used on a regular basis shortly after the war began. But what occurred in Foča was still more horrific, if measured by the scale of the atrocities.

Located within Republika Srpska, and thus relatively remote from external review and intervention, Serbs developed a quasi-formal set of rape camps in and near Foča. A systematized plan was set in motion. Muslim men would be rounded up in neighboring villages and taken for questioning. Women were ordered to stay in their homes, lest their loved ones be killed. After an interval ranging from a few days to a few months, armed men (perhaps police reserves, militiamen, or paramilitary Chetniks) would come to the neighborhoods where the women remained and begin a series of "interrogations."

Those interviewed by Gutman said these procedures quickly turned into rape at gunpoint.

The town's Partizan Sports Center became central to what further evolved into systematized gang rapes. Increasing numbers of women were transported there. Some were raped in the middle of the center's hall, in full view of others. As Gutman (1993) reported:

'Only the women over fifty were safe,' [one informant said]. ' They always took the ten youngest from the sports hall. . . .' There seemed to be a special regime for the prettiest and the smartest women, who were singled out for the most frequent raping. . . . ' When they take you away, they may kill you. So if you are raped, you feel lucky. At least you're alive,' [another informant said].

Yet many did not survive this abuse. Others simply disappeared. Nearby homes, apartments, and barracks also were used to carry out the rapes. Processions of women and Serb soldier "escorts" could be seen passing in and out of the town center on a regular basis. One woman reported that she and several other women were raped by twenty-nine men. Another woman estimated that she had been raped about 150 times during a two-month period. Still others reported becoming pregnant and later aborting their fetuses.

Compounding the problem is the shame associated with having been raped. Among more conservative Muslims, the notion that a woman has been violated is tantamount to suggesting she has become "disposable." Some victims will be secreted away, others shunned, still others expelled from their communities. This problem is reported with particular clarity by Gordana Igrić (1999). Based on her work with Kosovo's Albanian population, she learned that the traditions instilled by the fifteenth century Code of Leke Dukajini remain strong. Retention of honor is essential. Men are urged to protect their wives and daughters. A man who fails to exact "blood revenge" should a female member of his family be violated brings shame upon his kin.

Following Nordstrom (2004), why are the kinds of "spectacular violence" reported in this section enacted? Why is such cruelty seen? What possible use could it serve? One straightforward school of thought suggests that the aggressors are seeking to severely disrupt the social order. According to Ruth Seifert (1999), who bases some of her analysis on what has transpired in Bosnia, the outcomes of war have to do with the destruction of culture, the manipulation of symbols, and the altering of perceptions. Abusive tactics, such as concentration camp beatings and the raping of women, speed these results while terrifying the population. Submission is therefore more quickly achieved. Following Elaine Scarry, Seifert (1999: 149) stresses that women are disproportionately targeted and "have a particular place in this logic of destruction."

EFFECTIVE ACTION: THE ROLE OF
NONPROFIT AGENCIES AND NGOS

The symbolism of the bridge in Bosnia reaches a powerful apogee in the work of Michael Sells (1996). His book is titled *The Bridge Betrayed*, and in it he argues that Serbian atrocities, at least in part, can be traced to the notion of a Christian holy war. The defeat of the Serbs by the Ottoman Turks at the Battle of Kosovo in 1389 has been continually reemphasized and reframed through history. Its most important symbol is embodied in the death of Prince Lazar at the hands of the victorious Turks at *Kosovo polje* (the Kosovo battlefield) on June 28 of that year. If Lazar is viewed as a Christ-like figure, as some Serbs suggest, then Muslims come to be viewed as "Christ killers." Slobodan Milosević chose this exact date, six hundred years after the defeat, to deliver his powerful and inflammatory speech to the estimated 1 million Serbs who had gathered at the battlefield.

The Omarska and Foča complexes established by the Serbs during the civil war were not the only concentration camps in Bosnia and the surrounding territory. No exact count is available, but others were exemplified by those at Sušica, Trnopolje, and Manjača (Cohen 1998: 214ff.). Other tragedies were exemplified by the 1995 massacre of nearly 8,000 men and boys near Srebrenica. Yet the abuses that occurred at Omarska and Foča were extreme. They serve to remind us that a legacy of concern must be created by all of us. Using a metaphor based on the writings of Ivo Andrić (1977), as he considered the old bridge on the Drina River, we must "bridge the steep banks and the evil water" that separates people.

The lessons of concentration camps have been learned, relearned, and learned again. Will they ever penetrate our heads? Those excavating the remains of the deceased, both inside and outside former camp walls, offer poignant insights. Among the most useful are those of forensic anthropologist Clea Koff. Having worked in Bosnia, Kosovo, and Rwanda, she believes that the careful excavation of human remains is essential to the conceptual and emotional reintegration of the deceased into his or her family and community. No detail is too small. No bone should be left unexcavated. The empirical approach is essential—yet the humanness of the task appropriately asserts itself. She sometimes looks at a mass gravesite about to be excavated and thinks, "We're coming. We're coming to take you out" (2004: 46). Once, in 1996 while excavating the remains of a Bosnian boy who had been killed during the war, a remarkable image came into her mind:

I "saw" this young guy . . . on the hillside where we had just been digging, and I "felt" the pain of the bullet entering his thigh just above the knee; I could sense his youth and the tragedy of it all and I thought of his family and what they were missing, and I thought of what one of the Women [of Srebrenica] had said—how someone had told her they last saw her son getting on a bus with lots of other men and he was crying—and how that was the last she ever heard about him . . . and I lost an element of self-control. I felt so awful, so full of hurt and emotion, and mixed in with that was a knee-buckling sense of privilege that I was touching the bones of someone whose family was out there and wanted more than anything to have him back, no matter what condition he was in. . . . (2004: 153).

In Sarajevo I interviewed a forensic archaeologist who held much the same perspective. Working for the International Commission for Missing Persons, a transnational humanitarian agency, his ongoing work with human remains near Srebrenica forced him to try to remain objective and detached, yet this was not always possible. The humanness of the bones often leapt out at him, touching his soul. He was only able to remain at his job for a year. Staff turnover is always high. Maybe it is tied to the nightmares that some have; Koff (2004: 52) reported that, while in the field, she would occasionally dream of having dismembered legs in bed with her.

The forensic work in Bosnia will continue long into the future; as of late 2005 some 14,000 people still were listed as missing. Approximately 16,500 bodies had been exhumed from approximately 580 grave sites (Reuters 2005). The ICMP is engaging in an innovative effort to identify the remains already in storage, as well as those still being uncovered, from the several conflicts in the former Yugoslavia. In December 2005 its blood collection teams visited North America for the first time. Twelve states within the United States were targeted. Samples were collected from refugees and other immigrants thought to be related to missing persons. The blood samples are needed for DNA identification. Since DNA is used to trace genetic links among family members, samples are needed from several members of each family network. Since the year 2000, ICMP has collected over 75,000 samples from family members in various locales.

A legacy of concern is exemplified in the work of nongovernmental organizations (NGOs), intergovernmental organizations (IGOs), and private voluntary organizations (PVOs) in Bosnia. Although the total has dwindled since 2000, in the years immediately following the war the number of such organizations registered in the country exceeded 400 (ICVA 1998). By sector, they ranged from those like Mercy Corps working on infrastructural rehabilitation, to the International Rescue Committee working on IDP resettlement, to Catholic Relief Services working on community development, to the American Refugee Committee working on refugee resettlement, to Women to Women (*žene ženama*) working on adult education, to the United

Figure 4.1. The mass slaughter of civilians during the Bosnian civil war usually was accompanied by the burial of remains in unmarked grave sites. Here a forensic anthropologist begins the exhumation of two bodies near the town of Zvornik. (Photo by Ian Sethre)

Methodist Committee on Relief (UMCOR) working on language training for youngsters, to World Vision International working on psycho-social rehabilitation. The latter, among a number of Sarajevo-centered programs, was assisting women and children traumatized by the ominous events portrayed earlier in this chapter. Its psycho-social rehabilitation program utilized nonintrusive therapeutic techniques involving play therapy, community outings, and counseling. As Perin Arkun (2004) has emphasized, World Vision Inter-

Figure 4.2.   Several thousand unidentified bodies are stored in warehouses like this in northeastern Bosnia. Exhumation from mass grave sites by forensic specialists is followed by humane cataloging and storage procedures. Any subsequent identifications of remains are accompanied by their repatriation to family members. (Photo by Ian Sethre)

national works in Bosnia in the context of self-described and sincere "peacebuilding initiatives." The needs of an emergent civil society are taken into account. The University of Denver, through its service learning program which I directed, during the summer months was able to place student interns with each of the above-named organizations—as well as the International Commission for Missing Persons and the UNHCR—between 1996 and 2004.

Networking and systematic cooperation among agencies of this type is essential to long-term success and program sustainability. The Organization for Security and Cooperation in Europe (OSCE) mounted a fairly well-organized initiative intended to bridge the efforts of a number of European-based agencies operating in Bosnia. The International Federation of Red Cross and Red Crescent Societies similarly worked to bridge among NGOs working primarily in Republika Srpska. Yet many smaller and "disconnected" agencies operated in relative isolation. By contrast, Clea Koff worked in Bosnia for the

UN International Criminal Tribunal for the former Yugoslavia, a type of IGO.

Broadly speaking, the mission of humanitarian agencies—referring specifically to NGOs—is to work independent of formal governmental control in the provision of services to needy beneficiaries, in the most effective and efficient manner possible (Cole 1999: 30–31). Diffuse programmatic goals, poor accountability, and erratic funding streams are obvious deterrents to success. Agencies such as the American Refugee Committee that have paid attention to principles of total quality management (TQM) while working in Bosnia have achieved more. Working as a service learning intern for this agency, University of Denver student Keith Cole reported from Sarajevo that TQM ideally is enacted through a rigorous yet flexible organizational structure, one "that creates and allows for participation in the planning and implementation of a continuous quality improvement program by all the staff members of the organization and the beneficiaries who are involved" (Cole 1999: 14). Attention is paid to reflexive or real-time interactions, to subtleties in cross-cultural communication, and to ongoing processes of review, evaluation, and feedback.

The roles of extraordinary individuals within such organizations also must be recognized. Truly dynamic leaders are essential. Refugees International was among the most successful agencies to work in Bosnia during and after the war. Founded by Lionel Rosenblatt, it had—according to Richard Holbrooke (1998: 46)—built a reputation in places like Cambodia and Somalia by "pressuring [and] harassing" governments to do more for their populations of displaced persons. By working with the UNHCR, as well as with other humanitarian agencies and NGOs, Rosenblatt and his organization were able to provoke the creation of a network of service providers that improved service provision while minimizing interagency competition over resources. Like Rosenblatt, the late Fred Cuny also brought passion and persistence to his work in Bosnia. During the war, he almost single-handedly pressured and provoked various service providers and government agencies so that water filtration and natural gas services could be restored in Sarajevo (Weschler 1999: 36). Warren Harrity, a graduate of the University of Denver, worked through a German NGO to almost single-handedly restart and recharge infrastructural development in the small Roma village of Staro Selo, located in eastern Bosnia. As these people (who had fled as refugees) repatriated from Germany and other central and eastern European countries after the war, he took a leadership role in planning and supervising the reconstruction of their homes. From wrangling with building suppliers to wrangling with bureaucrats, he never let up. The people I met there raved about his persistence and determination in the face of all odds.

POSTSCRIPT: AT THE TOP OF THE HILL

During the summer of 2004, my colleagues Fehro Mehinović, Dajana Hudek and I wended our way to a small village located at the top of a hill near the once-prominent mining town of Vareš. Located some forty kilometers north-east of Sarajevo, the settlement of Brezik was known to be the home of a particularly dynamic woman. Over a meal of tea and cheese, Ivanka Malbarić told us of her dreams (which initially had been reported in a local non-profit organizational publication). She wanted to establish a viable volunteer-run woman's organization that could enhance community development within the area. She reasoned that an income-generation project involving chicken farming would be essential. But she needed funds, perhaps $250, to buy the starter chicks necessary. It was hoped that repatriating refugees and new immigrants to Vareš could become involved. No resources had been located. No network of nonprofit nor community-based agencies had expressed substantive interest. No prospects were on the horizon. While the mayor and deputy mayor of Vareš had noted their support, even they had nothing more than a spare office at town hall to offer. The primary mining operation in the town had dwindled from a high of nearly 4,500 employees to the current low of only 70.

While no concentration camps were established in Vareš during the civil war, large numbers of people were imprisoned in the central school building. Some were beaten and otherwise abused. Croat and Bosniac residents predominate in the town, and my interviews with them indicate that it is not interethnic relations but economic upheavals that now cause the primary tensions. While memories are still fresh of battles fought and atrocities committed by both these groups, as well as by Serbs, these are being put aside for the most part. An atmosphere of anticipation pervades the town and neighboring villages.

The people of the Vareš area could benefit from the type of networking being promoted by the Advocacy Institute. As reported by Jennifer Donaldson (2005), the institute was founded in 1985; it works on-site and electronically to build coalitions among individuals and community-service agencies seeking to enhance social justice. Workshops and training programs have been conducted in the United States, Latin America, Africa, Southeast Asia, and Europe. Capturing the spirit of Ivanka Malbarić and other Bosnians we have interviewed, the institute recommends that potentially isolated groups in an area work toward forming a coalition that (1) demonstrates a unified platform, (2) presents a transparent coalition structure, (3) exemplifies open communication, and (4) initiates a campaign with measurable short- and long-term outcomes. In a collaborative environment of this sort, funding then can be more readily secured.

People flee the horrific conditions of war and concentration camps if they are able. Many become refugees, others become IDPs. But most would prefer to remain if abuses diminished and local opportunities arose. Those Bosnians my colleagues and I have interviewed in Denver since 1996—Muslims, Croats, and Serbs—report a variety of experiences that confirm the human rights situation in their "refugee homeland."

> For genocide to happen, you need only killers and victims—and those who stand by and let it happen."
>
> —Peter Jennings, ABC News, March 30, 1994,
> reporting on Bosnia and the town of Prijedor

REFERENCES

ABC News. "While America Watched: The Bosnia Tragedy." Peter Jennings Reporting. March 30, 1994 at www.markdanner.com/interviews (accessed February 10, 2005).

Andrić, Ivo. *The Bridge on the Drina*. Chicago: University of Chicago Press, 1977 [orig. 1945].

Arkun, Perin H. *Bosnia: Civil Society, Sovereignty and Peace*. Unpublished Ph.D. dissertation. Graduate School of International Studies, University of Denver, Colorado, 2004.

Bell, Martin. *In Harm's Way*. London: Penguin, 1996.

Cohen, Roger. *Hearts Grown Brutal: Sagas of Sarajevo*. New York: Random House, 1998.

Cole, B. Keith. *The Myth of Successful Humanitarian Intervention? Development, International NGO Management, Intercultural Communication, Continuous Quality Improvement and Post-Communist Legacies in the Former Yugoslavia: An Attempt at a Synthesis*. Unpublished Master of Arts thesis, Graduate School of International Studies, University of Denver, Colorado, 1999.

Danner, Mark. "America and the Bosnia Genocide." *New York Review of Books* 44, no. 19 (December 4, 1997): 55–65.

Donaldson, Jennifer. "The Power of Coalitions." *The Advocacy Institute Newsletter*, April 2005 at www.advocacy.org (accessed May 14, 2005).

Glenny, Misha. *The Balkans: Nationalism, War, and the Great Powers, 1804–1999*. New York: Penguin Books, 1999.

Gutman, Roy. "A Daily Ritual of Sex Abuse." *Newsday*, April 19, 1993 at www.haverford.edu/relg/sells/rape (accessed May 15, 2005).

———. "Mass Rape: Muslim Recall Serb Attacks." *Newsday*, August 23, 1992 at www.haverford.edu/relg/sells/rape (accessed May 15, 2005).

Holbrooke, Richard. *To End a War*, revised ed. New York: Modern Library, 1998.

Hukanović, Rezak. *The Tenth Circle of Hell: A Memoir of Life in the Death Camps of Bosnia.* New York: Basic Books, 1996 [orig. 1993].

ICVA. *The ICVA Directory of Humanitarian and Development Agencies Operating in Bosnia and Herzegovina.* International Council of Voluntary Agencies, Sarajevo, 1998.

Koff, Clea. *The Bone Woman.* New York: Random House, 2004.

Malcolm, Noel. *Bosnia: A Short History,* revised ed. New York: New York University Press, 1996.

Martin, Claire. "Bosnian Horror is Hard to Comprehend." *Denver Post,* (January 28, 1996): E8–E9.

Nordstrom, Carolyn. *Shadows of War: Violence, Power, and International Profiteering in the Twenty-First Century.* Berkeley: University of California Press, 2004.

Reuters News Service. "Ten Years after the War, 14,000 Bosnians Still Missing," at www.alertnet.org/thenews/newsdesk/index.htm? (accessed December 6, 2005).

Seifert, Ruth. "The Second Front: The Logic of Sexual Violence in Wars." In Manfred B. Steger and Nancy S. Lind, eds., *Violence and Its Alternatives: An Interdisciplinary Reader.* New York: St. Martin's Press, 1999.

Sells, Michael A. *The Bridge Betrayed: Religion and Genocide in Bosnia.* Berkeley: University of California Press, 1996.

U.S. Holocaust Memorial Museum. "Extermination Camps." Unpublished manuscript, Wexner Learning Center, Washington, D.C., 2000.

Van Arsdale, Peter W. "Rehabilitation, Resistance, and Return: Service Learning and the Quest for Civil Society in Bosnia." In Madelyn Iris, ed., *Passages: The Ethnographic Field School and First Fieldwork Experiences.* NAPA Bulletin 22. Berkeley: American Anthropological Association/University of California Press, 2004.

Weschler, Lawrence. "Life and Death of a Hero." *New York Review of Books* 46, no. 19 (December 2, 1999): 33–36.

Chapter Five

El Salvador and the Issue of Disappearance

She saw *coselitos*. It was terrifying.

One of my colleagues was describing her friend's experience to me. To dispose of the bodies of those who had been killed, members of Salvadoran death squads would take them either to the Puerta del Diablo or the Santa Tecla dump. The dump was located near the capital, San Salvador. Regardless of whether it was day or night, the bodies would brazenly be deposited among the piles of trash. In some cases the corpses would be dismembered. A hand or a foot might then be tossed near one of the litter-strewn pathways. A member of a guerrilla organization, a farm labor organizer, or an indigenous village leader would then be coerced to visit the dump. His "guide" might proclaim: "Look there! That's your brother's foot. The same will happen to you if you don't cooperate." In virtually no case was the dismembered hand or foot actually that of the person's loved one. No matter. The fear had been instilled. The terror had been reinforced.

In other instances, those Salvadorans visiting the Santa Tecla dump did so on their own. Rumors circulated that the bodies of "the disappeared" were being disposed of there; perhaps the body could be located and taken to a cemetery for a proper burial. Whether murdered outright or "disappeared," many of the missing were civilians; among these were children. In El Salvador, *coselitos* are the chunks of meat and vegetable that float in a soup. At Santa Tecla, the term *coselitos* became an ominous euphemism for the body parts that "floated" in the dump.

The purpose of this chapter is threefold. First, an overview of El Salvador's history since European colonization is presented. Changes in the environmental landscape owing to socio-political factors are briefly emphasized. As the environment was transformed over a 500-year period, a remarkably homogeneous yet in many respects compelling Latin culture arose. However, unlike other emergent Central American nations, indigenous peoples only played minor roles. Second, the roots of rebellion and origins of the deadly civil war (spanning the years 1980 through 1991) are presented. The war can be tied to the efficient yet oppressive military that had emerged over a 150-year period, to an extraordinarily wealthy elite—epitomized by the oligarchic "Fourteen Families"—who also had come to power, and to the (often clandestine) intervention of the United States. Third, and of particular importance to my discussion of human rights, issues of forcible disappearance are addressed. During the civil war, military and paramilitary campaigns aimed at an array of labor leaders, peasant farm leaders, and guerrilla leaders left thousands dead, thousands more wounded, thousands more missing—including *los desaparecidos* ("the disappeared").

This chapter demonstrates how instability can become institutionalized. It indicates how refugees and internally displaced persons (IDPs) can be created in unprecedented numbers. Within the context of structural violence, it demonstrates how a culture of fear and "spectacular violence" can emerge.

GETTING THE LAY OF THE LAND

One of the smallest countries geographically in the Americas, El Salvador covers a mere 13,000 square miles, yet the landscape is remarkably diverse. Volcanoes (several active) dot the terrain; at one location a national park features them and at another location an ancient caldera over two miles wide is filled by a lake, the shore dotted with small homes and a resort hotel. Mayan outlier settlements had been established in the western portion of the country by 1000 A.D., the archaeological remnants being visited by tourists today. However, despite its semitropical location, the country is now relatively devoid of rain forests and wild animals. Early and intensive exploitation of the land by Spanish settlers resulted in dramatic changes in vegetation. It is estimated that by the late sixteenth century over half the indigenous vegetation had been destroyed or transformed into agricultural land. Today a quarter of the land is devoted to grazing.

Cuzcatlán was the term given to this area of Central America by early Spanish settlers. Their penetrations and predations were both rapid and intense. By the mid-1530s several towns of significance had been established, including San Miguel in the eastern region. The Pipil, a prominent Native American group, were able to mount little resistance and were quickly assimilated, killed, or enslaved. By the seventeenth century few remained. The Spanish colonial period came to feature an increasingly pervasive monocrop economy. Indian labor was gradually replaced by peasant or *mestizo* labor. As the early objectives of "gold, glory and God" came to be muted, colonists' aspirations turned to such products as cacao, indigo, coffee, and sugar cane. These products did relatively well in burgeoning circles of international trade. Small ports were developed on El Salvador's coast, but the export process also created a dependency on monocropping that carried through the twentieth century. Internal markets were weaker than external markets. Regional trade cycles at times worked to the country's great advantage and at times to its great disadvantage. As a result of this monocrop economy, over a 400-year period most of the arable land, and consequently most of the wealth, came to be concentrated in the hands of a relatively small group. A restrictive—and at times oppressive—military elite evolved in concert with the landed elite.

The volcanic soils, coupled with a generally conducive climate, created a favorable situation for agriculture and related business activities. Including farm-bounded arable land, grazing land, and wooded areas, nearly 75 percent of the landscape is now in active use. Of agricultural land, about 31 percent is in basic staples—beans, corn, and rice. About 20 percent is in exported crops such as coffee, sugar cane, and cotton. About 28 percent is in pasture and grazing land. About 18 percent is in forest and about 34 percent in minor crops such as okra (Van Arsdale 1991/92: 46). Intensive and exploitive land use practices have resulted in the highest levels of pesticide poisoning in Central America, and the endangering or extinction of approximately 75 percent of the country's mammal species (McReynolds et al. 2000).

Population growth has been fairly steady over the centuries. Population density (including war-displaced IDPs) reached a high of 600 persons per square mile during recent decades in some areas. The country's pre–civil war population was about 5 million.

The rainy season typically lasts for about six months, from May through October. Precipitation normally ranges from about 60 to 100 inches annually. The eastern region receives somewhat less. Although the country is small, temperature and rainfall variations can be distinguished between the lower coastal plains in the south and the more mountainous midland region further north. Exceptionally dry periods lasting fifteen to twenty days are not unusual, and in the extreme can affect agricultural production.

Crops such as rice, while reliant upon rainfall, also benefit from small-scale, intensive irrigation. Our 1984, USAID-funded assessment of smallholder irrigation and farming (for which I served as chief-of-party) found that knowledge of effective irrigation practices, both technical and cultural, was widespread. The tertiary (i.e., smallest size) canals used for irrigation and drainage were engineered and made of cement where resources permitted. Alternatively, well-constructed earthen embankments were used, but were subject to rapid seasonal degradation. Few smallholders had access to mechanized equipment. However, haciendas that recently had been "released" to the quasi-communal ownership of former landless laborers under the agrarian reform program did have tractors, trailers, and trucks.

Agricultural and marketing entrepreneurs were gaining increased footholds in the rural areas during the period of our fieldwork. This activity has continued, in fits and starts. Several of the most innovative businessmen were promoting the expanded production of okra. Smallholders were growing it as a secondary crop, while realizing substantial increments in their farm incomes. Most of the okra was being shipped to U.S. Gulf Coast states. In one bit of wry humor, one processing plant's manager—while confirming that profits were up—told me: "We have good markets in the U.S. for okra. We Salvadorans certainly wouldn't eat that slimy stuff!"

Agrarian Reform

Entrée to an understanding of Salvadoran politics, human displacement, and forcible disappearance is best gained by examining the country's agrarian system. In fact, the distant antecedents to the agrarian reform program begun in 1980 are traceable to the 1880s.

It was during that decade that a revised (and landowner friendly) constitution was promulgated, portents of the modern agro-economic era began surfacing, and labor leaders reiterated key claims on behalf of peasant farmers. By the mid-1880s it was clear that the state was committed to a liberal policy regarding land rights, a policy driven by "coffee economics." Communal properties were abolished by decree and indigenous people were evicted from ancestral lands. Within twenty years most of the best coffee-producing land was held by members of the oligarchic Fourteen Families ("Catorce Familias"). The rural police and mounted police were established as instruments of control (Montgomery 1995: 30). The conditions for structural violence were becoming entrenched.

By the 1980s this oligarchic system was under full socio-political attack. What transpired was built upon a politicized agrarian understanding and a neoliberal policy. The expropriation of land under agrarian reform began in phased fashion and (as noted below) was promoted by U.S. officials. Beginning in the 1980s, holders of properties larger than 500 hectares were involved in the first phase. Nearly 300 were impacted during the program's first few years. Subsequent phases—which proceeded in fits and starts—emphasized voluntary involvement and eventually engaged the proprietors of smaller estates. Coffee *fincas* were particularly difficult to engage. By the time of our 1984 reconnaissance study, a number of mid-sized estates were being managed by their former laborers, some of whom had been landless. The subsequent and more sweeping "land to the tiller" phase was envisioned as a true grassroots initiative (Applied Social Science and Health Consultants 1984). The United States pushed firmly for all phases of the reform, not merely to aid farmers, but to diminish the power of the left while not alienating the right. This intemperate balancing act was to continue for the remainder of the decade.

President José Napoleón Duarte, who held office from 1984 until 1988, was supportive of agrarian reform and the nationalization of the banks. As previous head of one of two opposing juntas, he received the support of the United States early on, this enhanced by the fact that his Christian Democrat Party had shed its more liberal members. His minister of agriculture worked with our team in 1984 as we conducted an assessment of smallholder irrigation systems and their production potential. Wrangling between Duarte and Roberto D'Abuisson, the increasingly powerful man behind the ARENA party (whose infamous exploits are noted later in this chapter), proved both constructive and destructive to the nation's overall integrity during the early 1980s. The agrarian reform program was buffeted about; there was little continuity.

Complementing agrarian reform, a mixed economy (as practiced at the household level) has held out the most promise for rural residents during the past few decades. Smallholders raising a diverse array of crops, in concert with family members supplementing aggregate household income by working, for example, in tourist crafts or light industry, can assure a modicum of economic stability for residents of Central American nations (Thomas-Slayter 2003: 191–93). While a large number of Salvadoran households do precisely this, others have been thwarted due to the historical hold of monocropping and the politicization of reform initiatives. A push toward the development of cooperatives has met with mixed results. That Decrees Number 153 and 154, which actually established the agrarian reform program, were passed in March 1980, just as the civil war was heating up, sent a mixed message to many smallholders.

Institutionalized Instability and Cultural Persistence

Instability can exist as part and parcel of a societal system without destroying it. This is the case in El Salvador. Oppositional processes not only have torn at the fabric of society over the past 125 years, they have shaped the society that has emerged. These processes work to reduce the variety of meaning associated with seemingly disparate activities, such as smallholder farming and large-scale agribusiness, and faction-producing events, such as civil war. The

Figure 5.1. Farmers working cornfields near San Miguel discuss the embattled countryside with the author's research team at the height of the civil war. One commented that rebel forces at that moment were regrouping from government assaults in the hills pictured in the background.

result is something I earlier termed institutionalized instability (Van Arsdale 1991/1992).

Cultural persistence is found in spite of—or because of—these seemingly destructive forces. This persistence in El Salvador is characterized by a society that has become ethnically homogenized over the span of several centuries. Driven by a monocrop economy, a dominant oligarchy, and an oppressive military/paramilitary force, a culture of fear arose that serves—even after the civil war—to perpetuate and paradoxically preserve this culture. That the interests of El Salvador and the United States became inextricably intertwined during the twentieth century further bolsters this interpretation. The Catholic Church has been both vilified and commended for the role it has played in El Salvador. While contributing mightily to the process of societal homogenization (and thus cultural persistence), it also contributed mightily to the process of advocacy for the oppressed. As liberation theology took hold, the Catholic Church came to define poverty and oppression as a sin. The plight of the urban and rural poor assumed much more prominence. Church leaders increasingly became outspoken—and increasingly became targets of assassination. Members of Protestant denominations also contributed to this awareness. Even street corner preachers were discussing the issues, as I saw in San Salvador in 1984.

THE ROOTS OF REBELLION

In counterresponse to what recently had been occurring in Mexico, the Federal Republic of Central America was created by representatives of five former colonies in 1823. Its first president was a Salvadoran. El Salvador became an independent nation in 1839, when the Federal Republic crumbled. By this time much of El Salvador's prime land was already concentrated in the hands of a few hundred hacienda owners, indigo being a primary crop. Economic inequities, exacerbated by class and ethnic hostilities, eventually led to the so-called First Peasant Revolt of 1832. Brutally suppressed, with the leader's head displayed on a pike, it would be another hundred years until peasants again arose so forcibly against "the system" (Montgomery 1995: 28–29).

By the end of the nineteenth century coffee had replaced indigo as the monocrop of choice, and members of the Fourteen Families had established control of the prime coffee-growing areas, as noted previously. (My sources indicate that some forty families actually came to comprise the oligarchy.) Labor organizers and laborers themselves played important roles in the country during the early twentieth century. Chief among these was Augustín Farabundo Martí. A one-time colleague of Augusto César Sandino (whose name later became world renowned as the Sandinistas of Nicaragua came to power), Martí's travels and travails in various countries had convinced him that socialist labor practices offered promise for the peasantry. Having been at odds with the conservative president, Romero Bosque, for several years, Martí helped stir an uprising still revered today in tales both factual and legendary. Coffee warehouses were attacked, government offices were sacked, and several towns were overrun (Stephen 1995: 809). Before it ended in January 1932, as many as 30,000 people had been killed, including Martí (by firing squad). The labor movement had been dealt an extreme blow. Unions were banned. Popular political participation was squelched, exacerbated by the military overthrown of Bosque's elected successor (Arturo Araujo) by General Maximiliano Martínez. Yet the massacre (known as the *matanza*) served as a springboard for the revolutionary events that followed during the next sixty years.

El Salvador's seeming penchant for political dramatics take an extreme, albeit brief, turn in the late 1930s. After the *matanza*, General Martínez instituted a de facto dictatorship. He and his colleagues became fascinated with fascism and the emergent regimes in Italy and Germany. As Montgomery (1995: 40) notes, this seemingly aberrant fascination "grew out of the failure of [earlier] liberal governments . . . the communist involvement in the 1932 insurrection, and the resulting belief that what the country needed was a more elitist government." Popular support for fascism was not forthcoming, however, and the Black Shirts who marched in San Salvador in 1940 were greeted with jeers. By late 1940 Martinez did an about-face, condemning totalitarianism and stating his support for the Allies. It was about this time that the United States pledged to provide 35,000 rifles, thus becoming El Salvador's primary arms supplier (Montgomery 1995: 40).

Constants throughout this period were the uses of repressive tactics to maintain order. When persuasion failed, military and paramilitary personnel exerted tremendous pressure on citizens in both urban and rural areas. Extrajudicial detentions, torture, and murders were not uncommon. Other constants were the efforts of rural leaders, complemented by some who were urban-based, to further solidify the grassroots support for the revolutionary movement and the activism of what eventually became the FMLN.

The formation of the Farabundo Martí Front for National Liberation (FMLN being the Spanish acronym) was one of the most significant developments in El Salvador. Itself growing from an array of revolutionary organizations that coalesced (along with the Salvadoran Communist Party) in 1980, after numerous iterations and decades of prodigious grassroots effort, the FMLN came to represent what analysts called "the guerrilla movement," "the rebel movement," or "the insurrection." While the movement by no means should be viewed retrospectively as homogeneous, its leaders were able to promulgate the two general terms "liberation" and "pluralism" as ideological watchwords. Several left-leaning political factions and self-identified groups ("Christians," "women activists," "communists") came under its rapidly expanding umbrella.

Parallel to this development was the increased role of the United States in countering the perceived communist threat. By the 1960s the United States had taken a more active role in the country's politics. The communist threat was seen to be increasing and counterinsurgency training was deemed essential. By the 1970s, and in partial response to outside pressures, effective community-based rebel groups had been established throughout much of the countryside. Consejos Farabundistas (rebel-related administrative councils) were well established in such departments as Usulután, Cuscatlán, and Chalatenango (Montgomery 1995: 118–22).

Oligarchs and "Garch-ettes"

In August 1984 a reporter who regularly covered El Salvador for *Newsday* told me how a group of war correspondents recently had been stopped and ordered out of their vehicles in the department of Chalatenango. With guns at their heads, unidentified combatants had ordered them to lie on the ground. After stern rebukes all were freed. Later, perhaps exhibiting nervous tension, they laughed at their brush with disaster and commented that the oligarchs and their girlfriends—loosely referred to as "garch-ettes"—might have played a role. It was claimed that the most prominent of the lot drove expensive "garch-mobiles."

The oligarchy has variously controlled and manipulated El Salvador for much of its postindependence life. The power that had been more openly in its hands prior to the 1932 rebellion passed to the military after that. However, the oligarches remained integral to overall control of the political process and to shaping El Salvador's economic future.

The maintenance of a favored position for the oligarchy, as well as that of the armed forces, therefore was central to much of what transpired between 1932 and 1992. An oligarch interviewed by Montgomery (1995: 37) put it bluntly: "We have traditionally bought the military's guns [since 1932] and have paid them to pull the trigger." A colleague of mine, herself with strained ties to the oligarchy and the Fourteen Families, told of their abuses of power and ominous record of political attacks. Her father, a prominent newspaper publisher, was twice injured in attacks. In the last, he was stabbed, run over by a car, and left for dead. His recovery was deemed amazing.

THE CIVIL WAR

The civil war in El Salvador lasted from 1980 until 1992. Government forces seen as representing the establishment battled guerrilla forces seen as representing everyday citizens. In this sense, some analysts portrayed it as a "battle of right against left." From its inception through 1983 it was primarily a violent war, characterized by state and parastate terrorism. From 1984 through 1991 it primarily was characterized by counterinsurgencies and guerrilla activity. In certain senses it was a classic proxy war, waged on behalf of the United States and the Soviet Union. The roles of smaller actors such as Nicaragua and Cuba were touted as significant by the larger actors. In fact, the reverse was true. To understand this is to understand the sharply delineated, bipolar way in which the world was painted by key individuals, none more important than William Casey.

William Casey and the CIA

William Casey joined Ronald Reagan's administration in 1980 as director of the CIA. Casey brought nearly forty years of international experience to the job. Some of it was in covert operations, dating to World War II, other in activities as diverse as securities regulation and tax shelter analysis. He was a hard-core anti-communist and it was said that in his capacity as director he became singularly focused on "helping rid the world of the communist threat." It also was said that his ardent Catholic beliefs were used to engage what he saw as a moral mission (Coll 2004: 90–93).

While this book takes an implicit systems-analytic approach throughout, on occasion dominant personalities must be featured. No one did more to shape what was transpiring on the ground in any of the six nations featured in this volume than Casey for El Salvador. This was, on the one hand, because of the dangers perceived in neighboring Nicaragua with the emergent Contra-Sandinista problem, on the other hand, because of the force of Casey's personality. In the early 1980s, senior U.S. officials—Casey prominent among them—perceived two key regional fronts where the United States and its proxies needed to confront the USSR and its proxies: Central America (as exemplified by El Salvador) and Southwest Asia (as exemplified by Afghanistan). During 1984, when I was in El Salvador, an infusion of additional covert military aid from the United States was correlated with an even greater infusion of aid into Afghanistan, via Pakistan (cf. Coll 2004: 101–2). Salvadoran army proxies battled guerrillas in El Salvador while *mujahedin* proxies battled Soviet troops in Afghanistan. To Casey, and apparently to Reagan, it was a relatively black-and-white, either-or struggle in both instances.

Casey's funneling of some covert action funds through the Catholic Church to anti-communists in Central America (Coll 2004: 92) not only created rifts within the church membership, but exacerbated the dangers many pro-guerrilla Catholics faced. Shortly before his assassination, Archbishop Oscar Romero was one of several Catholic leaders who had spoken out against the improper use of outside funds.

By the mid-1980s, the civil war had reached its apex. Well over 50,000 people already had been "disappeared" or killed outright; in total, some 80,000 eventually would perish by war's end. With the terms "guerrilla warfare" and "terrorism" coming to be equated or confused at a global level during this time, as Bruce Hoffman noted (Coll 2004: 145), it is not surprising that the CIA came to place still greater emphasis on the clandestine roles of operatives. Indeed, the CIA's Counterterrorism Center was born in February 1986. At that same time, through a classified document signed by President Reagan (National Security Decision Directive 207), covert action against terrorist groups throughout the world was formally authorized (Coll 2004: 140). By this time, according to Steve Coll (2004: 92), "Casey had established himself as perhaps the most influential man in the Reagan administration after the president." Although his covert Nicaraguan operations were souring, his covert Afghan initiatives were strengthening. Operations in El Salvador, in turn, increasingly came to revolve around party politics.

Death Squads

One of the ways the government fought against the insurgency was through so-called death squads. These squads apparently first made their appearance in El Salvador in the 1960s. Early on, the most notorious was known as Mano Blanca (White Hand). They quickly evolved to operate as informal, flexible and highly organized paramilitary organizations. During the first two years of the war their violent activity steered the course of much of what transpired among combatants overall.

Paradoxically, the U.S. government seemed to be supporting two opposing stances simultaneously. While on one hand supporting a more conservative course of action (which could be interpreted as implicit support for the death squads), on the other hand it began pressuring the Salvadoran government about the squads and their abusive conduct as early as 1983. Vice President George Bush visited the country in December of that year with a list of military and civilian officials thought to be involved. His ultimatum: Fire or cashier them within one month, or risk suspension of U.S. military aid. Although no officer subsequently was suspended, and aid eventually was increased, the political pressure apparently did contribute to a significant reduction in murders and disappearances during 1984 (Montgomery 1995: 177–78).

Death squad activity was supported by erstwhile politician Roberto D'Abuisson, among many others. His name repeatedly was mentioned in interviews I conducted. It is likely that death-squad funding was derived in part from the group of Miami-based Salvadoran exiles known informally as "Millionaires' Murder, Inc.," to which he was linked (Montgomery 1995: 132–33). It also is likely that D'Abuisson was involved in the 1981 assassination of Archbishop Romero. For a period of time he maintained headquarters, not coincidentally, near the infamous Santa Tecla dump (mentioned at the outset of this chapter).

The role of the Nationalist Republican Alliance (ARENA) party was key. It had come into existence in the late 1970s and was dominated by representatives of the extreme right. One of its prime objectives was to defend the interests of the Salvadoran economic elite. Martín-Baró and Cardenal (1995: 1–2) stress that, as it gained strength, it aggravated political tensions and complicated relations with the United States. Its early candidate for president was none other than Roberto D'Abuisson. ARENA's opponents in the Christian Democratic Party, recognized as more liberal reformers, continued to battle both the FMLN and ARENA, while internal corruption diminished their own effectiveness.

El Mozote Massacre

In February 1981, the U.S. Department of State proffered a "white paper" that claimed to provide definitive evidence that clandestine military support was being given El Salvador's "Marxist-Leninist guerrillas" by the Soviet Union, Cuba, and their allies. The overthrow of the established government of El Salvador was seemingly at hand, a situation deemed intolerable by the administration of Ronald Reagan (Montgomery 1995: 150).

Although the U.S. public and many members of Congress were expressing increased displeasure with the support their government was providing El Salvador, the support—as measured in terms of governmental proclamations, military aid, and economic assistance—continued unabated. Tommie Sue Montgomery believes that the regular six-month certifications from the United States that the Salvadoran government was meeting conditions designed to prevent human rights violations represented little more than a game between Washington and San Salvador. "Human rights abuses that were increasing every month declined in the weeks immediately preceding certification. Documented massacres by the army became events to cover up. . . ." (1995: 150).

Further funds were released by the U.S. government to assist the Salvadoran military in the following months. Approximately fifty additional military advisors and instructors had been sent by the late spring of 1981. They worked to train rapid-response battalions, or what one advisor later described to me as "the good-guy guerrillas." Some worked as government contractors in the same clandestine, freewheeling fashion more recently described for operatives in Afghanistan (Pelton 2004). Some in fact mutated into "death squads." Both overt and covert operations were expanded, with the support of the ARENA party. Counterresponses by the FMLN (which also included their kidnappings and brutal treatment of members of the Salvadoran elite) led to increased numbers of army offensives, especially in the eastern portions of the country near the city of San Miguel. As I was taking a tour of the San Miguel area three years later, farmers pointed to the low-lying hills where FMLN militias were regrouping. One told me: "Government and guerrilla warfare is of little concern to me. I support neither side. I only hope that I am not injured and can put food on the table to feed my family."

The army had made relatively little headway in its campaign against the FMLN by the autumn of 1981. A more aggressive series of attacks in rural areas seemed inevitable, and indeed, was predicted by a number of analysts (Danner 1993). The El Mozote Massacre took place on December 11 of that year, and came to symbolize army abuse at its most extreme. After capturing a large group of men, women, and children, by one estimate approximately 480 of these prisoners and other villagers were slaughtered (Montgomery 1995: 152). By another estimate, relayed second-hand, approximately 800 were killed (Finkbeiner 2005). Eerily similar to the grizzly reports from Darfur (see chapter 6), stories are told of babies being speared on the bayonets of marauding soldiers (Finkbeiner 2005). The U.S.-trained Atlacatl Battalion "swept through the region and initiated a bloodbath" (Gill 1999: 874). Despite warnings that an insurgence was imminent, most villagers remained at home. The alternatives—refugee camps in Honduras, poorly guarded IDP camps within the country, or life in the slums of San Salvador—were not attractive. Many residents also had placed what proved to be unwarranted faith in a well-known store owner. After receiving a false tip from the army, he assured his neighbors that nothing would happen if they remained in El Mozote. Leigh Binford found that none of the local people who had joined the guerrilla movement or backed the government died in the attack; many likely (and ironically) were evangelical Protestants "who bore none of the red taint associated with Catholic Christian base communities" (Gill 1999: 875).

The El Mozote Massacre serves as but one example of how the army and death squads, often working in concert, brutalized ordinary people (Gill 1999). It also served to galvanize anthropologists concerned with human rights issues in Central America (Schirmer 2000). Other killings also came to symbolize the escalating violence, some striking close to home. Several persons were gunned down at a café in San Salvador's Zona Rosa during the autumn of 1984. They had been sitting at the same table I had occupied a few weeks earlier.

Camps for IDPs

At the height of the civil war, there were an estimated 300,000 Salvadorans who were internally displaced. Most were living in the 117 camps that had been established in the central and western portions of the country (Van Arsdale 1991/1992: 45).

El Transito, Numero Tres (The Transit Place, Number Three) was one such camp. Despite the bland name, the camp was a relatively vibrant place. Scattered across about ten acres of fenced land, it was located on the outskirts of San Salvador. Approximately 600 people lived there at the time of our 1984 visit.

Most of the camp's residents had come from the central and western areas of the country. Intense battles between government and guerrilla forces were causing disruptions in farm activities; crops could not be planted, tended, or harvested on schedule. Other jobs also were being disrupted. Some residents had lost loved ones to the fighting. Others had deserted their homes when family members had been captured or "had been disappeared." Several said they had been terrorized. Some of those we visited had managed to move their entire nuclear families intact, but most noted how fragmented their families had become. The camp's extended families frequently were comprised of both IDPs and refugees.

The camp was structured so that IDPs could move about relatively freely. Using ID cards any resident aged sixteen or older could pass in and out on a daily basis. As one camp leader told me, "The fence is primarily to keep unwanted visitors out, not to keep us residents in." Rows of tin-roofed shacks constituted the living quarters. Each was approximately twelve feet by twelve feet square. Obviously impinging on the residents' human rights was the lack of privacy. Nothing but a curtain separated one small interior room from the next. Nothing but a thin wooden wall separated one dwelling from the next. Yet those managing the camp made sure that there was plenty of open space and that trash was removed on a regular basis. Outhouses were well maintained. The school consisted of four open rooms, neatly kept. The soccer field was filled with children. The United Nations, in concert with local mission organizations, provided the bulk of the camp's funding.

Camp leaders explained to our research team that the single greatest impediment, apart from separation from family members, was the lack of viable employment. "We are not unemployed, but underemployed. That is worse, because we cannot use our skills." Many of the men earned a modest income by chopping and hauling firewood in the metropolitan San Salvador area.

I met a boy about seventeen years old, with a broad smile on his face. "I've lived here for about five years," he said in Spanish. "I came from the north with my family; the fighting drove us off our farm. There isn't much work here, but the government gives us food and medical care." When I asked him about restrictions on the IDP camp's residents, he said: "There is a fence around the camp, but we're free to come and go. We have identification cards. I often go into San Salvador by bus to visit a friend who has an apartment

Figure 5.2. The three leaders of a Salvadoran IDP camp (right) joke with members of their families during a visit by the author's research team. Residents of the camp had made substantial strides in improving its potable water and sanitation systems. A Catholic charity most recently had assisted them.

there." I then asked what he would do if he were offered a job in the capital, a mere six miles distant. "It would have to be a good job. Things are very uncertain in our country. At least there is some security in this camp."

By most accounts, the situation for displaced persons within El Salvador's numerous camps was better than it was for those struggling to survive as refugees in camps in neighboring countries. Mexico, Honduras, and Nicaragua sponsored UNHCR-assisted camps where conditions could, at times, be stifling. At one Honduran camp, Salvadoran refugees were restricted to closed compounds guarded by military personnel. Some report having been locked away for more than a decade, "their newborn children for years [seeing] nothing but tents and the barbed wire perimeter as they grew up" (UNHCR 2004: 27).

SPECTACULAR VIOLENCE AND "THE DISAPPEARED"

The spectacular violence that enveloped El Salvador from 1980 to 1992 was part and parcel of the structural violence that had been evolving for decades. Militaristic, oligarchic, and large-scale agrarian enterprises had come to shape the country in ways more complicated than—but also including—what might simply be termed "oppression" (Schirmer 2000). Outside interests, especially those of the United States, had become extremely powerful. During the course of the civil war U.S. economic aid exceeded $3 billion and military aid $1 billion (Tomaševski 1998: 193). Smallholders finally began to gain more ground with the agrarian reform begun in 1980, but this program initially also co-evolved with the civil war, compromising its effectiveness. (It is estimated that midway through the war, a mere 2.9 percent of the landowners still held 46 percent of the nation's arable land [Montgomery 1995: 23]). As Martín-Baró and Cardenal (1995: 3) emphasize, unjust and oppressive socio-political structures had come to underpin Salvadoran society. In the words of Paul Farmer (2003), a "war on the poor" indeed had been initiated. The most obvious forms of structural violence came to be manifested in spectacular violence.

A culture of fear began emerging in El Salvador during the nineteenth century. It came to both manifest and symbolize the ever-evolving structural violence. By the time the civil war began a century later, both sides had learned well how to capitalize on it. For example, both the government and the FMLN forced innocent civilians to serve as informants, threatening family members if their targets did not cooperate. Concomitantly, a "sub-culture of weapons" also had begun emerging during the nineteenth century. This must be understood not only in terms of the use of weapons, but in terms of their pervasiveness. By the time of the civil war they were ubiquitous; it seemed that an armed man could be found on every street corner and at the entrance to every major building. Once I opened a door in my hotel to rush to a meeting and almost ran over a man standing armed with an AK-47. Today weapons still are widespread and poorly regulated.

The Disappeared

The war in El Salvador, like that in neighboring Guatemala, is infamously remembered for the many people "who were disappeared," that is, made to disappear. *Los desaparecidos*, as they are known in Spanish, are "the disappeared." The total number is unknown. The very nature of the act means that no tallies are kept. Based upon a review of several sources, plus discussions with colleagues, my conservative estimate is that at least 7,000 people—men, women, children—were disappeared during the civil war.

Death squads and government security forces such as the Treasury Police were primarily responsible for *los desaparecidos*. (Some kidnappings, usually of the elite, also were engaged by the FMLN.) As recounted by several of my colleagues and former students, people usually would be spirited away from their homes at night. However, it was not unusual for them to be kidnapped during the day, as they returned from work or from the market. From the perspective of the death squads, it was preferable to kidnap the person in his or her neighborhood, in front of family and friends; this exacerbated the feelings of fear and loss among those closest to the victim. While adults usually were the targets of kidnappings and forcible disappearance, children sometimes were ensnared. If perpetrators thought that a child had witnessed a murder they had committed, with the possibility of testifying or providing incriminating evidence, that child would be targeted. Some children were recruited as lookouts or couriers by members of the armed forces or the FMLN. If discovered, they also were at risk of forcible disappearance.

Co-Madres is a nongovernmental organization that was founded to provide support for mothers and other relatives of victims of politically motivated murders or disappearances. The full name of the organization is "Comité de Madres y Familiares de Presos Politicos, Desaparecidos y Asesinados de El Salvador" (Committee of Mothers and Relatives of the Political Prisoners, Disappeared, and Assassinated of El Salvador). It was founded in 1977 by impoverished women—many of whom were nonliterate—at the suggestion of Archbishop Romero (himself later assassinated). As the civil war heated up, the organization became increasingly critical of government policy, especially with regards to human rights violations. During the 1980s its office was frequently raided and its members were harassed. It endured a bombing at its headquarters on October 31, 1989, just hours before a similar bomb killed nine and injured forty at the office of FENASTRAS (a trade union and workers' rights organization). The UN Truth Commission later found that Salvadoran security forces had had several members of Co-Madres under constant surveillance. The commission also later found that the bomb attacks on the offices of both Co-Madres and FENASTRAS had been part of a systematic pattern of attacks. It stated that the government of El Salvador had failed in its duty to guarantee the human rights of the members of these organizations.

Involvement in Co-Madres became a transformative experience for many women. They saw themselves not only as concerned mothers but, increasingly, as human rights and women's rights activists (Stephen 1995). The single most gripping account of the work of Co-Madres is provided by one of its leaders, María Teresa Tula, who was interviewed by Kerry Kennedy for her award-winning book *Speak Truth to Power* (2004). Until 1978 Tula had never been involved in politics. Her husband's involvement in a labor strike, coupled with his murder in 1980, served as one impetus to the increasingly important role she came to play. Coevolving was her own impetus to assist others like herself in a two-pronged fashion: To speak out about human rights abuses and to search for those who had been "forcibly disappeared." Over the years she was kept under surveillance, arrested, detained, and—in one horrific instance, while blindfolded—raped by three men who had been interrogating her.

Tula reports that, as their organization became more well known, threats multiplied. After Archbishop Rivera y Damas offered them office space alongside that of the Human Rights Commission, death squad leader Maximiliano Hernandez was reported in a major newspaper as threatening the members of Co-Madres with forcible disappearance or decapitation. Just fifteen days later one of their members indeed was captured by security forces, taken to one of the stations manned by national police, tortured, and raped. She later was dumped by the side of the Santa Ana-San Salvador Highway and—although not initially able to talk because of damage to her mouth—later recovered. As I reflected on this account, I was reminded of the body I had seen by the side of the same highway in August 1984.

Perhaps El Salvador's best-known organization regarding *los desapareci-dos* is Pro-Búsqueda. It was formally founded in 1994 as "Asociación Pro-Búsqueda de Niñas y Niños Desaparecidos" (Pro-Search Association for Disappeared Girls and Boys). It is a nonprofit human-rights group whose mission is threefold: (1) Its investigation and juridical assistance unit is dedicated to the search for children who were disappeared during the war. It presents these cases to national and international courts. (2) Its psychological unit helps in the process of reintegrating traumatized families. It also provides psychological support to children who have been found, as well as to the families whose children still are missing. (3) Its educational unit works to raise awareness about the issue. Pro-Búsqueda's membership primarily consists of relatives of girls and boys who were disappeared, children who have been located, and activists who identify with the cause (Lucas 2005).

The investigation and juridical assistance unit had registered 754 cases as of September 2005. Of these, 301 had been resolved as follows: 172 had had reunions with their families, 90 had been located but not yet reunited with their families, and 39 had been determined to be deceased. The remaining 453 cases remained unresolved. At about this same time, the Inter-American Human Rights Court found the government of El Salvador guilty of human-rights violations in the case of two sisters from Chalatenango. This was the first time any court had condemned the Salvadoran government related to *los desaparecidos*.

Pro-Búsqueda publishes news of searches for and reunions of *los desaparecidos* and family members on its website, www.probusqueda.org.sv. A recent update presented the story of another pair of sisters, Imelda del Carmen Marroquin Ávalos and Heidi Noemí Marroquin Ávalos. Having spent years in the United States, they were reunited with family members on July 2, 2005 (Navarrete 2005). People who left as refugees can trace their loved ones aided by the organization's investigation and juridical assistance unit.

The work of activists in other Latin American nations has continued to benefit the cause of *los desaparecidos* as well. Architect Patricia Indiana Isasa was sixteen years old when she was kidnapped in 1976 in Argentina. Taken by a commando group of the state police, she was initially "disappeared" and then held for over two years without trial or due process. In 1997 she initiated an investigation into her kidnappers' identities; eight perpetrators eventually were located and jailed. As of late 2005 they were awaiting trial in Argentina. Isasa now lectures on issues of human-rights abuse and forcible disappearance throughout the United States and Latin America.

The forensic work of humanistic scientists who have been trained like Clea Koff (2004), whose spadework—both literally and figuratively—is featured in chapter 4, has gone a long way toward bringing closure to the status of *los desaparecidos*. The exhumed remains of a number of individuals have been identified, and (as in neighboring Guatemala) sensitively returned to family members for proper burial. I particularly was impressed by the comments of Clyde Snow, a pioneering forensic anthropologist, who told me several years ago that his work in Central America—aided by indigenous colleagues "who placed people in a cultural context"—was the most meaningful thing he could do with his life.

THE CARTAGENA DECLARATION

Lost in the hubris of multiple proclamations and multiple documents covering refugee human-rights issues is the Cartagena Declaration. With one in nine people in the Central American region having had to abandon their homes and flee during the early 1980s, the strains upon economic and political resources were tremendous. The civil war in El Salvador became both a literal and symbolic flashpoint. UNHCR representative Leonardo Franco was among those seeking to break new ground. The draft declaration he helped craft in 1984 allowed this to happen.

The Cartagena Declaration was innovative for several reasons. Regarding international refugee protection, it expanded the 1951 convention and 1967 protocol with operational definitions to include "refugee persons who have fled their country because their lives, safety or freedom have been threatened by generalized violence, foreign aggression, internal conflicts, massive violation of human rights or other circumstances which have seriously disturbed public order." It reiterated "the importance and meaning of the principle of *non-refoulement* (the nonforcible return of persons to a country where their lives might be endangered), including the prohibition of rejection at the frontier." It firmly expressed "concern at the situation of displaced persons within their own countries." It encouraged countries "which have a large number of refugees, of the possibilities of integrating them into the productive life of the [host] country by allocating to the creation or generation of employment the resources made available by the international community through UNHCR, thus making . . . economic, social and cultural rights [more attainable.]" The document stressed "the voluntary and individual character of repatriation of refugees and the need for it to be carried out under conditions of absolute safety, preferably to the place of residence of the refugee in his country of origin." It also stressed that the "reunification of families constitutes a fundamental principle" (UNHCR 2004: 26). That Latin Americans had played primary roles in the crafting of such an innovative document was important from a prestige standpoint as well, a situation reminiscent of the late 1960s when African representatives had done the same.

Unlike the Geneva Conventions, the Cartagena Declaration was nonbinding. This allowed affected Latin American countries to approve it more quickly and with fewer bureaucratic entanglements. It repeatedly has been endorsed by the Organization of American States. Since most states in Latin America are party to the 1951 UN Refugee Convention or its subsequent Protocol, most apply the declaration's broader definition as a matter of practice. Some have incorporated key elements into their own national legislation (Cutts 2000: 123). The U.S. government was initially apprehensive, fearing that thousands more displaced persons would flood the country owing to the broad definitions contained in the document.

EFFECTIVE ACTION: THE PURSUIT OF HEALING

By the mid-1980s, when the civil war was at its peak, it is estimated that from 10 to 20 percent of El Salvador's entire population had fled the country. One estimate I evaluated placed some half a million Salvadoran refugees in California alone. It is not known how many refugees have returned to their homeland since the peace accords of 1992, but the overall proportion is relatively small. Remittances sent by those abroad to family members that remained continue to serve as a mainstay of the Salvadoran economy.

The November 16, 1989, massacre of six Jesuits by a battalion trained by U.S. forces was a critical event to what became the last phase of the civil war. "This brutal murder appears to have opened the eyes of the architects of U.S. policy to the impossibility of professionalizing the Salvadorean army and of converting it into a pillar of democracy. . . . After November 1989, Washington began to look for a dignified way to disentangle itself from the chaotic situation that it helped create in one of its backyards" (Martín-Baró and Cardenal 1995: 5). The autumn of 1989 also saw the bombings of the Co-Madres and FENAS-TRAS offices noted previously. This same year also saw the ARENA party gain control of the state apparatus, in one sense a victory for more conservative factions and in another sense a victory for reformers, since the role of the Fourteen Families had been reduced and military authority was being transformed.

The "notion of negotiation," intended to move all parties toward peace, had been put forward as early as April 1989, when Alfredo Cristiani was elected president. Like D'Abuisson, he represented the ARENA party. Unlike D'Abuisson, he represented a more moderate, nonviolent platform. He did not carry the ominous baggage of his colleague. Representatives of the new regime and the FMLN began meeting in September.

In summarizing what ultimately transpired (from a longer account by Montgomery 1995: 215–24), it should be stressed that by 1989, the FMLN had begun promulgating a form of democratic socialism. It had abandoned its earlier and outdated Salvadoran version of Marxism-Leninism. While this change aided the emergent peace process, subsequent bombings and counter-offensives derailed it. United Nations shuttle diplomacy helped bring the parties back together a few months later; so did the U.S. congressionally supported decision to condition part of its future military aid on progress in the Jesuit murder investigation. Still more derailments (exacerbated by murders and a major FMLN offensive against the capital) took place, however, and it was not until 1991 that peace finally was assured. ONUSAL (United Nations Observer Mission in El Salvador) proved a helpful broker, among several external parties.

In 1992 the FMLN gained official status as a national political party. It continues in this position today. Several women who had played leading roles as guerrilla fighters have come to play leading roles as party politicians.

The Truth Commission

Cross-nationally, the post–World War II era has witnessed the development of human-rights tribunals, international criminal courts, and special councils dealing with rights issues such as torture and forcibly displaced persons. Intra-nationally, this era also has witnessed the development of councils and commissions dealing with internal abuse and atrocity. The *gacaca* of Rwanda are one example of the former; the various truth and reconciliation commissions are one example of the latter.

The United Nations Commission on the Truth in El Salvador (known colloquially as the Truth Commission) was formed in 1991 and released its last report in 1993. While there have been about twenty truth commissions established worldwide since the 1970s, that in El Salvador was modeled in certain ways on Latin America's first significant commission of this type, Argentina's National Commission on the Disappeared, which was created in 1983. As Buur (2001) notes, such commissions emphasize five essential features: (1) They exist for a predefined period and cease to exist with the submission of their findings; (2) they focus on past human rights violations; (3) they focus on individual human rights violations; (4) they are vested with some sort of authority by their sponsors, such as the power to search for and seize information; (5) they use scientific methods derived from human rights documentation as they access data, analyze information, and draw conclusions. Buur also emphasizes that such commissions usually serve to promote reconciliation and promote psycho-social healing.

As a UN-brokered and government-sanctioned body, El Salvador's Truth Commission was able to make much more headway than other types of investigative unit could have. As Hayner (1998: 207) emphasizes, its broad mandate was to investigate "serious acts of violence . . . [whose] impact on society urgently demands that the public should know the truth." Evidence was collected on disappearances, torture, political killings, massacres, and politically motivated rape during the civil war. Two of its most important findings were that members of the Atlacatl Battalion had participated in the El Mozote Massacre, and that FMLN commanders had approved a policy of assassinating mayors whom they had perceived to be working against them. The commission concluded that approximately 85 percent of the human-rights violations that had taken place during the civil war were attributable to state military and security forces, such as the Treasury Police.

The impacts of the Truth Commission and other investigative bodies continue to be significant. Most recently, in November 2005, former Salvadoran army colonel, Nicolas Carranza, was found responsible by a federal jury seated in Memphis, Tennessee, for murder and torture during the civil war. The verdict came in a lawsuit brought by five Salvadorans who stated that they had been tortured, or that their family members had been killed, by soldiers under Carranza's command. One former U.S. official testified that Carranza had been the "quarterback" in a campaign of terror. The lawsuit, following guidelines established through the Alien Tort Claims Act, emphasized his failure to stop crimes against humanity in his former role as commander of security forces. The judge ordered Carranza (who lives in Memphis) to pay $2 million in damages.

POSTSCRIPT: STEPS TOWARD STABILITY

The ramifications of the war's disruptions and long-imbedded structural violence are still being felt today. Institutionalized instability still persists. Discussions still harken back to the El Mozote Massacre and the much earlier *matanza*. Gang activity has increased in the major cities. The gang known as Mara Salvatrucha is particularly well organized and widespread; its network extends from Los Angeles (where it originated) back to El Salvador. Refugees who have come as far as Colorado report on the problems these groups are causing. Less experienced members of the Salvadoran police force are said to fear them, as Lance Finkbeiner (2005) told me. Coyotes still spirit immigrants across the Guatemalan, Mexican, and U.S. borders; the charge per person can run as high as $5,000.

It was estimated that, as of the mid-1990s, El Salvador had the lowest per capita calorie rate in Latin America; that the infant mortality rate was approaching 80 per 1,000; that half the houses consisted of one room, for families averaging 5.6 members each; and that 63 percent of the people had no sanitary facilities (Montgomery 1995: 24). Shortly after the turn of the twenty-first century, it was estimated that the country had the hemisphere's second-highest murder rate, exceeded only by Colombia (Dickson-Gómez 2002: 417).

The culture of fear, though diminished, stills persists. Spectacular violence does this. Recent field research conducted by Julia Dickson-Gómez among peasant parents who had lived in guerrilla encampments found the explicit transmission of trauma to their children, even though the children had not directly experienced the civil war. Sufferers of *nervios* (severe anxiety) were found to transmit the fear associated with the violence they had experienced to their children via narratives; thus a sociological symptom of *nervios* ironically becomes the very process of oral transmission itself. A "worldview of fear, pessimism, and violence" is passed on and resocialized (2002: 416).

Despite its problems, the nation's postwar situation offers cause for hope, as Montgomery (1997) first emphasized. The military has been reduced in size and former guerrilla leaders have won seats in the Legislative Assembly. In demilitarizing, the armed forces were able to exceed the threshold specified in the 1992 peace accords. They were reduced to one-third their former size, a mere 18,000 men. A number of officers have entered universities, both in El Salvador and elsewhere, to enhance their education; cadets are encouraged to seek college as well as academy certification. Spurred by FMLN demands, the National Civilian Police and the National Council for Human Rights were two new organizations emerging from the peace accords. Unfortunately, government funding for the latter organization has lagged, the result being overreliance on international donors. The Ministry of Education has expanded its outreach to favorable acclaim. Media outlets have again gained the confidence of the citizenry. The percentage of mayors who are women has risen dramatically. Most represent the ARENA party, which—in modified form—has continued to dominate the political scene.

Not surprisingly, developments at the municipal level have been extremely variable. As Montgomery (1997) and more recently Lucas (2005) have noted, some municipalities have become vibrant and others have become stagnant.

Innovatively, community forums have been instituted in a number of villages, representing what Montgomery terms "the most vital form of democracy being practiced in El Salvador today." Radio Venceremos, once a major irritant to the government as it broadcast from the mountains of Morazán, now is a pop music station.

Transnational corporate activity, while modest by international standards, is engaging relatively large numbers of workers. The garment industry is estimated to employ 70,000 Salvadorans, approximately 80 percent of whom are women. The Gap is one of the firms represented. Negotiations over contracts remain sensitive, since it is estimated that the minimum wage in El Salvador covers less than half the basic needs of a family of four (Thomas-Slayter 2003: 202–3). The progressive capitalist sector is forming an increasingly viable alliance with the social change movement. The latter is represented by a diverse and loosely knit group of former FMLN, NGO, and activist organizations.

Tourism is on the rebound. Adventure tourists aspire to climb the country's volcanoes, although some hikers still feel the need to be accompanied by armed guards. Surfing on the Pacific coast is enjoying a modest resurgence.

Despite having been buffeted by Hurricane Mitch in 1998 and a series of earthquakes, the people of El Salvador demonstrate remarkable resiliency. Former guerrilla fighters such as Comandante Pedro (David Pereira Rivera) have been elected to the Legislative Assembly; former refugees have returned from as far away as California; and the U.S. military presence has virtually disappeared.

REFERENCES

Applied Social Science and Health Consultants. *Evaluación del Proyecto No. 519–0184, USAID/El Salvador, Oficina de Pequeñas Obras de Riego.* San Salvador/ Denver, Colo.: ASSHC, 1984.

Buur, Lars. "Truth and Reconciliation: A Briefing." *Aid Policy & Practice Series.* Copenhagen: Centre for Development Research, 2001.

Coll, Steve. *Ghost Wars: The Secret History of the CIA, Afghanistan, and bin Laden, from the Soviet Invasion to September 10, 2001.* New York: Penguin, 2004.

Cutts, Mark, ed. *The State of the World's Refugees: Fifty Years of Humanitarian Action.* Oxford: United Nations High Commissioner for Refugees/Oxford University Press, 2000.

Danner, Mark. *The Massacre at El Mozote: A Parable of the Cold War.* New York: Vintage/Random House, 1993.

Dickson-Gómez, Julia. "The Sound of Barking Dogs: Violence and Terror among Salvadoran Families in the Postwar." *Medical Anthropology Quarterly* 16, no. 4 (December 2002): 415–38.

Farmer, Paul. *Pathologies of Power: Health, Human Rights, and the New War on the Poor*. Berkeley: University of California Press, 2003.

Finkbeiner, Lance. Interview with former teacher, Colegio Internacional de San Salvador (CISS), November 9, 2005.

Gill, Lesley. Review of *The El Mozote Massacre: Anthropology and Human Rights* by Leigh Binford and *We Wish to Inform You that Tomorrow We Will Be Killed with Our Families: Stories from Rwanda*, by Phillip Gourevitch. *American Anthropologist* 101, no. 4 (December 1999): 874–76.

Hayner, Priscilla B. "The Contribution of Truth Commissions." In *An End to Torture: Strategies for Its Eradication*, edited by Bertil Dunér. London: Zed, 1998.

Kennedy, Kerry, and Eddie Adams (photographs). *Speak Truth to Power: Human Rights Defenders Who Are Changing Our World*. New York: Crown, 2004.

Koff, Clea. *The Bone Woman*. New York: Random House, 2004.

Lucas, Kevin. Email interview with language instructor, accompanied by Pro-Búsqueda website information, via San Salvador, November 24, 2005.

Martín-Baró, Ignacio, and Rodolfo Cardenal. "Fifteen Years Later: Peace at Last." Introduction to Tommie Sue Montgomery, *Revolution in El Salvador: From Civil Strife to Civil Peace*. 2nd ed. Boulder, Colo.: Westview, 1995.

McReynolds, Samuel A., Thomas Johnston, and Charles Geisler. "The Relationship of Land Tenure to Agricultural Practices and the Environment in El Salvador." *Culture & Agriculture* 22, no. 1 (new series, Spring 2000): 9–28.

Montgomery, Tommie Sue. *Revolution in El Salvador: From Civil Strife to Civil Peace*. 2nd ed. Boulder, Colo.: Westview, 1995.

———. "Democracy in El Salvador." Unpublished circular, American Anthropological Association, Arlington, Va., 1997.

Navarrete, Marco Pérez. "Un Reencuentro: Es Volver a Nacer y a Vivir." Asociación Pro-Búsqueda de Niñas y Niños Desaparecidos at www.probusqueda.org.sv/modules (accessed December 8, 2005).

Pelton, Robert Young. "Into the Land of Bin Laden." *National Geographic Adventure* 6, no. 3 (April 2004): 74–78, 82–88.

Schirmer, Jennifer. Review of *The El Mozote Massacre: Anthropology and Human Rights'*, by Leigh Binford and *'Power, Ethics and Human Rights: Anthropological Studies of Refugee Research and Action*, edited by Ruth M. Krulfeld and Jeffrey L. MacDonald. *American Ethnologist* 20, no. 4 (November 2000): 980–82.

Stephen, Lynn. "Women's Rights are Human Rights: The Merging of Feminine and Feminist Interests among El Salvador's Mothers of the Disappeared (Co-Madres)." *American Ethnologist* 22, no. 4 (Winter 1995): 807–27.

Thomas-Slayter, Barbara P. *Southern Exposure: International Development and the Global South in the Twenty-First Century*. Bloomfield, Conn.: Kumarian, 2003.

Tomaševski, Katarina. "Foreign Policy and Torture." In *An End to Torture: Strategies for Its Eradication*," edited by Bertil Dunér. London: Zed, 1998.

UNHCR. "Cartagena: 20 Years Later." *Refugees* 4, no. 137 (Fall 2004): 22–31.

Van Arsdale, Peter W. "Cultural Persistence Despite Instability in El Salvador: An Anthropological Perspective." *High Plains Applied Anthropologist* 11/12 (1991/1992): 40–66.

Chapter Six

Sudan and the Issue of Genocide

The *janjaweed*'s acts aren't human. They're committing genocide in Darfur, absolutely.

This statement was made to me by a Masalit tribesman from Darfur. Having escaped several years ago and made his way to Denver as a refugee, he has become an eloquent spokesman for those still struggling in western Sudan and Chad. A friend of this man, also a refugee from Darfur, told me what had happened to his college classmate. A bright student, she had excelled at college in the town of Nyala. When he fled, he lost track of her. Through a colleague, he later learned that she had become pregnant and a few months later had been captured by the horseback raiders known as *janjaweed*. As an apparent "rite of passage," one *janjaweed* youth—earlier chastised for his lack of aggression—had chosen her as his victim. He killed her, slit open her belly, and removed her fetus. He then impaled it on a spear, to the acclaim of his fellows. In another report, relayed to me by the same person, another woman whom he had known also had been killed in western Darfur. She was hastily buried by members of her family. The next day, in an attempt to further terrorize the village, several members of the *janjaweed* dug up her body and decapitated it.

This chapter develops the theme that, in Sudan as elsewhere, statewide systemic dysfunction can lead to genocide. As of 2005 an "ambiguous genocide" was occurring in Sudan's western-most region, Darfur. Drought, famine, and civil war represent the interactive array of ecological, socio-economic, and political factors at play. Hundreds of thousands of refugees and internally displaced persons (IDPs) were created from 2003 through 2005—not a new phenomenon in the region when viewed historically. During the same short period, perhaps 300,000 people died as a result of predations, social upheaval,

and resource scarcities. During the past twenty years, as many as 2 million Sudanese have died under duress or been killed. An understanding of the long-
term resource exploitation strategies, and ever-increasing tensions, among
sedentary and pastoral/transhumant peoples is essential. An understanding of
the central government's role in the long-running civil war between north and
south also is essential, since it has reverberated in what came to be a new, east-
west civil war. Core-periphery relationships must be examined. This chapter
shows that the inhabitants' fear of ethnic cleansing and genocide is well
founded, although an absolute extermination is not underway. It also shows
that the residents of Darfur are tremendously resilient; strategies used to combat famine are useful in combating the adversities associated with massive predations. Well-organized negotiations aimed at peace and resource reallocation
among an array of parties are indicated to be critical.

GETTING THE LAY OF THE LAND

"The landscapes of Darfur are drawn on a vast scale" (de Waal 2005: 33). To
comprehend the genocide in Darfur is to comprehend this landscape, the diverse peoples who inhabit it, and the limited resources they share. The task of
our team from PRC Engineering Consultants more than two decades ago in
Darfur and neighboring Kordofan region was to assess the status of water
supplies for some forty villages and small towns, and in so doing, to assess
overall resource availability. Headquartered in Denver, our company had
been contracted to complete one of the most far-ranging scientific studies
ever conducted in western Sudan. Reports on water needs were to be prepared
for the government of Sudan; potential development agencies and funders
also would be reviewing our findings. My specific job was to work with a Sudanese counterpart (i.e., a colleague with skills similar to mine) to conduct a
reconnaissance of socio-economic and socio-environmental resources that
would impact proposed water development projects. This assignment also
gave me the opportunity to get the general lay of the land, and to gain a preliminary understanding of human-rights issues. What emerged of particular
importance was the interplay of transhumant (seminomadic) and sedentary
peoples, an at-times collaborative but also tension-filled dynamic that has
proven to be the crux of the recent genocidal crisis.

Darfur is approximately the size of Texas. Before the genocidal depopulat-
ing crisis associated with the recent east-west civil war, its population was estimated to be about 6 million. Virtually all are Muslims. The population had
grown fairly rapidly during the previous two decades, a phenomenon predicted by our PRC Engineering Consultants team in 1979 (despite politically

tainted complaints by the central government about what they labeled as our "demographic overestimations"). While crisscrossing the Darfur region in our team's two Land Rovers during 1979 and 1980, we were able to utilize the talents of a diverse array of professionals. Trained in the United States, western Europe, south Asia, and eastern Africa, these included people with the titles of administrative specialist (led by engineer Skip Kerr), regional planner, hydrologist, geologist, cartographer, surveyor, land use specialist, soil specialist, agro-economist, development economist, civil engineer, and socio-economist/socio-environmentalist (a complex label chosen for me and my Sudanese counterpart so that the politically sensitive titles of "anthropologist" and "sociologist," respectively, would not have to be used). The staff was rounded out by Sudanese ably assisting through their roles as administrative assistants, drivers, and cooks. Some remained at our base camp, while others traveled in teams of two, four, or more.

The landscape of Darfur is both desolate and beautiful. It also is topographically and physiographically diverse, and in many places difficult to traverse. For the most part, vast stretches of savannah are speckled with acacia and other scrubby vegetation. In central Darfur, the huge Jebel Marra mountain massif dominates the panorama. It is comprised of relatively recent volcanic materials. It holds both environmental and mystical power for the Sudanese of the region. In northern Darfur, expanses of sand and related *qoz* soils—outliers of the Libyan Desert, itself an outlier of the Sahara Desert—predominate. Watercourses are found at surprisingly frequent intervals; most are seasonally dry *wadi*. The landscape is dotted with oases. However, most are not the kind that stereotypically are used to characterize the Sahara. Palms, camels, and turbaned residents are rarely seen. These instead are nondescript "wet spots" that surround hand-dug wells or natural springs, themselves surrounded by low-lying vegetation and grasses. In most cases a small village is found nearby.

Rainfall varies from an annual average of only about one inch in extreme northern Darfur to over twenty-seven inches in extreme southwestern Darfur. The two wettest months, July and August, are characterized by short-duration, high-intensity rain storms in the mid-latitudes. *Wadi* will flood and roads will become impassable. With temperatures exceeding 40 degrees C during the summer, evaporation of water is extraordinarily rapid. Prevailing winds during the dry season emanate in the north. The hot, dry air that blows in from the Libyan desert diminishes agricultural productivity. Blinding dust storms (*haboob*) bring all activities to a halt (PRC Engineering Consultants 1979: III–2, 3).

Livestock raising and small-scale agricultural production are the predominant economic activities of Darfur. A limited amount of mechanized agriculture is seen. The most important crops, grown to various degrees of success in alluvial, clay, and sandy soils, are millet, dura, sesame, cotton, and sorghum. While millet and dura are primarily grown for subsistence purposes, the latter three serve as cash crops. The cash crop economy also benefits from groundnuts (exported internationally), gum arabic, roselle, and tobacco (Van Arsdale 1989: 69; PRC Engineering Consultants 1979: III–6, 7). Vegetable gardens and fruit orchards are tended in many areas. While most agricultural land is rain fed, aquifers supply most of the water needed for gardening and household use. Irrigation schemes, so well known from the Gezira region along the Nile south of Khartoum, are virtually nonexistent in western portions of Sudan.

CITIZENS, NOT TRIBESMEN

Darfur means "land of the Fur." Diverse yet amorphous ethnic groups inhabit this region. Old-school anthropologists and ethnographers referred to them as "tribes" as they attempted to sort, categorize, and describe their cultures and customs. However, as Alex de Waal (2005) emphasizes, the peoples of this region cannot be categorized readily into tribes or even peasantries. He believes it is better to refer to them as ethnic groups (while noting their permeable cultural nature) or even by a simple, all-encompassing term: "citizens."

The fluid nature of ethnicity also is emphasized by Gérard Prunier (2005), who has authored the single most comprehensive historical analysis yet of the situation leading to the atrocities in Darfur. Since the founding of the Sultanate of Darfur in the fourteenth century, a swirl of independent political operations combined with assimilationist practices, forced displacement, and slave raiding created a region both rife with problems and rich in prospects. Processes of Islamization were penetrating, stabilizing, and nominally all-encompassing. Mahdist revitalization movements reaffirmed the importance of indigenous religious leaders. Colonial benign neglect under Anglo-Egyptian condominium rule contributed to the marginalization of the region; neocolonial marginalizing practices since independence was gained in 1956 have continued to the present.

Our field research in 1979 and 1980 allowed us to derive a partial ethnodemographic profile. In addition to Nyala (then the largest city in southern Darfur) and El Fasher (then the largest city in northern Darfur), we visited smaller places with names like Habeila, Kutum, Mellit, Tawesha, and Rahad El Berdi (this last settlement being discussed below). Like most of the other villages and towns in the region, at the time of our visits these latter five ranged in size from about 3,000 to 12,000 persons. Many grew in subsequent years, several of these in turn laying claim to the unofficial title of "growth center." Where water resources allowed, gradually expanding populations of sedentary and transhumant peoples alike continued to take advantage of surprisingly large expanses of unused arable land. Residents of many settlements we studied called themselves Fur. Others classified themselves as Masalit, Zaghawa, Hawazma, Habannia, and by other ethnic labels. Ancient ancestries suggest ties to such diverse locations as Nigeria, Tunisia, and the Red Sea coast. Recent migrants come from Chad, Mauritania, Mali, and Niger.

Using the Fur as the prime example, they illustrate both ethnic fluidity and cultural complexity. Since neither their language nor religious practice can be used to readily categorize them, their pattern of livelihood becomes the de facto key to distinguishing them. Yet this is complicated. Many are farmers. Some are livestock herders. Some are both. Of those who maintain herds of cattle, some have been labeled as "Fur el Baggara" owing to their connections—putative and real—with "traditional" Baggara cattle Arabs, who themselves are not easy to categorize ethnically. To use a different example, it is possible to meet a member of the Berti "tribe" who also is "Fur" and "Baggara." Adoption of a migrant into a group also occurs with relative ease. One's current community membership usually is deemed more important than one's ancestry. Indeed, the original Fur state was founded by its indigenous residents on the principle of ethnic assimilation (de Waal 2005: 48).

Scattered amidst these peoples are others who are immigrants or itinerant traders. I met truck drivers from Libya and livestock herders from Chad. Some cross the international border on a regular basis with papers; some cross on a regular basis without papers. The so-called annual orbits of herders can span hundreds of miles; several of the most well-established cross the borders between Sudan, Chad, and Libya.

While there are extraordinarily poor people, there is not a class of landless laborers. While there are farmers who struggle to meet the minimal subsistence requirements of their families, there are not large numbers being dispossessed of their lands through established legal channels. Indeed, a system of usufruct theoretically assures that those who continue to till their lands can keep them. Even those without formal records noting established patterns of use can pass their lands to their descendents legally.

It is not a simple matter to categorize these citizens as either villagers or nomads. However, this dichotomization is frequently used (Khalifa 2006). In a now-classic study within Sudan, Ahmed (1976) effectively categorized herding into pastoral nomadism (involving herders who regularly move with their families in search of pasture and water), seminomadism (involving those who leave part of their family in the *dar* while the remainder move in search of pasture and water), and transhumance (involving the pastoralism practiced by sedentary people whose primary economic activity is agriculture). Many

Figure 6.1. Habannia herdsmen tend to a great amount of "mobile wealth." This boy assists his father, a respected sheikh, as their herd of about 100 camels moves through western Darfur. At the time this photograph was taken (1979), each adult camel was valued at about 1,000 Sudanese pounds.

people who regularly dwell in villages, such as the Berti, maintain herds of livestock that require occasional movement as new pasturage is sought. Many people who regularly move with their livestock, such as Baggara "cattle Arabs," maintain residences in villages. Some even split their families into two units, one that is "more mobile" and one that is "more sedentary."

It also is not a simple matter to categorize these citizens by their skin color, although this system is frequently used. Numerous classification schemes—some benign, some racist—have been attempted over the past several centuries (Prunier 2005). So-called Hamitic Arabs are said to be lighter skinned, and so-called Black Africans are said to be darker skinned. The blackness of some Fur is said to be "blue" because it is so intense. The term *zurga* for "blacks" is used in a derogatory manner (Power 2004: 61). As Chehade (2005) correctly emphasizes, in Sudan "being Arab" refers less to one's physical appearance and more to one's "state of mind." Further, the recent conflict has not been about religion per se. Virtually all of those involved are Muslims. It is, in part, about the beliefs and practices of those who are Arabized Muslims and those who are non-Arabized Muslims.

Therefore, what is important is not so much one's ethnic label as one's means of livelihood. To paraphrase Alex de Waal (2005: 51), economic necessities override cultural imperatives. As it plays out within Darfur in sedentary but especially transhumant situations, this amalgam of socio-economic activity clearly illustrates what I elsewhere have referred to as adaptive flux (Van Arsdale 1989: 72). It can be defined as that set of short-term tactics and long-term strategies that enable a group's survival under fluctuating, harsh, and erratic conditions in an area that is socio-economically peripheral in relation to the state's core. Adaptive flux reflects a group's own self-help capabilities and motivations; externally-derived strategies (and thus dependencies) are not central. The concept is particularly applicable to those who are able to "cope successfully with deprivation—in its interactive ecological, economic and political manifestations" (Hailu et al. 1994: 23).

PROMISES AND PROBLEMS OF DEVELOPMENT

"Since 1985 Darfur had been a time-bomb waiting for a fuse" (Prunier 2005: 86). Darfur's basic problem is one of resources, compounded by an ineffectual and oppressive state political system, itself more reactive than proactive in dealing with resource constraints. As I witnessed twenty-five years ago, and as is still seen today, there is tremendous tension between the centralizing tendencies of the Khartoum government and the decentralizing tendencies of the remote regions. A type of core-periphery relationship exists. Political forces are extremely imbalanced; the marginalization of peoples not linked to the Khartoum elite is significant. Power is exerted centrifugally from the core, while those in the periphery react centripetally. A swirl of ethnic identity plays out on this landscape, but it is only of secondary importance to the political economy. In Sudan's ethnically diverse society, diverse viewpoints are unwelcome. In Sudan's periphery, economic survival is paramount.

"Big-ticket" development projects have long appealed to Sudan's central government. The huge Gezira irrigation scheme along the Nile, south of Khartoum, has been relatively successful; cotton is one of the major crops grown there. Many Fur have migrated to the Gezira to benefit from labor opportunities (de Waal 2005: 231). By contrast, the Jonglei Canal has not been successful—and indeed, has not been completed. It was to be one of "the world's biggest ditches" and also was to have enhanced irrigation. While not directly impacting Darfur, it was to be a major technological showpiece for the country. Located in the swampy south-central region and intended to span nearly 250 miles, construction was initiated in 1980 by a joint Egyptian-Sudanese team. It was halted in 1983 as result of the civil war between north and south. Sa'oudi (2001) recently described its original intent as "a comprehensive engineering and environmental venture designed to make full use of the [White] Nile River, promote human and economic development in semi-populated regions and boost agricultural development in both countries." Over twenty years ago, a Shilluk resident of the region named Billy Madison told me of the technological promise of the canal draining the swamps, which his people thought would be more than countered by the sociological problem that such drainage would inflict upon their way of life. As it turned out, the civil war inflicted far more sociological damage than a completed canal ever could have.

The full promise of big-ticket oil production has yet to be realized. Chevron was exploring near the area where we worked in 1980; it identified several promising oil reserves. Darfur currently has three identified oil fields. Discoveries in the Kordofan region, bordering Darfur to the east, suggest significant production still could come about if the political environment stabilizes. Oil reserves in Sudan are estimated at 563 million barrels (Kotch 2005: 56). Exports from the country began in 1999; increased production in the south was largely responsible. President Omar al-Bashir thereafter agreed to a provisional arrangement where up to half the country's oil revenues would be shared with the south as attempts were again being made to end the long-running civil war. Establishment of a National Petroleum Commission was underway as of 2005, but existing concessions with other organizations (e.g., Nile Petroleum Corporation) were proving problematic. PetroChina Company Ltd. has expanded its petroleum holdings in the country. Natural gas resources in the western regions still are being investigated. Mineral resources in Darfur are thought to be modest; some copper deposits have been discovered.

On a more modest scale, a number of development programs have been initiated in Darfur during the past several decades. Several "integrated" livestock operations, so named because of the inclusion of meat marketing strategies, have been started. These primarily have targeted Sudanese, rather than external, customers. "Forestry plantations" have been opened in the Jebel Marra area and elsewhere. These were so named because a more systematic approach to tree farming was being touted. Basic infrastructure enhancement and cultivator support services also were included. Some expansion of mechanized farming capabilities has occurred. Most farmers continue to use hand tools. The Western Savannah Development Corporation was begun in 1978 to aid in coordination and oversight of these enterprises. Combinations of external donor aid and Sudanese government funds were utilized.

In terms of the region's transportation network, some expansion of the asphalt highway system has been achieved, but it remains rudimentary. Most roads are dirt and/or gravel, and many of these are unimproved. One major rail line crosses the region. Neither the line nor its spurs are well maintained. Air transport serves the three centers of El Fasher, Nyala, and El Geneina (the latter near the Chad border). Radio and satellite-linked communications systems have been in place for some time.

Small health clinics have dotted this rural landscape for decades. Most are staffed by nurses, paramedics, and/or college-trained health practitioners. Some also incorporate nutrition and nutrition education programs. Relatively few doctors are available in Darfur. The civil war has led to the establishment of several new clinics in conjunction with refugee and IDP camps. Doctors Without Borders is among the externally based organizations providing important medical services. Water resource development programs, like the one for which I provided data, have frequently been implemented—but favorable long-term outcomes have been few in number. The links between effective health care and effective water resource use (including sanitation) are well recognized. In contrast with the devastating diseases found in wetter southern Sudan, such as trypanosomiasis (sleeping sickness) and onchocerciasis (river blindness), the drier western part of the nation is better off.

As illustrated elsewhere in this book (e.g., chapter 2 on Papua), regional development projects and programs can be relatively easy to conceive, moderately easy to implement, and relatively difficult to bring to long-term fruition. Those in Darfur, such as the Jebel Marra Project, fit this pattern. External donors in the past few decades have been exemplified by the governments of Yugoslavia, Germany, Britain, and the United States. Most of their efforts were modified, curtailed, or aborted. Political turmoil and civil war can signal the death of initiatives tied heavily to external sources.

ECOLOGICAL TRANSITIONS AND THE IMPACTS OF FAMINE

From an historical perspective, it is very difficult to pinpoint a specific time period or series of events that led to the contemporary crisis in Darfur. Nor is this necessary. A systems perspective affords a comprehensive, interactive, and more appropriate analytic framework. Stated differently, it is not a series of events that are to blame, but rather, a dysfunctional system. Yet extreme events like genocide are tied to human motivations and decisions, intimately linked to the system, and cannot be minimized or explained away. Human culpability must be emphasized.

Consistently low rainfall and droughtlike conditions during the 1970–1985 period set the stage for ecological transitions—and political tensions—that have persisted to the present day. Our field research indicated that the major land use problem in Darfur has been tied to overcrowding in some areas. This is a seemingly paradoxical situation given the scarcity of available resources and low population density overall. Deterioration of both crop and grazing lands has been occurring for decades in these areas (PRC Engineering Consultants 1979). The relative paucity of potable water, in concert with polluted *hafir* (mini-reservoir) supplies, has been exacerbated by livestock herd growth that puts increasing pressure on water and grazing resources. Increased herd size is promoted by citizens as a buffer against the vagaries of drought and famine.

Desertification and Drought

The process of desertification is a problem with complex roots. Sudanese scientists interviewed by our team referred to it as a "phenomenon creeping from north to south," a "steady and expanding process," or "inevitable." Tied primarily to sweeping meteorological changes (and thus possible long-term warming associated with global greenhouse effects), population growth (and therefore resource depletion), and livestock herd growth (and thus overgrazing), it has been systematically recognized as a problem in western Sudan since about 1960 (cf. Ahmed 1976).

Drought is defined as a sustained period with less-than-adequate, accessible water resources. As Charles Hutchinson (1989: 5) stressed after a systematic review in the 1980s of conditions in the Sahelian zone of Africa, "it is easy to find drought with no famine, and conversely, famine without drought . . . [particularly in] parts of Sudan." Darfur experienced a significant drought during the 1980s. It only partially correlated with locally variable episodes of famine.

Favorable climatic conditions during the 1950s allowed the expansion of agricultural activities through much of the Sahel. As mechanized farming techniques were introduced, these lands were converted in ways not readily amenable to "adaptive retreat" when climatic conditions worsened (Hutchinson 1989). Gradual incursions by pastoralists such as the Kababish into previously "untapped" lands were less problematic when drought was not present, but extremely problematic when drought returned.

Further exacerbating the pressures on the socio-economic structure were the influx of refugees from Chad during the 1980s (Van Arsdale 1989: 66), which followed influxes of the early 1970s. Although the flow dramatically decreased as strife between Libya and Chad was brought under control, it can be inferred that the secondary impacts associated with the refugees' initially disruptive influence on Darfur's socio-economic structure never fully subsided. Wage labor demands were especially severe. In a real sense, the last Chadian refugee exodus from west to east was replaced years later by the recent exodus of Darfurian refugees from east to west.

Famine

Famine is a political—and politicizing—process. While in one extremely important way it refers to the systematic lack of food and nourishment for a population (Cuny 1999: 1), such that suffering and death might ensue, in another way it refers to a complex of political, ecological, and economic factors that impair a society. To state that famine always equates with prolonged and severe hunger is to oversimplify the analysis. To state that famine always leads to significant physical incapacitation and large numbers of deaths misdirects the analysis.

A large number of famines have been recorded in Sudan and Darfur over recent centuries. As summarized by de Waal (2005: 71–77 passim), over the 100-year period from 1885 to 1985 there were at least twelve famines that informants could discuss with some degree of clarity. That of 1888–1892 was especially devastating, with widespread fighting being the main cause. Each of the major famines was categorized by local residents in narratives that include areas impacted, groups involved, and perceived cause(s). Just as hurricanes are named, famines are named using evocative terms such as Ab Sotir ("father of the whip"). That of 1984–1985 was called by some people Ifza 'una ("save us"). Famines that kill, in the most powerful sense of the word (i.e., that devastate a population and create circumstances from which long-term recovery is difficult), are rare.

To reiterate, famine is a process or set of processes, not an event. It is appropriately associated with notions of political instability and war, food insecurity, and socio-economic disruption (Murphy 2003). It is a "social experience" much more than a "technical malfunction" (de Waal 2005: xii). It is my contention that famines have served to condition Darfur's residents to dealing with adversity, but have made the region more vulnerable to political turmoil. The adaptive flux that people demonstrate in coping with dramatic resource fluctuations at the local level cannot override the pressures associated with governmental oppression and dysfunction at the regional and national levels.

The most debilitating famine in Darfur's recent history was that of 1984–1985. It unfolded in several different ways within the region. Various ethnic groups were differentially impacted; the experiences of the Masalit, Zaghawa, and Fur confirm this. On average, rainfall had diminished throughout much of the Sahel since the late 1970s. Adjustments were made to planting and harvesting cycles. The quantities of grain produced continued apace. Refinements were made in annual orbits taken by herders as they moved through the savannah. Market fluctuations were significant and displacement of villagers extensive. Out-migration for supplemental labor increased.

The previous experiences of Darfur's citizens auger well as they make adjustments to adverse, localized drought and famine conditions. Adaptive flux is demonstrated as less acreage is planted, more seed crop is held back in reserve, slightly larger numbers of animals are sold, and differential schedules are implemented for the marketing of goods and engaging in supplemental wage labor. Market fluctuations, especially those tied to grain sales, reverberate powerfully; some of the most adverse effects are not experienced until well after the rains have returned. These phenomena were exaggerated during the 1984–1985 famine due to its severity, and of course, not all adaptive strategies succeeded. As noted by de Waal (2005: 176), excess death rates reached slightly over three times the normal in 1985.

RAHAD EL BERDI

After a delay of nearly a week owing to aircraft problems, in late 1979 I was able to return to the western part of the country to continue the reconnaissance work begun a few months earlier. My colleague Ismail Mohammed, both logistician and interpreter, met me at the remote airstrip outside of El Fasher (the nominal "northern capital" of Darfur). The airport itself consisted of nothing more than the asphalt airstrip, a fuel truck, a windsock, and a shed where two dreary men processed paperwork. Yet the guards whose job it was to protect the airport bristled when I tried to take a photograph. "Not allowed!" they yelled in English as they waved their rifles at me.

Flying in to El Fasher, I had been struck by the desolate landscape outside my window. As I looked down, all I could see was reddish-yellow sand and a scattering of low hills. The sand reminded me of the pictures that had been transmitted from the Viking landers on Mars a few years earlier. One village several miles outside the city was nestled against a low rim of hills. From the air it appeared to not have a single tree or bush.

My trip from El Fasher to the southwestern part of Darfur was relatively uneventful. It was the dry season and all roads were passable. Beginning our journey by pickup, one passenger's ribs were injured when high speed and a rough track caused him to fall from the truck's bed. The delay caused by our taking him to a clinic for treatment necessitated that Ismail and I catch a different ride. We hailed a huge cargo truck that was lumbering south. Six of us packed into the cab. Thirty more already were riding atop the cargo in the rear. Stopping only once, about 3 a.m. for two hours of fitful sleep in hammocks (with a temperature that had dropped to 40 degrees F.), the remainder of our trip to Nyala took about twelve hours. Having rejoined our team, we soon headed to Rahad El Berdi.

In 1979 the town of Rahad El Berdi had a population of about 12,000. Our field reconnaissance, focusing on water resources, was conducted in concert with local Sudanese. Our preliminary assessment indicated that the town had the potential to be a primary growth center (PRC Engineering Consultants

1979: Table I–4). Complemented by a contingent of merchants, most of the residents were Fur farmers. Their primary crops were millet and sorghum. Garden produce also was important and relatively abundant. The average annual rainfall during the late 1970s and early 1980s was about twenty-five inches in this area (de Waal 2005: 83). While some 15 percent less than the longer-term average, it was deemed adequate by those we spoke to. A relatively lush environment and good soils afforded better growing opportunities, and thus, better opportunities for employment. Migrants from other parts of Darfur came to Rahad El Berdi to obtain work as laborers. Camel herders also arrived seasonally, further complicating the pattern of resource use and decision making among locals (cf. Reeves and Frankenberger 1981).

When we arrived we found that tensions were high. Baggara cattle herders (many identified as Salamat) had recently been altering their orbits so that their herds could access better grazing land. Albeit temporary, new herding paths were being created near the gardens of Rahad El Berdi's residents; some cattle were straying and trampling crops. Others were contaminating the water in shallow ponds with excrement and urine.

One resident told me that problems among herders and farmers were escalating. Negotiations among the aggrieved parties were needed. However, little had been achieved. "I now am negotiating at the point of a gun," he said, showing me his shotgun and the bag of shells he was carrying. "I hope I don't have to use it, but I will if I have to." His comments were harbingers of things to come.

A QUESTION OF GENOCIDE

Genocide entails a purposeful and systematic campaign against a population or ethnic group, with the intent being its partial or total eradication. "Never again" became "once again" as the situation in Darfur unfolded (Genocide Intervention Fund 2005). Still another brutal cleansing was underway in the world. As in other nations and at other times, thousands again were being killed under conditions that violated human rights and commonly accepted standards of human decency. Beheadings, dismemberments, and excruciating torture of the living again became commonplace (Power 2004). Former U.S. secretary of state Colin Powell used the term "genocide" in his testimony to the Senate Foreign Affairs Committee, based on his on-site assessment of the Darfur situation in 2004. His successor, Condoleezza Rice, also used the term based on her on-site inspection in 2005. That United Nations emissary Antonio Cassese, acting at the behest of UN Secretary General Kofi Annan, did not deem the term "genocide"

Figure 6.2. Arguments can explode into violence in Darfur. The cattle of nomadic herdsmen, intruding on this man's property near Rahad El Berdi, caused him to pull out his shotgun. He said he was ready to negotiate, either over a table or at the point of a gun.

appropriate in his site report of January 2005 (Moorehead 2005: 56), does not diminish the devastation and suffering that have occurred.

Harkening back to the devastation in Bosnia, Kosovo, and Rwanda during the 1990s, politicians, military personnel, service providers, and academicians began debating the nature of the crisis emerging in western Sudan in early 2004. Reports of killings increased; they were mixed with reports of death owing to other causes associated with famine and disease. By early 2005 an aggregate death and casualty toll of 280,000 to 310,000 was being circulated by careful observers (Prunier 2005: 152). Alex de Waal (2005: xviii–xix) captured the situation adroitly when he stated that "genocidal intent" was evident. It was not *Genocide* (capital added) in the sense that absolute extermination of a people was occurring, but *genocide* in the sense specified by the 1948 Genocide Convention.

Gérard Prunier holds a similar, but not identical, view. Four key criteria are met in Darfur: (1) Massive casualties are present; (2) state involvement is present; (3) ethnic conflict is present; and (4) sustained violence is present. But a systematic state-based "intent to eradicate" is not present (2005: 152–8). He believes that violence reached "genocidal proportions" (2005: 109), but cannot be characterized in precisely the same way as that of Rwanda in the mid-1990s. Events in Darfur constitute an "ambiguous genocide."

Systematic, long-term planning of what variously has been termed "ethnic cleansing" or "genocide" in Darfur does not seem to have taken place (cf. Dubinsky 2005). As noted by the editorial staff of the UNHCR's flagship magazine, *Refugees* (Anon. 2004: 9–11), the *New York Times* was one of those publications that wrestled with how to make sense of the complex situation: "If this is a genocide, it doesn't look very much like those we've known before. Instead, it is shadowy, informal; the killings take place offstage. It is the destruction of a people in a place where it is virtually impossible to distinguish incompetence from conspiracy. Is that by design . . . or just more evidence of a government's utter haplessness?"

The Sudanese Liberation Army

The Sudanese Liberation Army (SLA) arose in response to grievances being expressed by citizens of Darfur. It is comprised mainly of the members of Darfurian farm families. It crosses ethnic lines and is primarily secular in ideology. At one level the grievances the SLA responded to are traceable to the political neglect shown by the government toward its residents in the western regions as the civil war between north and south was being fought. At another level they are socio-economic, traceable to the increasing tensions over land and related resources occurring intermittently since the late 1970s (Van Arsdale 1989). Significant battles between farmers and herders took place in 1987 and 1989 (Power 2004: 61). An insurgency of radical secularists arose, only to be aborted in 1991 (de Waal 2005: xvii). On April 25, 2003, members of the then two-month-old SLA attacked the airport and a military compound in the northern Darfur town of El Fasher. In addition to killing a number of Sudanese soldiers, they captured the commander of the Sudanese Air Force. It is likely that this move was designed to attract the attention of the central government, much as the late John Garang had done years earlier for rebels in the south.

The SLA's founding manifesto included its vehement protests against the central government's "policies of marginalization, racial discrimination, exclusion, exploitation, and divisiveness." Its objective was "to create a united democratic Sudan on a new basis of equality, complete restructuring and devolution of power [aimed at] political pluralism and moral and material prosperity for all Sudanese" (Power 2004: 62). Another organization, the Justice and Equality Movement (JEM), also recently arose and also claimed similar objectives on behalf of Darfur's residents.

The Janjaweed

There have been raiders and bandits of various types in Sudan for centuries (Bascom 1998: 118–120; Prunier 2005: 13). Sultans, colonialists, local leaders, and sheikhs all would use them. Some would operate quasi-independently, others would operate like mercenaries. In Darfur in recent decades so-called Arab cattle raiders occasionally would sweep into a non-Arab village and abscond with a few head. The now-infamous *janjaweed* of Darfur loosely trace their origins to such raiders, past and present. However, the tactics they employed beginning in 2003 also can be traced to the tactics used by the north in its battle with the south over a twenty-year period. Many likely were trained in militia camps during the 1990s. Government-sponsored air attacks against Dinka and other ethnic groups in the south would be complemented by ground attacks utilizing Arab raiders. The same pattern began to play out in the new battle, between east and west, in Darfur. As Anita Sanborn (2005) told me, many of the government's troops are from Darfur and could not be expected to fight their own people. As she also noted, many now regret the roles they played in the earlier battles against those in the south.

Various definitions have been offered for the term "janjaweed." Likely first coined in 1988 (Prunier 2005), its origins are traceable to the Arabic term *jinjaweit*, meaning "horse and gun" (Chehade 2005). Koerner (2005) expands upon this meaning, suggesting the Arabic colloquialism "man with a gun on a horse." He adds that the term long has been associated with the notion of "bandit." Khalifa (2006) confirms this point, and translates the term, based on a much longer derivation, as "devil on horseback with a machine-gun." Power (2004) suggests the rough translation "evil horsemen." Most of the *janjaweed* raiders are recruited from among the so-called Arab nomads. Yet, as the above analysis indicates, this is by no means a clearly definable group. What is increasingly clear is that through 2005 many of their activities were being coordinated by Sheikh Musa Hilal, who was working directly for the central Sudanese government (Power 2005). The *janjaweed* under his command, albeit operating loosely, ransacked and burned villages, pillaged supplies, and raped large numbers of women.

As the SLA's militancy and resolve became more clear, the central government's militancy and resolve to oppose them also became more clear. It became manifest in the increasing activity and brutality of the *janjaweed*.

REFUGEES AND IDPS

During the past twenty-five years, Sudan has been home to some of the world's largest refugee and IDP populations. While recognizing that from a demographic perspective, refugee and IDP totals cannot always be readily separated, as of 1980 the refugee total was about 500,000 (UNHCR 2000: 311). As of 1985 the total was about 1 million (Van Arsdale 1988: 1; Bulcha 1988: 19). As of 1995 the total was about 700,000 (UNHCR 1995: 251). As of early 2005, the total number of refugees from other countries within Sudan was about 142,000, but nearly five times that number were internally displaced owing to conflicts in the south and west (UNHCR 2005: 8).

For much of the last twenty-five years, Sudan has been in the somewhat unusual position of being both "major refugee producer/sender" and "major refugee receiver/assister." As of December 2004, the latest date for which complete statistics are available, Sudan had produced 730,600 persons who were currently refugees in other countries. The increase of 21 percent for the year 2004 alone was the largest for any sending country, and was directly attributable to the outflow from Darfur. Concomitantly, for 2004 alone Chad experienced a 78 percent increase in incoming refugees, reaching by late December a total of nearly 260,000—most having come from Sudan. This increase was the largest of any refugee-receiving country for that year (UNHCR 2005: 3). Subsequent field reports indicate the numbers continued to climb during 2005 (see, e.g., International Crisis Group 2005c).

Perhaps 2 million refugees and IDPs have been created by the recent conflict in Darfur. Most of those who fled have gone to Chad, with approximately 75,000 of those leaving earliest already there by the end of 2003 (Anon. 2004: 8). Refugee camps began to be established at that time. Anita Sanborn reported to me that those camps she visited in April 2005 were very overcrowded, at approximately twice capacity. She also reported that basic supplies were reaching a majority of those ensconced on-site. Those who have become IDPs within Darfur have been assisted at the many camps established in the region. Most facilities are relatively well organized.

Referring to another region of the Horn of Africa (i.e., the Sudan-Ethiopia corridor), Bulcha (1988) has noted the seeming paradox of refugees crossing borders in both directions. In a few instances, they even have passed one another on precisely the same paths. This also has occurred in the Chad-Sudan corridor, although in a more attenuated manner and over a longer period of time. Refugees from Chad have sought work in Darfur as laborers (de Waal 2005: 144), and others from the Central African Republic have sought similar opportunities. The recent surge in the outflow of refugees from Darfur has been accompanied by a concomitant reduction in the number entering the region.

EFFECTIVE ACTION: THE ROLES OF DIPLOMATS AND GOVERNMENT OFFICIALS

Sudan provided a safe harbor for Osama bin Laden from 1992 through 1996. While he had been on U.S. radar screens as early as 1984, American analysts had not then been clear as to his motives or allegiances. By the late 1980s several warning signals had emerged and been evaluated by the CIA's Counterterrorism Center. Bin Laden had become widely known as a jihadist warrior. Pressure came to be placed on the government of Sudan to remove him. In an effort to regain some measure of U.S. good graces, Sudanese government officials claim to have offered to turn bin Laden over to American officials in 1996. American officials claim otherwise (Coll 2004: 322–23). In any event, the United States stated it had no indictable evidence against him at that time, while readily recognizing even then his increasingly powerful support for terrorism.

Still, American pressure did force bin Laden to flee to Afghanistan in May of that year. Upon arrival he openly noted "the beginning of war between Muslims and the United States" (Coll 2004: 326). During his previous sojourn there he had inspired anti-Soviet jihadists and, although not immediately, became a key advisor to (and funder of) the Taliban. After his departure from Sudan, despite a Tomahawk missile attack on a Khartoum pharmaceutical factory thought to be engaged in lethal weapons activity, the Sudanese government claims to have redirected its political energies in more benign directions. While the east-west conflict might belie that notion, opportunities for diplomatic success nonetheless have emerged.

International diplomats and local government officials theoretically can play important roles in resolving conflicts of the sort seen in western Sudan. Not surprisingly, one key is common recognition by multiple actors of the nature of the foundational problem. While the central government might claim the problem is "suppression of the insurgency," this in fact is merely an objective (not shared by most "African" residents of Darfur). While the SLA might claim the problem is "equitable recognition and socio-economic integration into a wider Sudan," this in fact also is merely an objective (not shared by members of the Khartoum elite).

The case of Darfur is a prime example of subsystem dysfunction mirroring system dysfunction. What is happening in Darfur, as exemplified by the recent SLA insurgency and government-backed genocidal attacks, mirrors what is happening in Sudan as a whole, as exemplified by the recent north-south civil war. Viewed systemically, the peace process has been similarly intertwined regionally and nationally.

North-South Peace Negotiations

The north-south civil war extended from 1983 through 2004. (It followed an earlier civil war which lasted from 1956, shortly after Sudan claimed its independence, through 1973.) The final peace accord, primarily reflected through negotiations between the central Sudanese government and the Sudanese People's Liberation Army (SPLA), was completed on December 31, 2004, and signed on January 9, 2005. It is known as the Naivasha Agreement. Among its most important provisions is a move toward greater governmental decentralization (International Crisis Group 2005c), an issue raised by administrators with me and many others as early as 1979. The year 2005 brought substantive advances to the peace process in Sudan. Building upon an array of negotiated points, a new national constitution was proposed. A National Constitutional Review Commission, while delayed owing to various administrative pitfalls and tactical maneuvers by participants, moved toward the drafting of an interim document. Representatives of the south by no means presented a unified set of proposals, and indeed, several militias were in substantial disagreement among themselves. Several opposition groups from the north and west were not formally included in the early talks. As international donor assistance continued to be arranged for the country, the United States and Germany specified that such aid be linked to progress on Darfur.

An ever more complex web of negotiations enveloped political developments. North-south relations continued to affect east-west relations. Having experienced mixed diplomatic results in Sudan for years, the UN Security Council finally was able to negotiate deployment of its first peacekeeping contingent in the south in May 2005. African Union-backed talks continued. The union was complimented by some for what were seen as bold, intra-African initiatives, while criticized by others for inadequate proactivity and inept allocation of resources (particularly regarding Darfur). In a progressive move, in March 2005 the UN Security Council referred Darfur to the International Criminal Court (ICC). The names of more than fifty men suspected of war crimes then were sent to the ICC. The central Sudanese government balked. Picking up on a theme repeated endlessly over the past decade, President Omar al-Bashir and his deputees reasserted their perception of the need for "the internal handling of internal affairs." International Crisis Group representatives believe that the negotiated peace, while essential to Sudan's long-term political survival, poses a number of threats (International Crisis Group 2005a). Stated differently, a negotiated peace is necessary but not sufficient. True power sharing by the government has yet to be demonstrated. SPLA Chairman John Garang's negotiated promotion to the post of national vice president (ironically implemented just three weeks before his death in July 2005) was symbolically significant, but would have done little to effect needed internal governmental reform. A self-determination referendum proposed for the south in 2011, if passed, will radically restructure the state and undercut governmental access to the south's oil wealth. The west (represented by Darfur and Kordofan) hypothetically might seek similar autonomy. Some analysts believe that the influential National Congress Party signed the peace agreement under duress, in part to deflect international pressure over Darfur (International Crisis Group 2005a).

The importance of negotiations never can be underestimated. That former U.S. secretary of state Colin Powell was nominated for the 2005 Nobel Peace Prize for his efforts in Sudan attests to this.

East-West Peace Negotiations

Negotiations toward sustainable peace in Darfur must take broader developments in Sudan carefully into account. They must center on the foundational problem of the political marginalization of much of Darfur's citizenry by the central Sudanese government, this exacerbated by land use disputes among "Arab" and "African" ethnic groups. Structural inequalities between core and periphery are significant and demonstrable, yet with substantial effort, negotiations could reduce certain of the economic gaps. Food security could be improved.

Paradoxically, the central government was identified with "the north" during the 1983–2004 war, but with "the east" during the recent war involving Darfur. These dichotomies further accentuate the marginalization of southern and western populations, while reaffirming structural inequalities within the country. They should serve to remind negotiators of the gaps to be bridged.

In my opinion, negotiations should focus on the following actors and actions. Building upon what had transpired through early 2006, discussions should engage leaders of the SLA (especially those representing the large Fur, Masalit, and Zaghawa populations); leaders of JEM (who at times have been at odds with the SLA); so-called Arab tribes such as the Baggara; refugee and

IDP camp leaders; Darfur's gubernatorial staff; Khartoum's defense and interior ministries; Sheikh Musa Hilal (as de facto leader of the *janjaweed*); and African Union representatives. Representatives of the United Nations and the European Union's Africa Peace Facility should be present as observers. Representatives of groups such as the Sudan Council of Churches USA and Doctors Without Borders, exemplifying agencies active in humanitarian outreach, should also be included as observers. The on-site documentation of atrocities by specialists such as the ICG's John Prendergast and Harvard University's Samantha Power, in concert with the anonymous testimonies of survivors, should be made readily available to all participants.

Negotiations of this type should focus on both process and product, that is, on "what to do" and "what the outcomes should be." Mohamed El Baradei, 2005 Nobel Peace Prize laureate, has taken much this same approach in other regions as negotiator and chief United Nations nuclear inspector. Whatever the arena, even the toughest negotiations should emphasize "righting the system" rather than on "wronging the government." The first priority for negotiations in Sudan is elimination of predations by the *janjaweed*. As Nuti (2004) stresses, following interviews with Human Rights Watch, accountability for the inhumane actions of the *janjaweed* must be pushed without respite. As of mid-2005, an international presence of at least 12,000 (primarily African) troops had been projected as necessary for the region (International Crisis Group 2005b). Other officials later increased the figure. As peacekeepers, the troops' capacity for humanitarian intervention should not be compromised (see next section). An ideal longer-term scenario would station 20,000 or more, from several African nations, at key towns like Nyala and El Fasher, at border checkpoints, and at refugee and IDP camps. A stronger stance by the African Union's Peace and Security Council against *janjaweed* pillaging and brutality, supported by the UN Security Council, would be necessary. In turn, the international community should strongly support the Union as it becomes more grounded in its work. The Sudanese government should be persuaded to assure the protection of humanitarian workers in Darfur, both expatriate (e.g., Doctors Without Borders) and indigenous (e.g., Sudan Mercy). Negotiations also should include a parallel track to improve networking and service coordination among the numerous NGOs working in Darfur.

As of late 2005, the African Union's Mission in Sudan (AMIS) had been emplaced and was working to monitor peace negotiations. A majority of its funding comes from the European Union's Africa Peace Facility. Negotiations also likely will be influenced by the recent decision of both Harvard University and Stanford University to divest from PetroChina Company Ltd., a firm (as noted previously) with extensive petroleum holdings in Sudan. The International Crisis Group is pushing for other major universities to review their investment portfolios as well, and if holdings are confirmed for companies operating in Sudan, to divest.

Babiker Ali Khalifa, whom I interviewed in January 2006, is among the Sudanese government officials who believe the United States can play an ongoing, conciliatory role.

Humanitarianism and Humanitarian Intervention

The nation of Sudan is by no means bereft of humanitarian interests or humanitarian activities. While the processes currently are embattled, as Prunier (2005) stresses, a number of initiatives are underway. Persons I interviewed on-site as early as 1979 and in Denver as recently as 2005 stressed their concerns with rights violations and their eagerness to help their fellow Sudanese, including those in Darfur. Agencies such as Save the Children and Doctors Without Borders have had long-standing operations in the country. The U.S. Agency for International Development had begun trying to deliver humanitarian assistance to Darfur as early as February 2003 (Power 2004: 68). Officials interviewed on-site in April 2005 by Anita Sanborn (representing the Colorado Episcopal Foundation) proved adept at tracking the various needs of local people, keeping close watch on incoming and warehoused supplies, and negotiating with relief agency representatives. As she noted, the Episcopal Church is among those actively working to facilitate both the delivery of supplies and the improvement of transnational communications. It is not a coincidence that former senator John Danforth, an ordained Episcopal minister, was named President George W. Bush's special envoy to Sudan in 2001.

Humanitarianism is not the sole prerogative of Western powers or professionals. Throughout the years that the late John Garang led the Sudanese People's Liberation Army in the south, he had fought oppressive strategies of the north and sought an alliance of all of Sudan's marginalized "African peoples." As described by his colleagues to Anita Sanborn (2005), he was perceived as "the father and the shepherd" of his people. While exerting substantial power both on and off the battlefield, he nonetheless presented himself as an everyman, as a carpenter and a farmer. On occasion he would cook for his troops, making sure that he ate last. He was widely admired and after his death, briefly eulogized by President George Bush.

Humanitarian intervention involves the use of troops, as noted above. Because the premises are complex and the prospects are encouraging for this type of intervention, it is covered in detail in chapter 8. One key for some humanitarian interventionists concerned with Darfur has been the emerging role of the African Union. Beginning in 2004, representatives of the union came to seek a larger role, including the use of troops. Rwanda, perhaps ironically, was among those nations offering soldiers for Darfur. It is possible that the African Union also will be able to address the nagging problem of slavery in Sudan, in a manner perceived as complementary to its humanitarian intervention and as nonthreatening to local leaders.

Humanitarian intervention can be enhanced by the advice and advocacy of the International Crisis Group. The ICG is one of the world's leading on-site, human rights monitoring and advocacy organizations. Its data collection network is extensive. It has a special expertise in African conflicts. ICG representatives have been critical of the UN Security Council regarding Darfur (2005c), but also of certain tactics of the African Union (2005b). The ICG stressed that, through mid-2005, both organizations had variously exhibited indecisiveness and a lack of bold initiative. Both also had offered a number of potentially useful ideas, such as asset freezes and travel bans on anyone who impedes the peace process.

Long-Term Strategies

Long-term socio-economic development and humanitarianism go hand in hand. Sustained agricultural growth, complemented by "integrated" livestock programs (with some reduction in herd sizes), is essential to the restabilization of Darfur's socio-economic structure. Careful attention must be paid to the voices—and thus ideas—of everyday farmers and herders. Perceptions of "being Arab" or "being African" ultimately are not nearly as important as, for example, "being a millet farmer." Citizens' abilities to calculate annual risk-yield ratios, hedge against drought, restructure their planting and migration cycles, and engage in mid-range planning must be affirmed (Van Arsdale 1989; Hutchinson 1989; de Waal 2005). The idea of circumscribed and fenced "nomad ranches," as proposed to me by Darfur's governor in 1979, fortunately was abandoned; I was one of several researchers and agency officials who told him how economically dysfunctional and sociologically problematic these would be.

It is not the elimination of an "ambiguous genocide" that holds the key to Darfur's future, although atrocities must cease. It is not the elimination of famine, drought, and desertification. It is not ancestry that holds the key. Rather, it is these citizen's own efforts at enhancing security, effecting a rights-oriented civil society that embraces decentralized governance and community-based development, and the depoliticizing of socio-economic relations. As Michael Ignatieff repeatedly stresses, rights evolve through deliberative process (Gutmann 2001). Land rights and creative land use strategies are essential. A focus on self-defined livelihoods is critical. Diplomats and local government officials can, and must, focus on these points.

POSTSCRIPT: DENVER FOR DARFUR

During the spring of 2005, students associated with the University of Denver's Center On Rights Development (CORD) organized a major rally. It was held on the steps of the Colorado capitol building. The rally sought to bring to the public's attention the ongoing human-rights abuses in Darfur. In parallel with rallies and petition drives held elsewhere in the country, speakers from the United States and Sudan discussed the legal, political, economic, and cultural ramifications of the conflict. Emerging from among the approximately 200 participants was an implied consensus that a genocide indeed was taking place. Standing quietly near the first row of steps (without overcoats, despite the freezing drizzle) were four Masalit refugees displaying a carefully lettered banner decrying the Sudanese government's recent actions.

The Denver for Darfur rally was an example of what can be done to promote greater awareness of genocidal situations. Such rallies can even help spur negotiations. Publicity on the problem has been extensive within the United States. A mid-2005 International Crisis Group/Zogby poll found that over 80 percent of Americans supported a tougher international response to the situation in Darfur.

REFERENCES

Ahmed, Abdel Ghaffar M. "The Question of Pastoral Nomadism in the Sudan." In *Some Aspects of Pastoral Nomadism in the Sudan,* edited by Abdel Ghaffar M. Ahmed. Khartoum: Khartoum University Press, 1976.

Anonymous. "A Reasonably Good Year in a Troublesome World." *Refugees* 4, no. 137 (2004): 6–15, 18–21.

Bascom, Johnathan B. *Losing Place: Refugee Populations and Rural Transformations in East Africa.* New York: Berghahn, 1998.

Bulcha, Mekuria. *Flight and Integration: Causes of Mass Exodus from Ethiopia and Problems of Integration in the Sudan.* Uppsala, Sweden: Scandinavian Institute of African Studies, 1988.

Chehade, Carol. "Darfur: The Color of Genocide." *Sudan Tribune*, March 31, 2005 at www.sudantribune.com/article.php3?id_article=8786 (accessed June 30, 2005).

Coll, Steve. *Ghost Wars: The Secret History of the CIA, Afghanistan, and bin Laden, from the Soviet Invasion to September 10, 2001.* New York: Penguin, 2004.

Cuny, Frederick C. with Richard B. Hill. *Famine, Conflict, and Response: A Basic Guide.* West Hartford, Conn.: Kumarian Press, 1999.

de Waal, Alex. *Famine That Kills: Darfur, Sudan.* Rev. ed. Oxford: Oxford University Press, 2005.

Dubinsky, Zach. "The Lessons of Genocide." *Essex Human Rights Review* 2, no. 1 (Spring 2005): 112–17.

Genocide Intervention Fund. "Creating a Genocide Intervention Fund to Support African Troops in Darfur." *Media Release,* February 5, 2005 at www.genocide interventionfund.org/about/proposal (accessed July 6, 2005).

Gutmann, Amy, ed. *Michael Ignatieff: Human Rights as Politics and Idolatry.* Princeton, N.J.: Princeton University Press, 2001.

Hailu, Tsegaye, Tsegay Wolde-Georgis, and Peter W. Van Arsdale. "Resource Depletion, Famine, and Refugees in Tigray." In *African Refugees: Development Aid and Repatriation*, edited by Howard Adelman and John Sorenson. Boulder, Colo.: Westview, 1994.

Hutchinson, Charles F. "Will Climate Change Complicate African Famine?" *Resources* (Resources for the Future) 95 (Spring 1989): 5–7.

International Crisis Group. "The Khartoum-SPLM Agreement: Sudan's Uncertain Peace." *ICG Africa Report*, No. 96, July 25, 2005a.

———. "Darfur Needs Bolder International Intervention." *ICG Media Release*, May 25, 2005b at notification@crisisgroup (accessed July 21, 2005).

———. "Sudan." *ICG Crisis Watch*, May 2, 2005, at www.crisisgroup.org/home/index.cfm (accessed July 21, 2005).

Khalifa, Babiker Ali. Interview with former Sudanese ambassador to South Korea, Denver, Colo. January 10, 2006.

Koerner, Brendan I. "Who are the Janjaweed?" *Slate Explainer*, July 19, 2005 at www.slate.com/id/2104210 (accessed July 21, 2005).

Kotch, Nick. "African Oil: Whose Bonanza?" *National Geographic* 208, no. 3 (September 2005): 50–65.

Moorehead, Caroline. "Letter from Darfur." *New York Review of Books* 52, no. 13 (August 11, 2005): 55–57.

Murphy, T. Craig. "Cyclical Linkages between War and Hunger in Africa." Unpublished manuscript, Graduate School of International Studies, University of Denver, Denver, Colo., 2003.

Nuti, Paul. "Perspectives on the Crisis in Darfur." *Anthropology News* 45, no. 9 (December 2004): 12–13.

Power, Samantha. "Dying in Darfur: Can the Ethnic Cleansing in Sudan be Stopped?" *New Yorker* (August 30, 2004): 56–73.

PRC Engineering Consultants. *Western Sudan Water Supply Project: Phase I Report.* Denver, Colo.: PRC Engineering Consultants Inc., 1979.

Prendergast, John. *Frontline Diplomacy: Humanitarian Aid and Conflict in Africa.* Boulder, Colo.: Lynne Rienner, 1996.

Prunier, Gérard. *Darfur: The Ambiguous Genocide.* Ithaca, N.Y.: Cornell University Press, 2005.

Reeves, Edward B., and Timothy Frankenberger. *Socio-Economic Constraints to the Production, Distribution, and Consumption of Millet, Sorghum, and Cash Crops in North Kordofan, Sudan.* Report No. 1, Department of Sociology/College of Agriculture, University of Kentucky, Lexington, 1981.

Sanborn, Anita. Interview with the president of the Colorado Episcopal Foundation, August 3, 2005.

Sa'oudi, Mohammed Abdel-Ghani. "An Overview of the Egyptian-Sudanese Jonglei Canal Project." *The International Politics Journal: Al-Siyassa, Al-Dawliya*. January, 2001 at www.siyassa.org.eg (accessed July 15, 2005).

UNHCR. "2004 Global Refugee Trends: Overview of Refugee Populations, New Arrivals, Durable Solutions, Asylum-Seekers, Stateless and Other Persons of Concern to UNHCR." *Population and Geographical Data Section Report*, Division of Operational Support, United Nations High Commissioner for Refugees, Geneva, June 17, 2005 at www.unhcr.ch/statistics (accessed July 30, 2005).

———. *The State of the World's Refugees: Fifty Years of Humanitarian Action*. Oxford: Oxford University Press/United Nations High Commissioner for Refugees, 2000.

———. *The State of the World's Refugees: In Search of Solutions*. Oxford: Oxford University Press/United Nations High Commissioner for Refugees, 1995.

Van Arsdale, Peter W. "The Ecology of Survival in Sudan's Periphery: Short-Term Tactics and Long-Term Strategies." *Africa Today* 36, no. 3/4 (Fall/Winter 1989): 65–78.

———. "Resource Scarcity in Western Sudan: The Impacts of Nomads and Refugees." Paper presented at the conference *Ending Hunger in Africa*, University of Denver, Colo., February 1988.

Chapter Seven

Palestine and the Issue of Internal Displacement

Please help me. I am absolutely desperate!

A Palestinian man grabbed me by the arm and shouted these words in my ear. I was walking with friends on a street in Bethlehem, toward the church built on the site where many Christians believe that Jesus was born. The man went on to explain that his family's livelihood depended on tourism, and that the current Intifada (Palestinian uprising) had caused a tense situation where the flow of tourists had been reduced to virtually nothing. Another man told me how he had attended college in Bethlehem, hoping to get a job as a teacher. Yet no such jobs were available and he also had become dependent on tourism, selling cheap jewelry on the street corner. Still another man told me that by posing for photographs and selling bracelets, he could make the equivalent of ten dollars a day.

This chapter is more broadly historical than any other in the volume. Palestine has experienced three millennia of forced migration, deportation, and displacement. Palestinian refugees and internally displaced persons (IDPs) have been created in extraordinary numbers since 1948, the year that Israel was proclaimed a state. Many of those who remain within Israel and the disputed West Bank and Gaza territories are second- and third-generation refugees living in restructured homelands. The chapter also is about the construction of narratives by Arabs and Jews. "Right of return" has become central; it also has become reified. The chapter is not about diminishing the achievements and aspirations of Israelis. It is not about blame nor moral judgment. Taking an implicit systems perspective, the situation confronting displaced Palestinians is intimately related to the situation confronting formerly displaced Israelis. Just as modern Palestine has been shaped, in large part, by the emergence of modern Israel, modern Israel has been shaped, in large part, by the emergence of modern Palestine.

GETTING THE LAY OF THE LAND

Palestine is the geographic term for the region that incorporates most of the nations of Palestine, Israel, and Lebanon today. In both geographic and environmental senses, Palestine (south of Lebanon) is comprised of what I would term "four countries." To the east is the lake-and-river country, as indeed the Sea of Galilee and the Dead Sea are lakes, interconnected by the south-flowing Jordan River. To the west is the plains country, bordering the Mediterranean Sea and traversed for thousands of years by the Via Maris and other trade routes. The fertile Jezreel Valley can be thought of as a northern extension of this country. The central portion of Palestine is dominated by the hill country. The Judean Wilderness is key to this; Jerusalem is also located here. To the south, and extending beyond Palestine proper, is the desert country. The Negev is being developed by Israel, and while still desolate, extensive irrigation and farm schemes can be found. Annual rates of precipitation range from forty inches in the north, near Lebanon, to less than four inches in the south, near Egypt.

From the perspective of some in Israel, the land itself is so important that it is known colloquially as "the Fifth Gospel." In the northern part of Israel, standing atop Mount Carmel near a statue dedicated to the prophet Elijah, I was able to see a long way. Toward the southwest I saw haze floating over what I knew were Mediterranean waters, even though I could not spot the sea itself. Far to the south I saw steam rising, perhaps from a hydroelectric plant near Tel Aviv. Toward the east I saw indistinct hills. A view from another spot further down the mountain's flank proved them to be the hills of Nazareth. Dropping down the southeast flank still further, I was able to get a clear view of the verdant Jezreel Valley. The ruins of the ancient, multitiered city of Megiddo stood nearby.

On the Mediterranean coast, I walked along the remarkably well-preserved walls of an Arab fortress. I was reminded of the frequent Middle Eastern superimposition of wall upon wall, building upon building, city upon city. A small Hellenistic site known as Straton's Tower (established as early as 400 B.C.E.), had been superceded by the imposing Roman city and arena of Caesarea Maritima (established by Herod about 20 B.C.E.), which had been partially superceded by the fortress. Islamic rulers had built it about 640 A.D.

Early one morning I arose early so as to be able to see the sun rise over the hills flanking the eastern shore of the Sea of Galilee. The rays first glinted off buildings in the city of Tiberias, on the western shore. Really just a medium-sized lake, this "sea" and the nearby Golan Heights have variously served as symbols of trans-ethnic passage and interethnic conflict for more than three millennia.

On a pleasant day in early March I hiked through the Kidron Valley, skirting old Jerusalem's east side. Walls and towers demarcating the Old City dominated the skyline. On the valley's eastern rim I chatted with a Palestinian boy who was babysitting his two-year-old twin sisters. He lived nearby, in the settlement of Silwan. A mile further south, at the entrance to the Hinnom Valley, I came to long-abandoned caves that had been used as tombs, scattered along cliff walls near an apartment complex.

Thirty-five miles further south, from the top of the Masada massif, as I looked toward the east—toward Jordan—I again saw haze floating over water. But in this case, it was floating over the Dead Sea. On the top of this massive butte Herod built an extensive palace complex. Of greater historical importance, as noted below, some 960 people had engaged in an act of group suicide on this same spot as the final Jewish battles with Rome wound down.

The city of Beersheva is located equidistant between the southwestern shore of the Dead Sea and the southern Gaza settlement of Rafah, on the Mediterranean coast. Now a bustling metropolis containing everything from McDonald's Restaurants to shopping malls, where Hebrew, Arabic, Amharic, Russian, and English all can be heard (Markowitz and Uriely 2002), the site has been inhabited for over 4,000 years. It marks the approximate southern boundary of ancient Palestine. From a desolate hill southeast of Beersheva, I was able to see a considerable expanse of the Negev Desert, which extends south to the Sinai Peninsula. The outpost that once stood on this rise had been used by Nabataean traders some 2,000 years ago, on their treks between Gaza and Petra in southern Jordan. Not far away I hiked through the Wilderness of Zin. This is a beautiful yet arid area with towering cliffs reminiscent of those in southern Utah. It was through here that Moses is said to have passed as his exodus drew to a close. Nearby is the southern home of David Ben-Gurion, Israel's first prime minister.

In a real sense, I had been able to see Palestine and Israel from north to south, from east to west. This compact landscape contains lush valleys, rocky hills, large lakes (known as "seas"), irrigated farmlands, and deserts. Deserts and wildernesses are emphasized in much of the written history, serving to symbolize the difficulties confronting people then and now.

THREE THOUSAND YEARS OF FORCED MIGRATION AND DISPLACEMENT

The land of Palestine, as noted previously, encompasses the nations of Palestine, Israel, and Lebanon today. Some twenty-five to thirty centuries ago such nations as Phoenicia, Philistia, Samaria, and Judea were included. The transjordanian region east of the Jordan River, while essential to an understanding of political developments, is not a part of Palestine per se.

Palestine is at the geographic crossroads of northeast Africa, the Near East, and southeast Europe. The prehistory and history of Palestine was shaped by "crossroads migrants." Well over 3,000 years ago, as the Bronze Age came to a close, seafaring peoples from as far away as Sardinia, Mycenaea, and Cyprus came to populate the coastal plains adjacent to the Mediterranean. Others arrived from Mesopotamia, perhaps mixing with indigenous peoples. Diverse cultures evolved, coming to encompass the nations of Canaan, Philistia, Phoenicia, Moab, Judah, Samaria, Galilee, Israel, and others. More than five millennia before this, seminomadic peoples with tribal names unknown to us had begun to take advantage of the ecologically diverse Fertile Crescent and Levant regions to domesticate crops and animals, and to establish settlements that grew into the world's first major towns. More than thirty millennia before this, at least one branch of early-modern humans had made their debut in this region. Their lineage truly was "out of Africa."

Forced migration and displacement (deportation) must be viewed as countervailing forces to those of migration. While not easy to decipher, these processes are not a new phenomenon in Palestine. Useful records are available from the eighth century B.C.E. on. Moving in from the northeast, the Assyrians invaded the region in 734 B.C.E. Under kings Tiglath-Pileser III, Shalmaneser V, and Sargon II, the destruction of Israelite, Philistinian, and other peoples' cities was brutal and far ranging. Forcible deportation was used to rid the Assyrians of a potentially problematic citizenry as new administrative structures were put in place. It also was used "to populate cities and settlements in Assyria itself while at the same time weakening the enemy's country by destroying its national framework" (Stern 2001: 11). Initially, as many as 50,000 people may have been deported from Palestine and resettled in Mesopotamian towns; subsequently 200,000 more may have followed. In the next eight decades, as Ephraim Stern notes, many of the cities and towns that had come under Assyrian control were repopulated with peoples from Babylon and beyond.

The Israelite deportation from the northern kingdom of Israel, beginning in 734 B.C.E., became known in popular lore as the displacement of the "Ten Lost Tribes." Inadequate scholarship, augmented by the wishful thinking of zealous "tribal locationists," subsequently came to place the descendants of these tribes in such remarkably diverse but improbable locales as western Burma, Britain, and South America (Gonen 2003). In fact, many of the Israelites had been assimilated into Assyrian society. Some had been deported to locations as far east as Persia. A diaspora had been created (Younger 2003).

The Assyrian occupation was followed by that of the Babylonians. Although it only lasted for about seventy years (604–538 B.C.E.), it also was characterized by deportations. Most famous was the forced exile to Babylon of members of the upper classes, upon the capture of Jerusalem in 586 B.C.E. In subsequent years additional deportations took place—including those of Philistines—all these during the reign of King Nebuchadnezzar. Unlike the earlier Assyrian plan, the Babylonians apparently did not repopulate Jerusalem and other occupied towns with people from other regions under their control (Stern 2001: 305; Jacobson 2001: 44).

Deportees from throughout Palestine were established in communities near Nippur. They lived in towns named after their own hometowns in Palestine, like Ashkelon and Gaza. Most were well treated. Some even assumed important offices (Stern 2001: 306). Most of those who had been deported from Jerusalem later repatriated. To some this cycle was seen as a recapitulation of the exile to Egypt of proto-Israelite tribes and their subsequent return to Palestine under Moses some 700 years earlier. In a very real sense these early forced migrants, deportees, and exiles were refugees.

Population realignment, reassessment, and replacement continued to characterize Palestine during the Greek and Roman periods. Philistine and post-Phoenician coastal peoples, many thought to be ancestral to contemporary Palestinians, continued with robust trade by land and sea. Their societies were built partially upon those of earlier Canaanites, dating perhaps to 3000 B.C.E. Some Canaanites established settlements in the West Bank region early on. They likely were the original inhabitants of Jerusalem (Shanks 1995: 1). As Jalal Kazzouh, head of the archaeology department at al-Najah University, has stressed: "[West Bank excavations reveal] our ancestors. These are our roots" (Anon. 1998: 25).

Forcible displacement has continued to characterize Palestine (and thus Israel) during much of the past 2,000 years. The so-called First Jewish Revolt against Roman rule began in 66 A.D. The destruction of the Second Temple of the Jews in Jerusalem in 70 A.D., along with much of the city, was accompanied by large displacements. It is estimated that under the Emperor Vespasian some 12,000 were transported to Rome alone, to help in the construction of the coliseum. While the Romans believed that they finally had terminated the uprising in Judea, some rebels fought on. They likely were headquartered on top of the Masada massif at the southern extreme of the Judean Wilderness.

The likely suicide of some 960 refugees on Masada's rim in 73 A.D. served to symbolize the ongoing intercultural strife in the region northwest of the Dead Sea. Rather than succumb to the siege being mounted by Roman troops, a pact among the holdouts led to the deaths of all but seven persons (Ben-Yehuda 1998). Masada has subsequently become an ideological symbol for the state of Israel, the subject of movies, a site venerated by Israeli soldiers, and one of the region's most popular tourist attractions (Ben-Yehuda 1996). Its importance is enhanced by its ever-evolving narrative.

The Second Jewish Revolt against Rome took place over a three-year period, from 132 to 135 A.D. It was led by Simon Bar-Kokhba (aka Simeon Bar-Kosiba). He was assisted by a large group of rebels. Recent excavations in four caves within the Ein Gedi Nature Reserve, near the western shore of the

Dead Sea, located coins, arrows, and spears. These indicate that, as their cause became more hopeless and they were forced to retreat from Roman forces, some of the rebels took refuge here. Noncombatants also were taking refuge elsewhere, with still others being forcibly displaced from their towns. The ensuing Roman victory under Emperor Hadrian led to the exile of Jews from Jerusalem and Judea (Sudilovsky and Feinberg Vamosh 2003). Other Palestinian peoples also were negatively impacted.

Upon final suppression of the revolt, the name of the province of Judea was changed to Syria Palaestina. Caesarea Maritima served as its capital during the remainder of the Roman and subsequent Byzantine/Christian periods (Porath 2004; Jacobson 2001). Gaza was invaded by Arab forces in 634 A.D.; most of Palestina (including Jerusalem) had been captured by 638 A.D. A foothold for Islam was readily established. Nonetheless, the area continued to serve as a center for Jewish and Christian faithful. Jerusalem's Temple Mount, once the site of Jewish temples, had become home to the Dome of the Rock by the late seventh century. Thus, the literal displacement of peoples in Palestine has been complemented by the symbolic displacement of holy sites. From Hershel Shanks's perspective, this octagonal domed Omayyad mosque "is not only one of the most beautiful achievements of Islamic architecture, it is also the earliest dated building extant in the Moslem world. And it is unique" (1995: 234). It has remained virtually unchanged to the present day.

The Crusades were mounted under the auspices of Euro-Christian hegemony. In 1099 A.D., after a lengthy siege, Crusaders under the leadership of Godfrey de Bouillon conquered Jerusalem. Moslems and Jews alike were tortured and murdered. Both groups were then barred from the Holy City. The Dome of the Rock and other mosques were converted into churches. After the Moslem general Saladin retook the region in 1187 A.D., this and other churches were again converted into mosques (Shanks 1995: 238–40). Saladin permitted Jews and Christians to return peacefully. Two later onslaughts by Crusaders during the first half of the thirteenth century did not result in sustained occupations of Jerusalem or other Palestinian locales. The displaced continued to establish and reestablish themselves within the greater Palestine, Syria, and Transjordan regions.

It is claimed that Jerusalem was conquered twenty-three times over the past 3,000 years (Shanks 1995: xiii). At one point its official name was even changed to Aelia Capitolina. Yet the city has continued to serve as a nexus of Jewish, Christian, and Islamic politico-religious systems. Its Old City has continued to serve as a symbol. Its four quarters—Moslem, Christian, Armenian, Jewish—serve as reminders that persons of diverse views can live side by side.

When assessing the region's current geopolitical checkerboard, the processes of forced migration and displacement open one window into what is impacting Palestinians and Israelis alike.

THE CREATION OF MODERN PALESTINE AND ISRAEL

The etymology of the term "Palestine" and its derivatives is subject to debate. As Jacobson (2001) notes, many people assume that the term derives from the biblical term *Peleshet*, "Land of the Philistines," thus linking it philologically to the Greek *Palaistinê* and the Latin *Palaestina*. Viewed from historical and archaeological perspectives, the Philistines likely descended from Mycenaeans of the Aegean region. They were one of the so-called Sea Peoples who populated the eastern Mediterranean coast's Canaanite region as early as 1300 B.C.E. Although withstanding the incursions of Assyrians during the eighth century B.C.E., and adopting certain cultural characteristics of other peoples, the Philistines (as an ethnic entity) could not withstand the onslaughts of the Babylonians during the seventh and sixth centuries B.C.E. Even the citadel of Ekron was finally destroyed by Nebuchadnezzar of Babylonia (Gitin 2005). During the fifth century B.C.E., the term "Palaistinê" was being used to describe the entire area between Phoenicia and Egypt, thus encompassing Israel. Roman writers continued to use this term. The widely regarded historian Josephus Flavius, writing during the second century A.D., refers to the Philistines as Palaistinoi, but also uses it in a wider geographic/demographic sense.

By contrast, the term "Israel" is said to have arisen from an incident in which Jacob, son of Isaac and grandson of Abraham, wrestled with an angel (as reported in the biblical book of Genesis). The first archaeological reference to Israel is found on a victory stelae commissioned by the Egyptian pharaoh Merneptah about 1200 B.C.E. The early post-exodus inhabitants of Canaan are variously referred to as proto-Israelites or Hebrews.

Like other peoples of the Middle East, Palestinians represent an amalgam of cultural, ethnic, and biological lineages. Therefore it is identity, and how that identity is interpreted by a people and its neighbors, that is paramount. It is the Nation of Palestine, in concert with the Nation of Israel, which then takes on primary importance. When considering the creation of refugees and IDPs, the Palestinian diaspora must be interpreted interactively with the Jewish diaspora. In a real sense, the interactions of Middle Eastern peoples have transformed cultures, created new ethnic labels, and produced multiple diasporas.

Early Controversy and Conflict

Modern Palestine is, in part, a creation of modern Israel. Modern Israel is, in part, a creation of modern Palestine. Building upon a plan first put forth by Britain's Lord Arthur James Balfour (1848–1930), the creation of a national Jewish homeland in Palestine proceeded in fits and starts. Dawn Chatty and Gillian Lewando Hundt, in *Children of Palestine* (2005), provide a comprehensive synthesis of what transpired. After the controversial and ill-fated

Sykes-Picot agreement of 1916, which aimed at dividing lands under the control of the rapidly collapsing Ottoman Empire, the Balfour Declaration was revealed. As Balfour noted in a letter dated November 2, 1917, to Lord Nathan Rothschild, a British leader of the Zionist movement in London (and the first Jew to be seated in the House of Lords): "His Majesty's Government view with favour the establishment in Palestine of a national home for the Jewish people, and will use their best endeavours to facilitate the achievement of this objective." Britain's colonial role remained central throughout the next thirty years.

The League of Nations was created in 1919 and formally came into existence in 1920. In the league covenant, the Palestinian populace was recognized as an independent nation, placed "provisionally" under British mandate. Numerous complications and contradictions arose after the Balfour Declaration was incorporated into the League's Mandate for Palestine, not least of which allowed consultancy with the Jewish Agency regarding lands, immigration, and settlement, without consultancy with the indigenous Palestinians. Immigration of European (and other) Jews to Palestine was fairly extensive during the several decades following the declaration. A Palestinian revolt took place in the mid-1930s. By 1947 some 700,000 Jews were resident, of a total population of about 2.1 million.

The newly created United Nations sent a special commission to the Middle East in 1947. After evaluating data in the field, it recommended the formal partition of Palestine. This was incorporated into General Assembly Resolution 181, which was passed. According to the resultant plan, the new Jewish state was to encompass 56.4 percent of the territory and the Palestinian Arab state 42.8 percent. Jerusalem was to be an international zone. At this time, Jews owned only 7 percent of Palestine's land.

Within days of the announcement, Arabs had rejected the resolution and partition plan, and armed conflict had spread throughout Palestine. Jewish and Arab paramilitaries battled town to town, village to village, farm to farm. The Haganah (later renamed the Israeli Defense Force) proved superior to Arab militias, and—even though the Arab League eventually sent troops—ultimately prevailed. On May 15, 1948, David Ben-Gurion proclaimed the establishment of the state of Israel. Hundreds of thousands of Palestinians fled, variously becoming (depending on destination and definition) refugees or IDPs.

While the Israeli cabinet moved to block their return, fearing reprisals and violence, Arab governments refused to formally integrate the displaced persons, believing this would weaken their right to return. Many of the refugees sought safe haven in the West Bank (under Jordanian control) and Gaza (under Egyptian control). "Many had left their doors open, while others took their keys. Today many hold on to the keys to their homes as a symbol of hope and resistance in exile" (Chatty and Hundt 2005: 15). Some of these persons were doubly displaced, being forced to move again nearly twenty years later during the Arab-Israeli war of 1967. Israel's victory in 1967 resulted in its occupation of the West Bank, Gaza, and East Jerusalem, which constituted the remaining 22 percent of Palestine.

The notion of creating a Jewish state gained widespread, justifiable support as the survivors of the Holocaust, its concentration camps and pogroms, and other oppressive circumstances sought to carve out a homeland in the very region where their ancestors had done the same thing almost 3,000 years before. Yet the re-creation of a Jewish homeland "continues to epitomize the dilemma of self-determination in areas under previous colonial mandates. Even if an oppressed nationality deserves a right to a safe homeland, its existence within new borders is often realized at the expense of other groups, imposing on them economic hardship and the loss of self-governance" (Ishay 2004: 241–42).

Substantive attempts to create a governing body for Palestinians began in 1964, aided by Egypt and the Arab League. The Palestine Liberation Organization (PLO) was established in May of that year during a meeting in Jerusalem. At that time the structures of the Palestine National Council (PNC), the PLO Executive Committee, the National Fund, and the Palestine Liberation Army, as well as a national covenant, were laid out. With the subsequent ascendance of Yasser Arafat and the militant Fatah group, which joined the PLO in 1968 and assumed the leadership role in 1969, the PLO evolved into a kind of organizational umbrella. A modern Palestinian state was claimed in Gaza and the West Bank in 1974. The UN General Assembly recognized the PNC as official representative of the Palestinian people through Resolution 3210, passed on October 14 of that year. A PLO permanent observer mission to the United Nations also was established at that time. Gaza and Jericho were among the first areas to be formally incorporated into the new state.

Recent Controversy and Conflict

Revenge and retaliation are unfortunate hallmarks of the recent era. Reconciliation and rehabilitation seem to occur too infrequently. Within historical Palestine, the disputed territories of Gaza, the West Bank, and East Jerusalem now represent the nation "on the ground." So do the various refugee camps and settlements. Intermittent attacks continue among Israelis and Palestinians. Some involve the camps. For example, on November 1, 2005, a pilotless Israeli drone overflying Gaza's Jabaliya refugee camp fired automated missiles at a car whose occupants included Hassan Madhoun, a senior commander of the Fatah-affiliated Al-Aqsa Martyrs Brigade in northern Gaza, and Fawzi Karah, a local leader of the militant group Hamas' armed wing. Both were killed. Israeli authorities stated that Madhoun had played a role in a suicide bombing in Ashdod in 2004 that had killed ten Israelis (King 2005).

The first Intifada (Palestinian uprising) lasted from 1987 to 1994. The second Intifada (known popularly as the Al-Aqsa Intifada) began in 2000 and continues to the present. B'tselem, the Israeli human-rights information center, calculates that during the first two years of the Al-Aqsa Intifada the number of Israelis killed by Palestinians was 640. Of those, 440 were civilians, including 82 children. Approximately 335 were killed inside Israel proper, the rest in the disputed territories. Palestinians also killed twenty-seven foreigners during this period. The first suicide bombings in the Middle East were undertaken by the Hezbollah in Lebanon during the early 1980s. In the ten-year span from 1993 through 2002 there were 198 suicide bombing missions undertaken by Palestinians. Of these, 136 resulted in the attackers being blown up along with multiple victims. Several attacks were carried out by women. By contrast, the number of Palestinians killed by Israelis during the first two years of the Al-Aqsa Intifada was 1,597, of whom 300 were minors (Margalit 2003: 36). A number were killed as advanced weaponry was being employed in the pursuit of militants. Others were injured as homes of suspected militants were bulldozed.

Suicide bombings and bulldozing operations have been condemned by a variety of human-rights groups, as well as by Palestinian and Jewish activists I have interviewed.

IDENTITIES AND CLAIMS

Historical fact, legend, and myth are intertwined in the Middle East. That is, this region is much like any other vibrant and volatile region in the world. Dates become more than dates, they become benchmarks (or watersheds). Demographics become more than demographics, they become powerful or ominous statistics. Events become more than events, they become celebrations or issues. Leaders become more than leaders, they become icons or villains. Processes of depopulation, repopulation, migration, and internal displacement mold this system. The identity of one group helps shape the identity of the other.

The Palestinian refugee and IDP population worldwide totals about 4 million persons. Yet the fears expressed by some Israelis that a swelling Palestinian population (both in Israel and the disputed territories) will make Israel politically untenable are proving overblown. Recent demographic analyses indicate the Palestinian population is growing far less than the 5 percent per annum once projected, and that the West Bank and Gaza are experiencing net emigration. Palestinian birth rates are declining. The Jewish share of the aggregate population in Israel, Gaza, and the West Bank has remained fairly constant for forty years, at about 60 percent (Zimmerman and Ettinger 2005). The Palestinian Christian population has been decreasing. Such persons comprise less than 3 percent of the region's total population.

The overall population of Israel and Palestine is about 6.6 million. Just as diverse and at times fragmented groups have been incorporated as "Palestinian/Muslim," similarly diverse groups have been accommodated

Figure 7.1. Palestinian and Israeli youth usually mingle peacefully. This Palestinian teenager works alongside Israeli teenagers in Nazareth's bustling market district.

as "Israeli/Jewish." None have been more numerous than the Jews who emigrated from the former Soviet Union. None have been more interesting than the Ethiopian Jews; some 80,000 currently reside in Israel. They have immigrated to Israel over the past two decades, initiated by two major waves. The first wave, via Sudan in 1984, was known as Operation Moses; the second, via Ethiopia proper in 1991, was termed Operation Solomon. Some rabbinical authorities in Israel have questioned their status as Jews, and many have found it difficult to adapt to life in their new homeland. The controversial Fares Mura, who had converted to Christianity, also have continued to arrive from Ethiopia (Shabtay 2000: 982; see also chapter 3, herein).

The contemporary cartographic and geographic landscapes are overlaid with a confusing array of lines. These help shape identities and claims. The "green line" forms the border between Israel and the West Bank. It is not marked on the ground for most of its nearly 200-mile length, confusing those who might inadvertently wander across (Widzer 2005b). A formidable security wall is being built by Israel along or near most of this boundary. A boundary line demarcates Gaza (also known as the Gaza Strip) as well. It runs for about forty miles. Prior to the Israeli pullout from Gaza, various other lines, boundaries, and fences delineated its settlements there. These kinds of markers still are found, either cartographically or on the ground, around Jewish settlements in the West Bank. Zones A, B, and C represent still different kinds of lines, as noted below.

Resolutions and the "Right to Return"

Identities and claims are linked to the long and rocky series of negotiations, resolutions, and accords that have characterized the modern Israeli-Palestinian relationship. The "right to return" has emerged as a core claim.

Al-Nakba underpins the claim of "right to return." This term (meaning "the catastrophe") was applied to the 1947–1948 disruption, war, and flight. Having been forced to flee, the idea of returning to Palestine became central to the national struggle and to a narrative that suggests that repopulating the homeland is essential. From the Palestinian perspective, as Hassan (1998: 52–53) notes, expulsion from the ancestral landscape marked the beginning of a series of injustices that can be ended when they return. For this reason, many Palestinians have rejected the label of "refugee." In a 1964 meeting held in Jerusalem, the Palestinian National Council passed a resolution to replace the term "refugee" as used in this context with the term "returner." Since 1968, the right to return for refugees and IDPs also has become key to the Palestinian narrative of liberation. In 1974, spurred by the Palestine Liberation Organization, the right to return was placed at the forefront of claimed rights. For those choosing not to return, the notion of compensation was reinforced.

Resolutions passed by the United Nations General Assembly and Security Council have become important to the Palestinian narrative, both pro and con. Early in 1948, Count Bernadote of Sweden was engaged as a UN mediator. He was assisted by the America's Ralph Bunche. Little time had passed before they expressed their concern regarding the displacement of Palestinian refugees. Bernadote proposed to the emergent Israeli government that a limited number be permitted to return immediately. In what was a first in terms of intended Middle Eastern refugee agency involvement, he also proposed to systematically enlist the assistance of international organizations in the resettlement, and in the economic and social rehabilitation of the returnees. Although Bernadote was tragically assassinated shortly thereafter, the UN General Assembly followed his lead and adopted Resolution 194 later that year (Hassan 1998: 46–48).

Paragraph 11 of the resolution has frequently been referenced by Palestinian activists ever since. It states that "the refugees wishing to return to their homes and live at peace . . . should be permitted to do so . . . and that compensation should be paid for the property of those choosing not to return and for [any] loss . . . which . . . should be made good by the Governments or authorities responsible." The UN's new Conciliation Commission for Palestine (CCP) was charged with following through.

Many individual Israelis, for their part, were not opposed to the return of some refugees. However, Israeli Prime Minister David Ben-Gurion emphasized to the CCP that the resettlement of most should preferably be accommodated by, and in, Arab states. As negotiations were attempted, Arab representatives refused to meet with the Israeli delegates, setting a precedent for further stalemates that have occurred intermittently ever since.

UN Security Council Resolution 237 was passed in June 1967. Mirroring certain of the language used nearly twenty years earlier, it called on Israel to facilitate the return of those inhabitants who had fled during the so-called Six Day War. It was followed a few months later by Resolution 242. This explicitly stressed the need to achieve a just settlement to the refugee problem. As Hassan (1998: 54) points out, during this period Article 13 of the Universal Declaration of Human Rights (covering the right to leave and return to one's country), Article 12 of the International Covenant on Civil and Political Rights (covering the right to enter one's country), and the Geneva Conventions (discussed in chapter 8) were frequently used by the Palestinians to support their claims. Of equal importance were Resolution 181 (perceived negatively by Palestinians) and Resolution 3210 (perceived positively). These were previously discussed.

The several resolutions have been paralleled by several accords. Paramount were the Oslo Accords, drafted in 1993. They were seen by optimists as harbingers of peace. Laying out a phased series of steps and benchmarks, the accords called for the PLO to renounce violence and fight terrorism; for Israeli withdrawal from most of Gaza (except for Jewish settlements) and from Jericho; and for subsequent Israeli redeployments. The newly established Palestinian Authority would assume increased control. The Oslo II Agreement of 1995 specified further details about redeployment in the West Bank, as Robert Malley (2004) notes. That year the West Bank was divided into three zones. Zone A is under full Palestinian control and consists only of the biggest towns. Zone B is under Palestinian civil and Israeli military/security control. Zone C is under full Israeli control and covers most of the West Bank.

The Oslo Accords, however, did not focus on long-term outcomes: The ultimate disposition of Palestinian and Israeli territories; the fate of Jewish settlements within Gaza and the West Bank; the future of Jerusalem; nor the status of refugees and IDPs. Subsequent attempts by President Bill Clinton to deal with the refugee problem more directly, and to place "right to return" in a more viable position vis-à-vis the negotiating table, also led to little substantive change.

Post-Oslo talks, which would have led to extensive jurisdiction by the Palestinian Authority and further modifications of Israeli territorial control, met numerous hurdles. That Fatah had gained a central position within the authority caused consternation on the part of many Israelis. Nonetheless, periodic cooperation between Palestinians and Israelis on security matters did take place, the Palestinians were given nominal jurisdiction over 90 percent of their people in Gaza and the West Bank, and some Israeli redeployments occurred. But, deadlines were missed, deadly attacks by Palestinians continued, Jewish settlements in the West Bank grew, and—by 2000—Israel still held approximately 30 percent of Gaza and 60 percent of West Bank territory (Malley 2004). The fragile working relationship that had been established by Yitzhak Rabin and Yasser Arafat in the early 1990s, prior to Rabin's assassination, did not produce long-term results. Significant had been Rabin's 1993 formal recognition of the PLO. As of 2005, the spirit of Oslo seemed to have been lost. Former U.S. envoy Dennis Ross believes these efforts failed because "neither Israelis nor Palestinians underwent the necessary transformations" (Malley 2004: 20).

The Dangers of Politicization

One key complication for those working in this region is the danger of having one's research politicized. In concert with the challenge of presenting identities and claims in balanced perspective, this has nowhere been better exemplified than in the pioneering historical analyses of Bennie Morris. As Schwarz (2004) emphasizes, Morris's carefully researched conclusions regarding the creation of Palestinian refugees led him to be excoriated both as a PLO supporter and a Zionist propagandist. Morris demonstrated that neither the extreme Arab version nor extreme Jewish version is accurate; Palestinians fled or were expelled from their land as a result of war, not Zionist or Arab design. Reasons vary widely, being intertwined with complex social/familial, economic, and military factors. Arabs were angered at his assertions that expulsions were not the consequence of an ominous Zionist strategy, but more a collapse of morale owing to a lack of strong leadership and lack of national cohesion. Some Palestinians are shown to have abandoned their homes on the advice of their leaders, who saw the propaganda value of an exodus. Jews were angered at his assertions that incidents of Israeli valor were paralleled by incidents of atrocity and massacre. His analysis demonstrated that, from 1948 on, Israeli policy "unambiguously and often brutally sought to bar [refugee return]" (2004: 110). While Israeli security and safety concerns were genuinely pursued, Palestinians often suffered as, for example, a road was secured or a garrison established. Fears were genuinely expressed by people on both sides, as Morris stresses. Each side "could point to a history of grievous wrongs committed by the other."

The dangers of politicization, in the context of identity development, are demonstrated in a different way by Fatah. This organization was formed in the 1950s and by 1969 had taken control of the PLO. As Agha and Malley (2005: 20) stress, Fatah became the "big tent" that Yasser Arafat used to accommodate different perspectives and diverse actors. "Fatah was an extension of him [and] it mimicked him." Later, its members became key players within the Palestinian Authority. Everyday citizens were prodded to take sides, to choose between Fatah and Hamas. Questions of identity began to be asked, and as they were, began to be politicized: Is Fatah more secular or religious? Is it a liberation movement, whose objective is independence and whose currency is resistance? Is it a political party, whose leaders are emergent statesmen? Is it a terrorist organization, whose modus operandi is violence?

One's choice of organizational membership helps shape one's identity. The coalescence of a singular Palestinian identity is a relatively recent phenomenon, as Martin Widzer (2005a) points out. There was little sense of nationalism or homogenization during the last decades of the Ottoman Empire. Inhabitants of the region were more likely to think of themselves as Arab, Muslim, or Christian, as a Jaffen or a Nubulsi. It was not until a 1914 editorial published in the newspaper *Filastin* stressed the notion of a "Palestinian

nation" that the idea became a rally cry. In reality, identities have been relatively fluid in the Middle East for millennia, yet in the twentieth and twenty-
first centuries have become more politicized. Conflict hardens boundaries
and reshapes identities, even as just claims regarding ethnic safety and security are being made by people on both sides.

DIASPORAS, REFUGEES, AND CAMPS

A diaspora is a nation dispersed. Yet a homeland, a social cohesion, and a
strong identity all remain. Many of those who have been forcibly displaced,
or who have chosen to leave, maintain contact with others who have been dispersed, as well as with those in the homeland. Narratives that bind members
of the group are created. This has been the case with both Palestinians and
Jews. The diaspora of the one has directly influenced, and been influenced by,
the diaspora of the other.

The Palestinian diaspora becomes extraordinarily difficult to define when
landscape rather than people are considered. It exists both outside Palestine
proper and within the geographical territory of Palestine. It consists of citizens of the state of Israel who are Palestinian, of citizens of the state of Palestine (or the quasi-state represented by the Palestinian Authority), of residents
of West Bank and Gaza towns, of residents of West Bank and Gaza camps, of
those living in camps in neighboring countries such as Syria, and of those
Palestinians who have left the Middle East as refugees and immigrants and
reside in such places as Detroit, London, and Paris.

Refugees and IDPs

To many everyday observers, as influenced by the media, the Palestinian diaspora is best symbolized by refugees and IDPs. A Palestinian who has been displaced and is now living within Israel, Syria, or any other country can be considered a refugee. A Palestinian who is displaced and living within Gaza or the
West Bank can be considered an IDP. Yet this seemingly straightforward categorization becomes blurred in practice. This is due to issues of identity, nationalism, and mobility. The "right to return" and "the refugee problem" have become more than issues, they have become slogans and, in that sense, often have
been misused by ideologues on both sides.

Most of the Palestinians who became first-generation refugees or IDPs fled
in 1948 (during the war associated with the creation of the state of Israel) or
during 1967 (during the war when the West Bank and Gaza emerged as disputed territories). Second-generation and third-generation refugees live in
camps that have evolved into towns and villages. In some cases three con-

Figure 7.2.   Palestinian police supervise various checkpoints, religious sites, and facilities within the West Bank and Gaza. This officer is checking a visitor's credentials. His badge is pinned, rather than sewn, to a temporary jacket, one sign of the shortfall in the Palestinian Authority's clothing supplies budget.

secutive generations of Palestinians have occupied the same property within a camp for over fifty years. Many of the services first brought to the camps were through the International Red Cross and the United Nations Relief and Works Agency [for Palestine Refugees] (UNRWA), established in 1950. Food, shelter, health care, and education were its mandates.

A useful demographic summary recently was provided by Chatty and Hundt (2005: 11–12). Gaza has a total population of over 1 million. Of this number, about 75 percent are refugees or IDPs, half of whom live in its eight refugee camps. The West Bank has a total population of over 1.5 million approximately 37 percent of whom are refugees or IDPs. About a quarter of this number live in its twenty camps. Jordan is home to the largest Palestinian population in the diaspora. Over half the populace are of Palestinian descent; approximately 32 percent of the overall population are refugees. The ten primary camps are in the northwest portion of Jordan. Approximately 42 percent of the entire region's refugees live in this single country, which is about the same size as the state of Indiana. Refugees from the so-called first wave (1948) have full citizenship entitlements; those from 1967 and later waves do not.

As of 2001 the number of registered refugees living in Lebanon was 370,000. In 1949 the total had been 110,000. Currently about 53 percent live in one of Lebanon's ten official camps, another 20 percent in unofficial camps, and the remainder in various cities, towns, and villages. In Syria there are an estimated 400,000 refugees. A majority are first-generation and their descendants. Of Syria's eight refugee camps, Yarmouk is among the most well known. It houses about 90,000 refugees, making it one of the largest in the Middle East.

The Palestinian diaspora is not only defined by mobility and displacement, but also by confinement for those in camps (Kelly 2004). Although not entirely accurate, the perception held by many camp residents is that Israelis hold all the cards—metaphorically and literally—regarding employment, transportation, and identity.

The Dheisheh Camp

My 2001 trip through the West Bank and the town of Bethlehem took me to the outskirts of the Dheisheh refugee camp. It is one of three within the District of Bethlehem, the others being Aida and Beit Jebren. As of 2001 the camp had a population of about 11,000. It was first opened in 1949 and initially hosted those who had fled the many Palestinian villages located west of Jerusalem and Hebron. It sits on less than a square mile of land; until 1995 it was surrounded by a barbed wire fence. Dheisheh is a well-developed settlement. It belies the stereotype of a tent landscape as seen in Darfur or a hut landscape as seen in El Salvador. Most of the houses and apartments are built of wood, brick, and concrete. Cinderblocks are employed widely in construction. T.V. antennas line the rooftops. Flower pots dot many windowsills (Hamzeh 2001). Electrical, water, rubbish removal, and sewage systems are in place, although not always fully functional. Streets are paved. There are fourteen entrances to the settlement. Dheisheh is not only a camp, but a town. It is not only "temporary," but "permanent." It is not only "confined," but "open."

Life bustles in the camp. Many people run small businesses. Others work outside the camp in the Israeli service sector or on construction projects. Although there has been what Alzaroo (2005: 130) terms "minimum funding" by the Israeli government for public schools, they operate relatively efficiently. During the first Intifada, Israeli authorities closed many of the West Bank camps' schools and universities, the latter for up to four years. Approximately fifty days of curfews were imposed on Dheisheh; similar restrictions were imposed on other camps such as Al-Fawwar. Even kindergartens were closed briefly. Teachers were restricted by an array of regulations and low salaries. That said, nonformal education programs are widespread in Dheisheh and other West Bank camps. They include adult literacy, distance education, health programming (including midwifery), business and secretarial training, and arts education (Alzaroo 2005: 131). Funds are derived from NGOs, charitable Palestinian and Jewish organizations, religious institutions, and governmental sources.

Most of the camp residents who work outside work in metropolitan Jerusalem. Identity cards are required for all transit and transportation. As Widzer (2005b) emphasizes, such cards are seen as insulting since they are issued not by a Palestinian authority but by an Israeli authority.

Israeli military personnel invaded Dheisheh during the first Intifada. Tear gas was used (Hamzeh 2001). Israelis were concerned about protecting the main road near the camp that settlers use daily in journeys to and from Jerusalem. Many people say they feel safer in the camp than when traveling outside, and visit distant relatives infrequently as a result. Some own property outside the camp, in places such as Bethlehem and Hebron. Having earlier dominated portions of the service sector within Gaza, Hamas has gained stature as it has provided social services in camps like Dheisheh; the West Bank traditionally has been more the province of Fatah.

Early on, West Bank camp residents had characterized their lives as unbearable owing to poverty, unemployment, difficult housing conditions, and heavy dependency on United Nations donations (Alzaroo 2005). The poverty that characterized camp life early on has abated somewhat, but still persists for many.

ADAPTATION THROUGH NARRATIVES

Applied research of this type must strike the proper balance between understandings of order and disorder, of organization and chaos. While the circumstances are unfortunate, displacement and disorder should not be viewed as anomalous (cf. Hammond 2004: 207–17 passim). What refugees and IDPs do to survive in new homelands—or in the case of Palestine, restructured homelands—must be viewed as adaptive, "warts and all." Some strategies work better than others. An analytic dichotomy that simplistically describes "victims" and "survivors" is not appropriate, unless it is intended to reflect the voices and emically defined perceptions of those living these lives. An analytic dichotomy that simplistically describes "Palestinians" and "Israelis" (or Muslims and Jews) also is not appropriate, unless it is intended to highlight the stereotypes that exist.

Narratives are developed, whether explicitly or implicitly, to help the process of adaptation under stress. This occurred with events at Masada nearly 2,000 years ago, as noted previously. Most of those involving contemporary Palestine have developed around events taking place since World War II. The 1947–1948 war resulted in significant displacement and carnage. It became known to Palestinians as *al-Nakba* and, as mentioned earlier the notion of catastrophe took hold. The April 9, 1948, massacre at Deir Yassin village—near Jerusalem—led to creation of a powerful narrative, one that has become reified. So did the 1982 massacre at Sabra and Shatila. The first-wave refugee flight from mandated Palestine involved some 750,000 people and led to an exodus narrative. The 1967 Arab-Israeli war and West Bank annexation of land that had belonged to Jordan was accompanied by creation of a kind of "west of River Jordan/east of River Jordan" narrative. The 1967 event is known as *al-Naksa*. A similar narrative arose after Moses' descendants and tribesmen traveled through Canaan and approached the river 3,200 years ago. Forcible displacements and popular uprisings therefore have come to comprise key narratives.

Of prime importance in both the unfolding of history and the creation of narrative are the several resolutions and accords that have been promulgated and passed by various bodies since 1948. The most important were covered earlier. Each contributed to what has become an interlocking set of meta-narratives of rights and responsibilities. These interactively engage Palestinians, other Arabs, Israelis, and Americans; other parties are seen to play lesser roles.

A different form of adaptive narrative has been developed by residents of refugee camps. In camps such as Dheisheh and Jenin, posters are made from the photographic portraits of martyrs. The term "martyr" here is used in the Arabic sense, as in "witness," thus a poster can be made for anyone who has been killed in a confrontation, including accidentally. They are by no means restricted to suicide bombers. Some of the posters are professionally made and widely distributed; others are handmade, one-of-a-kind creations. It is believed that connectivity with Palestinians in the diaspora can be enhanced by poster use, while identities are reaffirmed. Some family members perform *haj* pilgrimages in the name of those pictured. Respected Christians also can be featured, as occurred with Jenin camp director Ian Hook after he was killed in 2002 (Higgins 2005).

Narratives build as much on opinions and lore as on knowledge and fact. As Widzer (2005a: 1) states, "Past peace efforts . . . have operated within the realm of *opinions* rather than *knowledge*. Making the transition from opinion to knowledge then, requires the negotiators to have a comprehensive understanding of what it means to the individual making his or her way through life as a Palestinian, an Israeli, a Jew, a Muslim . . . awash in the sea of contradictions." It will be interesting to see what type of narrative is built around 9/11 by Palestinians and Israelis. This date now is beginning to reverberate in the Middle East, as it already has in the United States. It was September 11, 2005, when Israel officially terminated its presence in Gaza.

EFFECTIVE ACTION: ENGAGING AN ARRAY OF RESOURCES

For decades barley, corn, and wheat have been the three crops of primary importance to residents of Palestine. As a former farmer told Salah Alzaroo (2005: 124), "God blesses these three seeds." Vineyards and olive groves have been essential for millennia. In recent years tourism, diamond cutting, mining and phosphates, and high-tech product development have emerged as central to the Israeli economy. Natural gas development is gaining a foothold. (Nuclear power is not used.) Palestinians have been the marginal beneficiaries of these modern enterprises.

Archaeological sites attract a great deal of interest and significant inflows of capital. Those I have visited, such as Megiddo, are of international significance. Relatively few Palestinian university teams are involved, compared to the large number of Israeli and foreign researchers.

Following the recent withdrawal of Israeli forces from Gaza (as well as from four West Bank settlements), the issue of resource availability again became crucial. Control and administration did not immediately become clear. Hamas and Palestinian security forces found themselves at odds. Economic activities that had been co-dependent upon Palestinians and Israelis were undercut. Trucking operations were adversely affected. Some businesses and market facilities were destroyed during the post-withdrawal celebrations. The flow of Palestinian laborers into Israel was reduced. The situation for most refugees and IDPs remained unchanged.

Gaza's extensive greenhouse system emerged as a kind of bellwether for development. Some of the greenhouses and crop distribution systems that had been developed by Israelis, often in conjunction with Palestinians, were destroyed as the Israelis left. Others were retained intact and taken over exclusively by Palestinian entrepreneurs. Some produce was successfully distributed internally; other produce could not be, since an open border does not exist between Gaza and Israel.

Resource disparities are reflected in the patterns of housing development within the West Bank. A kind of "ecological verticality" exists. Weizman and

Segal (cited in Roy and Al Sayyad 2005: 150–51) note how Jewish settlements strategically located in the West Bank occupy hillside sites, "suburban enclaves separated from the much poorer Palestinian neighbors but also enjoying a vertical sovereignty of surveillance and infrastructure." My own discussions with specialists in the region covered water resource access disparities. The ratio varies from about 5:1 to about 10:1 in favor of Israelis.

The European Union (EU) has been a substantial provider of economic aid to the Palestinians. In recent years this has included emergency aid for salaries. On November 7, 2005, the EU began to play a different role. It agreed to monitor a Gaza-Egypt border crossing that serves as a major gateway to the outside world for Palestinians living in the coastal strip. Foreign inspectors will be deployed at the Rafah terminal. Israel had closed Rafah before the September 2005 pullout, with the terminal open only sporadically to allow the passage of hardship cases.

Having spent seven years in the region, Martin Widzer (2005b) summarized it best when he told me that virtually all understandings of resource use must be shaped by understandings of risk and vulnerability. The risk is palpable, ever present, and perceived by all residents, not just Palestinians.

Employment and Unemployment

Unemployment among Palestinian refugees living in Lebanon is estimated at 40 percent; among those in Syria it is estimated that 26 percent live below the poverty line (Chatty and Hundt 2005: 11). The United Nations reports that the number of Palestinians in the West Bank and Gaza living below the poverty line (about $2.20 per day) has climbed to nearly two-thirds despite Israel's withdrawal from Gaza in September 2005 (Teibel 2005).

Some promising signs are on the horizon. According to the World Bank, the Palestinian economy expanded by about 8 percent during 2005; the unemployment rate fell. Personal incomes rose by an average of 12 percent. The increases were attributed to increased government spending, Israeli demand for merchandise and labor, and a relaxation of border closings as violence subsided. Palestinian laborers and goods do not flow smoothly when borders are restricted. However, after the Gaza withdrawal the pace cooled down (Teibel 2005).

The more liberal West Bank has generally been considered Fatah's base. Hamas has been more popular in more conservative Gaza. Both organizations have promoted economic development activities, although their follow-through has been spotty. The corruption that has characterized the PLO has had an overall dampening effect. Both Fatah and Hamas have variously attempted to gain overall control of Palestine. On December 16, 2005, Hamas achieved significant victories in local Palestinian elections in several of the

West Bank's largest cities, including Nablus and Jenin. By the spring of 2006 its influence had extended much further.

POSTSCRIPT: INNOVATIONS AND ADAPTATIONS

The political landscape has changed without Yasser Arafat and Ariel Sharon in positions of leadership. Creative, conciliatory, and compassionate actions have been taken by many Palestinians and Israelis who are opposed to division and conflict. Representatives of outside governments, agencies, and human-rights organizations also have been involved. As peace proponent Khalid Mansour (2005) told me, moderation is required; pragmatic solutions are welcomed; discussion is encouraged. Rather than a "holy war," a "holy peace" is needed. Following are several activities that strike me as both innovative and adaptive.

- The United Nations Relief and Works Agency (UNRWA) laid the cornerstone for the "Saudi Project to Rehouse Homeless Refugee Families" on December 11, 2005. Located in Rafah, within Gaza, it is being funded through a $20 million contribution from the Saudi Arabian government. The grant covers the cost of constructing shelters for approximately 800 refugee families, three schools, a health center, a mosque, a community center, a market center, and related infrastructure. Land was donated by the Palestinian Authority. Temporary jobs will be created for several thousand persons as the construction proceeds. Recent UNRWA projects have provided housing for nearly 1,000 other families in Gaza. Despite the criticism it has received on several fronts, the UNRWA continues to assist large numbers of people.
- The Israel/Palestine Center for Research and Information (IPCRI) was founded by Gershon Baskin in 1988. He now serves as its codirector, sharing duties with a Palestinian colleague. The center promotes dialogue around issues of scientific and political importance between representatives of Israeli and Palestinian civil society. Among the topics addressed is water resource development; this is important to all peoples of the Middle East but carries the added complication that as much as 30 percent of Israel's water is drawn from West Bank sources. As he told me when we met in Jerusalem in 2001, he believes that the sharing of information on topics of technical interest is a good way to bridge the cultural and ethnic divide. Persistence and seat-of-the-pants creativity also are keys. At one point, when it looked like the Palestinian and Israeli delegates headed to a scientific conference that ICPRI had arranged would be barred from meeting, he made certain that they were

seated near one another on the same aircraft. Valuable conversations, although informal, were opened long before the conference was to begin.

- A number of Muslim, Jewish, and Christian activists work together to bring Palestinian children in need of specialized surgery to the United States. Group member Omar Mansour told me on March 10, 2001, by cell phone from Ramallah: "The needs of a child transcend cultural boundaries." Most of the surgical services are provided pro bono. Several refugee and IDP children have benefited during the past decade.

- New and renewed communication strategies may be among the most useful innovations and adaptations. Local theater has been used creatively by Palestinians to present issues to a wide variety of audiences, including Jews. Since 1997, the Ashtar Theater Group (a Palestinian NGO) has produced one play a year, covering topics as challenging as sexual abuse and gender inequality. In stark contrast, but also helpful, broadcast e-mail messages have been sent from the West Bank city of Hebron on a regular basis. These serve to update U.S. activists on developments in that area. Displaced Palestinian Christians in Bethlehem also have benefited from broadcast e-mail appeals sent internationally. Various websites have been created by those seeking to mend bridges and broker improved relations. An example is that created by Ami Isseroff on behalf of the PEACE Middle East Dialogue Group. Still a different communication medium involves live musical performance. A tripartite ensemble of musicians representing Arabic, Hebraic, and Aramaic vocal traditions toured the United States in 2005. They believe music can serve as a vehicle for cross-cultural understanding. Finally, I would add that my colleagues Mark Levy and Khalid Mansour joined me in a "tri-alogue" on Middle Eastern issues that was published in the *Denver Post* in 2001. Jewish, Muslim, and Christian perspectives were presented and debated.

Ancient Palestinian ancestors certainly demonstrated the ability to adapt and compromise. Gitin (2005: 47) refers to "a thoroughly acculturated, hybrid Philistine culture" 2,600 years ago. Modern Palestinians whom I have met have demonstrated the same ability, as have Israelis. As Bill Moyers (2005: 10) recently wrote: "We must match [modern science] to what the ancient Israelites called *hochma*—the science of the heart, the capacity to see and feel and then to act as if the future depended on us."

REFERENCES

Agha, Hussein, and Robert Malley. "The Lost Palestinians." *New York Review of Books* 52, no. 10 (June 9, 2005): 20–24.

Alzaroo, Salah. "Palestinian Refugee Children and Caregivers in the West Bank." In *Children of Palestine: Experiencing Forced Migration in the Middle East*, edited by Dawn Chatty and Gillian Lewando Hundt. New York: Berghahn, 2005.

Anonymous. "Palestinian Archaeologists Uncover Canaanite Dwellings." *Biblical Archaeology Review* 24, no. 6 (November/December 1998): 25.

Ben-Yehuda, Nachman. "Where Masada's Defenders Fell." *Biblical Archaeology Review* 24, no. 6 (November/December 1998): 32–39.

———. *The Masada Myth: Collective Memory and Mythmaking in Israel*. Madison: University of Wisconsin Press, 1996.

Chatty, Dawn, and Gillian Lewando Hundt, eds. *Children of Palestine: Experiencing Forced Migration in the Middle East*. New York: Berghahn, 2005.

Gitin, Seymour. "Excavating Ekron." *Biblical Archaeology Review* 31, no. 6 (November/December 2005): 40–56.

Gonen, Rivka. Review of *Across the Sabbath River: In Search of a Lost Tribe of Israel*, by Hillel Halkin. *Biblical Archaeology Review* 29, no. 5 (September/October 2003): 78–80.

Hammond, Laura C. *This Place Will Become Home: Refugee Repatriation to Ethiopia*. Ithaca, N.Y.: Cornell University Press, 2004.

Hamzeh, Muna. *Refugees in Our Own Land: Chronicles from a Palestinian Refugee Camp in Bethlehem*. London: Pluto, 2001.

Hassan, Bassem. *The Palestinian Refugees Problem: The Past, the Present and the Future*. Unpublished masters thesis, Graduate School of International Studies, University of Denver, Colorado, 1998.

Higgins, Annie C. "Clamoring with Portraits: Memorial Posters in Palestinian Refugee Camps." Paper presented at the annual meeting of the American Anthropological Association, Washington, D.C., December 2005.

Ishay, Micheline R. *The History of Human Rights: From Ancient Times to the Globalization Era*. Berkeley: University of California Press, 2004.

Jacobson, David. "When Palestine Meant Israel." *Biblical Archaeology Review* 27, no. 3 (May/June 2001): 42–47.

Kelly, Tobias. "Returning Home? Law, Violence, and Displacement among West Bank Palestinians." *PoLAR: Political and Legal Anthropology Review* 27, no. 2 (November 2004): 95–112.

King, Laura. "Israeli Missiles Kill 2 Top Militants." *Denver Post*, November 2, 2005, 2A.

Malley, Robert. "Israel and the Arafat Question." *New York Review of Books* 51, no. 15 (October 7, 2004): 19–23.

Mansour, Khalid. Interview with Vice President, Ciber Inc., Denver, Colo. September 14, 2005.

Margalit, Avishai. "The Suicide Bombers." *New York Review of Books* 50, no. 1 (January 16, 2003): 36–39.

Markowitz, Fran, and Natan Uriely. "Shopping in the Negev: Global Flows and Local Contingencies." *City & Society* 14, no. 2 (Fall 2002): 211–36.

Moyers, Bill. "Welcome to Doomsday." *New York Review of Books* 52, no. 5 (March 24, 2005): 8–10.

Porath, Yosef. "Vegas on the Med." *Biblical Archaeology Review* 30, no. 5 (September/October 2004): 24–35.

Roy, Ananya, and Nezar Al Sayyad. "Medieval Modernity: Citizenship in Contemporary Urbanism." *Applied Anthropologist* 25, no. 2 (Fall 2005): 147–65.

Schwarz, Benjamin. Review of *The Birth of the Palestinian Refugee Problem Revisited*, by Bennie Morris. *Atlantic Monthly* 293, no. 3 (April 2004): 109–11.

Shabtay, Malka. Review of *The Hyena People: Ethiopian Jews in Christian Ethiopia*, by Hagar Salamon. *American Ethnologist* 27, no. 4 (November 2000): 982–84.

Shanks, Hershel. *Jerusalem: An Archaeological Biography*. New York: Random House, 1995.

Sottas, Eric. "Perpetrators of Torture." In *An End to Torture: Strategies for Its Eradication*, edited by Bertil Dunér. London: Zed, 1998.

Stern, Ephraim. *Archaeology of the Land of the Bible, Volume II: The Assyrian, Babylonian, and Persian Periods 732–332 B.C.E.* New York: Doubleday, 2001.

Sudilovsky, Judith, and Miriam Feinberg Vamosh. "New Finds in Ein Gedi." *Biblical Archaeology Review* 29, no. 2 (March/April 2003): 18–20.

Teibel, Amy. "Palestinian Economy Growing." *Denver Post*, (December 15, 2005): 16A.

Widzer, Martin. "Palestinian Political Fragmentation: Determining the Barriers to a Synthesized Government." Unpublished manuscript, Graduate School of International Studies, University of Denver, Colorado, 2005a.

———. Interview with doctoral candidate, Graduate School of International Studies, University of Denver, Colorado. December 14, 2005b.

Zimmerman, Bennett, and Yoram Ettinger. "Overestimating the Palestinians." *Atlantic Monthly* 295, no. 3 (April 2005): 44, 46.

Chapter Eight

Interventions that Work

Shall I kill you, or shall I give you a glass of schnapps?

Matters of life and death can be extraordinarily capricious for refugees. A Bosnian Muslim colleague of mine was asked the above question at gunpoint by a Bosnian Serb. Having been captured in Sarajevo during the 1992–1995 Bosnian war, my colleague had been conscripted to dig graves for Serbian soldiers killed in battle. In the preceding months he already had witnessed the capricious nature of humans at war. A teacher himself, he had seen fellow teachers and other captured professionals live and die, seemingly at random. On one occasion, he witnessed a dozen Muslim professionals being lined up by enemy troops. Two were chosen to die, for no apparent reason; the others were spared. On another occasion, a soldier grabbed my colleague's young son by the hair and held a knife to his neck. Another soldier yelled, "don't do that," and the boy was released.

Conversely, during the course of the war—prior to his escape and eventual resettlement in the United States—my colleague witnessed acts of bravery and generosity by Serbs as well. Several assisted his family while he still was in-country. Several aided his escape, at risk to themselves. The Serb soldier who had so capriciously given him the "death or schnapps" choice was a man of his word; he spared his life and offered him the drink.

The overall human-rights field is emergent, and with it, viable human rights and refugee regimes. Uncertainties remain, yet certain absolutes can clearly be specified. Freedom from torture, rendition, psychological abuse, arbitrary detention, and enslavement (including that of child soldiers) must be universally supported. When these acts occur, they must be universally condemned. In the pursuit of peace and democracy, even in the face of terrorism, there can be no shortcuts in this regard.

As demonstrated in this concluding chapter, understandings of interventions benefiting refugees and those living in refugee homelands must be framed with an understanding of ethics. These can be understood, in turn, by reviewing key developments in the history of human rights. Stated differently, to appreciate human rights one must study human wrongs; to appreciate useful humanitarian approaches one must study the historical antecedents. I turn first to selected antecedents, a number of which are linked to warfare. This includes the Geneva Conventions. I then turn to selected behaviors (including torture) and institutions (including truth commissions) influencing the development of contemporary humanitarianism. The emphasis is on the contributions of the West. Pragmatic humanitarianism, couched within a theory of obligation, is introduced as a framework to guide intervention and refugee assistance. In concluding, the contributions of expected and unexpected heroes are emphasized.

ETHICAL FOUNDATIONS

A thorough review of the history of human rights has recently been authored by my colleague, Micheline Ishay (2004). It is not my intent to reiterate her main points here, but rather, to build upon several that are seminal when viewed through the lens of vulnerable populations and processes of humanitarian assistance. "Just war" theory, although only covered briefly here, is foundational. Moral premises also must be examined. To the degree to which these contribute to my notion of "deep justice" (discussed near chapter's end), a bridge between theory and practice can be constructed.

Ethics is the science of morals. Contributions to ethics—and ultimately the arena of human rights—can be traced to major traditions as seemingly diverse as those reflected in Judeo-Christian, Islamic, Hindu, Buddhist, and Confucian belief systems. In the West, these are underlain by the writings of Greek and Roman philosophers. Numerous threads and strands can be traced, by no means reflecting uniformity over time or among traditions. However, the issue of equal moral status among diverse types of people, and by implication entitlement to equal assistance under times of stress, emerges as a common theme. The status of slaves, war captives, homosexuals, and women were most frequently at the heart of historical debates (Ishay 2004). Refugees and other types of displaced persons had been recognized for centuries, but not in categorical ways that could systematically benefit them. With few exceptions, status inequalities—while debated, adjudicated, and adjusted—were perpetuated. Questions of human need often were overridden by the practicalities of resource distribution under the control of oppressive elites.

Prominent in moving the discourse toward a conceptualization of deep justice are the central tenets of just war theory. These are traceable to the work of the thirteenth-century scholar Thomas Aquinas.

Wars were just, he claimed, when waged with self-restraint by sovereign authorities for self-defense, for the sake of the common good, and with peaceful ends. Provided that the ends were just, wars could be waged either openly or by means of ambushes. On the other hand, Aquinas perceived that wars were unjust if they were motivated by self-aggrandizement or the lust for power, or were conducted with cruelty. . . . [As revised later by various scholars], Aquinas's *jus bellum* view set the stage for a new way of thinking about morality in such inevitably "sinful" human situations as wars (Ishay 2004: 45).

Avoidance of desecration, passive resistance, and nonviolence all have emerged as increasingly important forms of counteraction. Most recently, so has humanitarian intervention. Given current expressions of misgiving and distrust on many fronts toward the purported aggression of Muslims, it is essential to note as Ishay does [2004: 46], the notion of just war as defensive— on grounds of pure necessity—is found in Islamic doctrine.

HISTORICAL BENCHMARKS AND
THE ROLE OF WARFARE

"War is a nasty business. It sears the soul." Pennsylvania congressman John Murtha, a Marine veteran, made this remark on the CBS television program "60 Minutes" early in 2006 as he discussed the war in Iraq. Wars indeed sear the soul, while simultaneously providing remarkable opportunities for historical analysis. The historical benchmarks derived from the study of conflict prove far more useful than numerical benchmarks in the study of human rights and humanitarianism. Numbers indeed can serve as powerful advocacy tools: "800,000 massacred in 100 days in Rwanda," "6 million Jews exterminated during the ten-year Holocaust," "200,000 Bosnian residents killed during the four-year civil war." However, numbers like this come to be idolized, that is, reified and "placed on pedestals" by even the most well-intended pacifists. On one hand, the danger is that the numbers might be inaccurate, as recent research in Bosnia has suggested (closer to 100,000 rather than the widely quoted figure of 200,000 may actually have perished). On the other hand, the danger is that individual traumas and abuses are unintentionally minimized.

Historical benchmarks prove useful as ethical principles related to human rights are analyzed. They add substance to what some would see as abstract notions. They provide touchstones as the rights of forcibly displaced persons are considered. When viewed from a Euro-American perspective, many of these benchmarks can be correlated with wars and resulting peace treaties, multinational proclamations and covenants, and postwar rehabilitative actions. The period of importance to this account covers some 350 years, from the mid-seventeenth century to the present. Notions of the contemporary nation-state, principles of social justice, and strategies for modern warfare emerged. The writings of Nevzat Soguk go so far as to emphasize that the modern nation-state—at least as defined by those in the West—has been shaped in large part by a statecraft that has had to wrestle with displaced populations (Van Arsdale 2001). While on one hand the emergent "modern refugee" has been marginalized socio-politically, on the other hand this kind of person has gained a central place in the theoretic discourse.

The Thirty Years' War (1618–1648) serves as my first benchmark. As Amnesty International's William Schulz (2003) reminds us, this war sounded the death knell of the Holy Roman Empire. Before the war, the empire had stretched across most of central and western Europe. The agreement that ended the conflict, the so-called Peace of Westphalia, ended the universal monarchy and established (or substantively clarified) the principle of national sovereignty. Putting aside the chaos that subsequently ensued in many of the petty states of the region, Schulz goes on to point out that the Peace of Westphalia was revolutionary. Yet it triggered repercussions. These were manifested over subsequent centuries as tensions increased between respect for a state's right to make decisions deemed beneficial for its citizens and recognition that "some common ground rules that apply to all may be necessary for the flourishing, if not survival, of civilization" (2003: 132).

Hallmarks of battle in the premodern era for presumably just causes obviously included the American Revolution and the French Revolution. As Ishay (2004: 96) states, the former "inspired people to fight tyrannical regimes and to spread the human rights credo of an emerging liberal age." In fact, these were European ideas being put into practice. The latter revolution "opened the gates for the arrival of new civic rights, and the Declaration of the Rights of Man and of the Citizen hailed universal rights previously acclaimed by the Americans" (2004: 97). These concepts continued to evolve in a parallel but dissociated fashion from those of other powers. For example, during this same period the Ottoman Empire was proclaiming the benefits of collectivities rather than those of individuals (as noted in chapter 4 regarding Bosnia), while emphasizing the principle of justice over the principle of freedom. Nonetheless, here too certain individual rights were given credence (Aral 2004).

Modern Warfare and the Geneva Conventions

The 1859 Battle of Solferino proved to be a key historical benchmark in the transition to modern warfare and the transition to modern humanitarianism. Indeed, from the perspective of understanding the evolution of principles of humane treatment, it is the most important precursor. Fought on Italian soil, armies representing Piedmont-Sardinia and France battled those of Austria in a sixteen-hour clash that resulted in some 40,000 casualties. It was one of the greatest land battles in Europe during the middle decades of the nineteenth century, and one of the most savage.

Witnessing what he judged to be unnecessary human carnage and lack of humane intervention at the battle, Swiss businessman Henri Dunant wrote a short pamphlet, "A Memory of Solferino." As he noted, injured civilians and soldiers alike often were offered little assistance at battles like this. Some were abandoned. Others (including prisoners of war) were mistreated or executed without cause. He proposed that societies of volunteers be set up in peacetime so as to be available to help the wounded in wartime. He also proposed that principles be laid down and codified to ensure that those treating the wounded would be afforded safety and neutrality. Dunant's initiative provided the organizational incentive for what became the Red Cross Society (founded in 1864) and later, the International Red Cross (Van Arsdale 1999). Of equal importance, his work laid the foundation for the first Geneva Convention, so-named because it was signed by fourteen nations at a meeting in Geneva, Switzerland.

Another benchmark occurred during this same period on another front. The U.S. Civil War, lasting from 1860 to 1865, resulted in the deaths of 620,000 soldiers and the incapacitation or injury of nearly 500,000 more (Kelso and Majkowski 2005). Most doctors had never seen such conditions, did not have battlefield medical training, and were ill equipped to assist the wounded. The situation confronting the estimated 400,000 prisoners of war was especially brutal. Systematic medical care was not provided, sanitation was inadequate, and food and water were scarce. Camp Sumter, located in Andersonville, Georgia, came to epitomize the worst of the worst, with 45,000 men in confinement and 13,000 ultimately dying in a fourteen-month period. Overall, approximately 56,000 men died in captivity during the Civil War, nearly the same number of Americans who died fighting in Vietnam a century later. Yet, following the innovations occurring in Europe, post–Civil War humanitarians and scientists spurred needed changes in ethics and medicine. Innovations promulgated by the Red Cross made their way into U.S. practice. With the passage of key constitutional provisions such as the 14th Amendment, promising equal treatment under law to all citizens, the federal government's role was strengthened in protecting individual rights against encroachment by the states.

The original Geneva Convention, which evolved into four primary conventions, signifies another benchmark. Following efforts at clarification that spanned the first half of the twentieth century, the current versions came to be codified in 1949. As before, they continued to relate to the humane treatment of persons in times of war. From the perspective of this book, of particular importance are the sections dealing with the humane treatment of POWs and those who have surrendered (many of whom—as in recent West African conflicts—also have been internally displaced or have attempted to flee as refugees). These documents provide a transnational legal framework for humane treatment that is to be followed by all signatories in times of war. They also provide a conceptual framework that, if followed, would promote more humane treatment by nonsignatories as well. They suggest universally applicable principles, complementing the transnational legal norms and human-rights laws that extend beyond conditions of war and also have developed significantly since World War II.

A number of analysts, myself included, believe that consideration of the broader implications of the Geneva Conventions should lead to moral judgments. Freeman Dyson (2005) is among these. Working as an analyst for the Royal Air Force Bomber Command during World War II, he tracked statistics that confirmed the great loss of life of British flight squadrons. Loss was often disproportionate to gain as he saw it, even though the British were on the side that ultimately was victorious. Tackling the sticky issue of moral justification head-on, today he uses a kind of calculus to weigh the costs and benefits of various military strategies. Economics, politics, and "greater good" (the latter best perceived, I would contend, through the lens of just war theory) all weigh in. Dyson is not opposed to war, just to inexplicable and tragic conflicts that do not lead to improvement in the human condition. Defensive battles are preferable to offensive battles.

During the first half of the twentieth century, a new kind of demographic transition was seen: The involvement of civilians in wars became far greater than ever before. Not only were more recruited to auxiliary and logistical support positions, but more were killed or injured in the course of battle. As Seifert (1999: 148–49) notes, far more civilians than soldiers were killed in World War I. (Despite proclamations to the contrary, it can be argued that little progress in the humane treatment of injured civilians and prisoners of war occurred during the Great War. On the western front in Europe, as stressed by Alistair Horne [1993] regarding 1916's famous Battle of Verdun, extremely deadly "wars of attrition" were being waged.) In World War II, the former Soviet Union lost approximately 9 million soldiers and 16 million civilians. While proportions were not as extreme, the numbers of civilians lost in other European and Asian nations also were severe. Japan lost several hundred thousand to firebombing raids of its cities during 1945 alone.

Benchmarks of the Cold War Era

Since World War II, about 90 percent of all war-related victims have been civilians (Seifert 1999, quoting UNICEF data). A large proportion have been women and children. As proxy wars in Asia, Africa, and Central America continued to unfold, the impact on civilians became an unfortunate benchmark of the Cold War era. At one point during this period, ten such wars were being fought worldwide at the same time.

The Cold War era saw the opening of refugee and internally displaced persons (IDP) camps in Asia, Africa, Central America, and Europe. A few were opened in the Southwest Pacific, including Australia. At various points in time it is estimated that as many as 300 UN sponsored or affiliated camps were in operation simultaneously. The earlier east-west flow of refugees gradually (although not entirely) was replaced by a south-north flow, which itself has come to be partially replaced by a south-south flow.

The year 1979 became a threshold year. As Pulitzer Prize–winning author Steve Coll stresses in his book *Ghost Wars* (2004), a series of chaotic events occurred that year. While at the time only seeming to be loosely connected (if at all), riots and hostage-taking in Iran, Pakistan, Afghanistan, and Saudi Arabia presaged the current era of global drama and post–Cold War conflict. The takeover of the U.S. embassy in Tehran, where forty-nine American hostages were held for an extended period, is well remembered; the riot and sacking of the U.S. embassy in Islamabad is not. Islam's diverse roles and transnational impacts emerged as key, as did reactions to U.S. hegemony. Resource imbalances among the have's and have-not's (while stressed less by Coll) also surfaced powerfully.

During the Cold War era, many national/ethnic homelands were "converted" into refugee homelands in the context of bilateral wrangling between the United States and the Soviet Union. As noted earlier, proxy wars were fought in Africa, Asia, and Central America, in countries like Ethiopia, Afghanistan, and El Salvador. These conflicts paralleled those being contested among diplomats representing the super powers. The fighting occurred on the ground in these refugee homelands; the fighting occurred through wars of words, saber rattling, and blatant shows of military weaponry in the two dominant states. With only a single exception (briefly involving the USSR's southern flank), actual attacks were mounted outside the superpowers' borders. Several million refugees and IDPs were created through these proxy wars. Several hundred thousand even came from among the Soviet Union's own Jewish and Pentacostal populations.

At several points of time during the Cold War era, the number of UNHCR-identified "persons of concern" approached 25 million worldwide. As demonstrated in El Salvador, war during this era also became an ominous and institutionalized learning experience. A respondent of Julia Dickson-Gómez told her: "One who doesn't know war, doesn't know anything" (2004: 145).

A Summary of Premises and Achievements

During the three-century period discussed above, warfare in the West evolved more fully into an instrument of statecraft. It reached its most re-fined and ominous form during World War II (and thereafter, during the 1949–1989 Cold War period). Armed forces attained a remarkably well-or-ganized, heavily funded, monolithic status. With a token nod of the hat to-ward just war theorists, these forces came to be housed in departments of de-fense, rather than departments of offense. During this period, as the modern nation-state evolved, notions of sovereignty and protection of the populace were clarified. Aided by the writings of social philosophers and the work of social activists, the field of human rights fully emerged. The notion of "just war" was applied to various conflicts—including the U.S. Civil War by some northern partisans—with varying degrees of accuracy and success. "Service to innocents" gained traction. The need to provide substantive assistance to injured civilians, noncombatants, and POWs became codified. Refugees as a category of innocent also gained traction, but remained amorphous in terms of actual humanitarian assistance through World War I. When viewed from the perspective of overall numbers of casualties, suffering during the period since the Thirty Years War was in no way reduced, but instead substantially increased.

During the first ninety years of the twentieth century, most refugees came from homelands involved in international conflicts and proxy wars. During the last ten years of the century, and through the present, most refugees have come from homelands involved in internal battles and civil wars. The two civil wars of the post–Cold War period most frequently cited as pivotal to our understanding of a new humanitarianism—a topic covered later in this chap-ter—were those fought in Bosnia and Rwanda (see, e.g., Judt 2005; Weiss 2005). While exceptions to this trend are notable (e.g., the Papuan refugees covered in chapter 2), this dramatic shift is correlated with socio-political changes in the relations among super powers and to socio-economic changes in regional alliances. Processes of globalization, while generally important, cannot easily be correlated with the processes currently producing refugees and IDPs.

TRIBUNALS, COMMISSIONS, AND COMMITTEES

Wars obviously have continued during the post–World War II period. As discussed later in this chapter, they have continued to mold the faces of humanitarians and the fates of refugees. Yet the period between 1945 and 1950 was unique. A shift began in the way transnational negotiation, business, and human service were conducted. While augmented by a leap in global communication capabilities, it more importantly signaled a leap in transnational perspective (Ishay 2004: 241–47). The creation of the United Nations was a seminal structural achievement; the creation of the first tribunal was a seminal functional achievement.

Emerging favorably in the post–World War II period, to borrow a phrase from Blau and Moncada (2005: 18), was the understanding that "the human rights project . . . makes ordinary people a priority." The five-year, immediate postwar period witnessed the parallel emergence of definable human rights and refugee regimes. Both regimes began to be characterized by norms that reflect widely held values about the human condition; by transnational rules and guidelines shaped through debate and negotiation; and by institutions, agencies, and individuals intent on actualizing the guidelines. Both built upon the innovative Universal Declaration of Human Rights, promulgated in 1948 as a tool to clarify and broaden rights-related international rules (Donnelly 2003). The human rights and refugee regimes have come to intersect in a number of important ways, which involve notions of deep justice and obligation, as information presented later in this chapter makes clear.

From a variety of perspectives, covering authors as diverse as Dyson (2005), Paxton (as cited in Lyttlelton 2004), and Muggeridge (2002), the Holocaust—viewed in the context of fascism—was the defining event of the World War II era. Dealing boldly with its ramifications, and becoming central to the emergence of the modern human rights regime, was the Nuremberg Tribunal. Convened immediately after World War II, it initiated a new era of international justice. As Ved Nanda (2005: 1E) emphasizes, the issue of personal accountability for crimes committed during war was brought front and center. The trials of twenty-two high-ranking Nazis "set a precedent that individuals, regardless of their status, from low-ranking military personnel to heads of state, will be prosecuted for war crimes and crimes against humanity." Categorically rejected were defendants' claims to "just have been following orders" or to "just have been doing what was necessary to preserve national unity." The Nuremberg Tribunal laid the groundwork for humane, legalistic interventions that contravene traditional (some would say sacred) notions of national sovereignty and individual impunity. As Tom Farer (1999: 10) stresses, the authors of the Nuremberg Tribunal's charter creatively included a category of criminality to cover the slaughter of entire cohorts of people by Germans on Germany's own soil. Yet it was in no way intended to take over or supplant all state juridical functions regarding war crimes.

This initiative was followed in recent decades by ad hoc war crimes tribunals in such places as Bosnia, Rwanda, and Cambodia. The recently established International Criminal Court, with offices in The Hague, has had its jurisdiction accepted by more than 100 countries (but not the United States). As of early 2006 the court was investigating atrocities committed in Uganda, the Congo, and Darfur.

An array of commissions and committees have been developed during the past sixty years. Only a few of the most important are discussed here. Most have proven innovative, some have proven effective, and a few have proven exemplary. A number are offshoots of UN mandates or of regional regimes, like the Organization of American States (OAS). An example is the Inter-American Commission and Court of Human Rights. Actually two complementary and interlocking entities, its operations began in the 1960s and came into full force in the 1970s. (The commission had existed on paper since 1948.) Like the European Commission and Court of Human Rights, it came to acquire a significant quasi-judicial function. It conducts its examinations and investigations in the form of proceedings between two opposing parties who make submissions in oral hearings. Proceedings are concluded with legally binding appraisals (i.e., judgments) of facts. Key investigations have been conducted in El Salvador, Colombia, and the United States, among other locales. Resulting reports have been widely circulated (Kellberg 1998; Farer 1997).

So-called truth and reconciliation commissions have been formed in about twenty countries since the 1970s, as noted in chapter 5. They usually have been established after the cessation of civil war, or in the case of South Africa, after the cessation of apartheid. They have achieved a high degree of success. Their hearings often have clarified issues involving refugee and IDP status, as occurred in El Salvador. Once their investigative work has been completed and reports issued, truth commissions are disbanded.

A different kind of commission was created in 1949: The United Nations High Commissioner for Refugees (UNHCR). It began operating in 1951 from offices in Geneva, Switzerland. As a subsidiary organ of the UN General Assembly, it was intended to serve as a kind of legal advocate and service representative for refugees worldwide. Its roots can be traced to the time thirty years earlier when the League of Nations appointed Norwegian explorer and humanitarian Fridtjof Nansen its first high commissioner for refugees. The so-called Nansen Commission innovated services for many of those displaced during World War I, from Germany to Armenia. In the eyes of many in the West, it came to symbolize the emergent world refugee regime; the UNHCR was built upon this tradition. Article 2 of the UNHCR Statute states that the work of the High Commissioner shall be of an entirely nonpolitical nature, being humanitarian and social. With few exceptions, it shall relate to groups and categories of refugees rather than to individuals. This mandate allowed it initially to move forward within the Cold War environment without becoming hamstrung bureaucratically (Cutts 2000: 18–19).

The UNHCR is structured in unusual fashion, as Loescher (2003) notes. It represents both an individual, the commissioner (currently António Guterres, the tenth in its history), and a bureaucracy, the commission. In the year 1999 its budget surpassed the $1 billion threshold (Cutts 2000: 3). To accomplish its mission, it must work cross-nationally, with a variety of governments, and cross-institutionally, with a variety of NGOs and service organizations. It must cajole, persuade, and assist without offending. It must be "on the ground" and "in the office" simultaneously. Having struggled to maintain a viable budget and relevant mandate since 2000, it even has been suggested by Richard Holbrooke and other internationalists that the UNHCR officially take on IDP protection.

The Human Rights Committee of the United Nations was established in 1977. A decade earlier, the UN had adopted the Covenant on Civil and Political Rights (CCPR), which provided the treaty-based mandate for the committee's eventual formation and operation. This process of formation was clearly to be distinguished from that associated with the UN Commission on Human Rights, which is charter based and was established in 1946. The committee was granted the power (a) to accept reports submitted by participating states as to measures being adopted to give effect to the rights recognized by the CCPR, (b) to deal with interstate complaints, so long as the involved parties recognize its jurisdictional competence, and (c) to receive and consider complaints from individuals alleging violations of the CCPR by states that had accepted its mandate through their ratification of the associated protocol.

Unfortunately, as Kellberg (1998) emphasizes, the Human Rights Committee has not been able to actualize its full potential. A number of states that ratified the covenant have refused to accept the interstate complaints procedure or the right of individual petition. Paradoxically, this has allowed the Universal Declaration of Human Rights to gain greater credence and juridical status. Most recently, the committee has been accused of becoming a home for representatives of repressive regimes (including Zimbabwe and Sudan) who, by virtue of their committee membership, can steer eyes in other directions.

TORTURE AND THE CULTURES OF VIOLENCE

"The main purpose of human rights—to prevent the abuse of power—requires those who wield power to police themselves" (Tomaševski 1998: 187). This straightforward admonition is particularly germane to the following brief consideration of torture and the culture of violence.

From the perspective of those living in refugee homelands, as well as refugees and other displaced persons themselves, the single human rights violation framing the most substantive debate in the first decade of the twenty-first century is torture. (Specific types of torture are covered in chapter 3.) This is not only because of its horrific effects on victims, nor the increased attention brought by the media, but because of its *sub rosa* pervasiveness. As Farer (1997: 528) aptly notes: "No government claim[s] that torture and summary execution [are] permissible even in states of emergency; they simply [deny] torturing and killing."

Torture is one manifestation of spectacular violence, itself a correlate of structural violence. Allegations of torture imply both legal and moral judgments. From allegations of physical abuse and humiliation of detainees by American personnel in Iraq's Abu Ghraib prison, to allegations of Canadian complicity in acquiring information from its own citizens under torture by foreign intelligence agencies, to allegations of torture condoned by former Yugoslavian leader Slobodan Milosević as he stood trial, this arcane practice is still very much in use. Worldwide, there clearly is no inverse correlation between "degree of democratic involvement" and "extent to which torture is used." The way in which humanitarians and politicians deal with torture during this century will serve as an explicit benchmark for the human-rights field, and an implicit benchmark for the refugee field.

A number of protocols, covenants, and conventions again torture and related types of abuse have been instituted during the post–World War II period. Its prohibition is specified in the Universal Declaration of Human Rights. Detailed information about these documents can be found in the writings of Ishay (2004), Donnelly (2003), and Kellberg (1998). Here it is important to stress the 1984 Convention Against Torture and Other Cruel, Inhuman, or Degrading Treatment or Punishment. This landmark document came into force in 1987. The convention was the first UN instrument to systematically take up the issues of non-*refoulement* (nonforcible return), nonextradition, and nonexpulsion, all potentially on the table not only as the statuses of high-profile refugees are considered but as possible rendition programs by the United States are being debated.

The Committee Against Torture was established according to Article 17 of the convention. It came into existence in 1988. Its members are elected by

States Parties, just as are those who serve on the Human Rights Committee. It can address interstate complaints and individual allegations, just as can the Human Rights Committee. As Rodley (2004) and Kellberg (1998) note, the committee has attracted a number of cases related to expulsion. In several of these instances it has been maintained that the complainant will be tortured if sent back to his or her country of origin in violation of Article 3 of the convention. Successful redress has been attained for most of these individuals, some of whom have been refugees or IDPs.

The role of the UN Special Rapporteur on Torture must be emphasized. No similar role had existed anywhere in the world, in any context, prior to 1985 when it was authorized by the UN Commission on Human Rights. Investigative procedures linked to emergent human rights understandings, while grounded in legal precedent, have allowed the four persons who thus far have served as Special Rapporteur to inquire into a wide range of allegations brought forth by individuals and organizations. The mandate covers all countries, irrespective of whether the state in question has ratified the 1984 convention. The work entails fact-finding missions (one of the most recent being to Georgia), the transmission of urgent appeals, and the submission of investigative reports to the commission and the UN General Assembly. One of the major issues that has been addressed is rape as a form of torture. In a speech delivered in 2005 at the University of Denver, former rapporteur Nigel Rodley adamantly stated that no quarter can be given to the practice of torture. It simply cannot be condoned in any way, in any situation. This follows his earlier statement (1998: ix) that "torture can be stopped . . . if states are willing to do so. . . . In the end, it boils down to a matter of political will."

Cultures of violence have emerged and become institutionalized in terrible ways. Seemingly new and horrific types of torture and abuse have gained notoriety, from the forcible amputations inflicted upon civilians in Sierra Leone to the sexual humiliations inflicted upon prisoners in Iraq. Both guerrillas and government agents in Colombia are blamed for the exacerbation of the IDP situation there, the most severe in the Western Hemisphere. The torture of civilians is a regular occurrence. As emphasized in chapter 3, Ethiopia's Red Terror created a culture of violence that led to the deaths of thousands and the displacement of hundreds of thousands. The conflict in El Salvador, covered in chapter 5, demonstrated at the societal level violence's powerful reshaping effects and at the personal level the chaos and fear that ensue. El Salvador has yet to recover. As emphasized in chapter 6, the *janjaweed* are creating havoc in Darfur; while genocide (in the strictest sense of the term) may yet be ambiguous, a culture of violence is firmly entrenched.

CIVIL-MILITARY COOPERATION AND
HUMANITARIAN INTERVENTION

Humanitarianism can be defined as "crossing a boundary" to help someone in need. The boundary can be geopolitical, economic, cultural, or psycho-social. The utilization of scarce resources is indicated. Risk to both beneficiary and service provider is involved. A moral imperative is implied. The successful actualization of assistance in complex humanitarian emergencies outside one's own geopolitical boundaries also suggests that a successful balance between sovereignty and individual rights, between security and freedom, has been negotiated.

The 350-year period since this chapter's first benchmark, the Thirty Years' War, has witnessed the evolution of innovative forms of humanitarianism in the West. Pragmatic understandings of military engagements (especially regarding the treatment of POWs and injured civilians) and theoretic understandings of just war have helped shape the types of actions now being taken. The human-rights regime, and its attendant covenant and commission-oriented approach, has played a major role. The refugee regime has played a minor role. One of the most recent dynamics, associated with the post–Cold War period, has not only been the downsizing of most armed forces but their virtually simultaneous reassignment in new roles involving humanitarian crises. An insightful summary, some of which is referenced here, has been provided by Thomas Weiss (2005).

An initial benchmark for this new type of civil-military humanitarianism was the intervention undertaken in northern Iraq after the first Gulf War, from 1991 through 1996. Vulnerable Kurdish populations were made safer, resources were stabilized, and no-fly zones were established. Representatives of the Western military and Western NGOs assumed prominent on-the-ground posts with Kurds as consultants. Other instances, with variable results, have included Somalia (1992–1995), Bosnia (1992–1995), East Timor (1999–2000), and Darfur (2004–present). The African Union's involvement in Darfur, if successful, could come to represent another benchmark: Non-Western troops shouldering the load.

A military intervention deemed appropriate by some observers and inappropriate by others was that undertaken by U.S.-led forces against Serbia in 1999. It lacked the formal support of the UN Security Council, was uninvited, and violated the boundaries of a sovereign state. It was preemptive. However, it was premised on the unfolding actions of Slobodan Milosević against Kosovo's Albanian majority. His prior actions against Bosnian Muslims and Croats indicated ominous repercussions might ensue if decisive actions were not taken.

Since the early 1990s, the Western world has been moving beyond what Weiss calls "Pollyannaish humanitarianism." He offers poignant observations about civil-military operations and the emergent role of twenty-first century humanitarians. Building upon the work—and admonitions—of pragmatic humanitarians like Fred Cuny, he stresses the need to engage military actors in creative ways that promote both effective intervention and peace. No longer should those militaries capable of effective assistance be labeled as aggressive interventionists (or oppressors). No longer should NGO personnel attempt to steer clear of military operatives carte blanche. No longer should sophisticated military forces such as those of the Western powers emphasize attack operations at the expense of humanitarian assistance.

Defined broadly, humanitarian intervention therefore is a new kind of civil-military cooperation that involves the use of external military personnel, working in concert with civilians, in rendering assistance to those at risk. At one extreme is a more conventional variant, where humanitarian intervention is seen as the use of coercive measures by outside military forces in times of crisis to ensure access to civilians or the protection of rights without the consent of local political authorities (Weiss 2005: xxix). At the other extreme is a newer and more fluid variant, where it is seen as the use of external troops, working in concert with civilian NGO/IGO specialists, to stabilize a crisis, reduce the risk to vulnerable populations such as refugees, and assist in the provision of short-term relief. Troops are seen to take on more of a nonaggressive peacekeeping and logistical support role. Harold Koh (cited in Mertus 2004: 49) adds that the country sponsoring the humanitarian intervention should be promoting human rights without promoting its own discernible political interests. My colleague Derrin Smith and I worked with members of the Romanian Land Forces Academy to provide training for this type of intervention to University of Denver graduate students in Transylvania during the summer of 2004.

Effective humanitarian intervention is dependent upon the proper training of military personnel (including logisticians), ideally in concert with civilian personnel (including NGO workers). This training must include courses in medical ethics. Nearly 125 years after the Battle of Solferino, the UN General Assembly adopted the *Principles of Medical Ethics*. These bear upon the roles of health personnel, particularly physicians, charged with the medical care of war prisoners and detainees. Principle 2, as Kellberg (1998: 15) notes, declares that it is a gross violation of medical ethics for such personnel to engage in acts that constitute participation in, or support of, torture or other degrading treatment. The 1975 *Tokyo Declaration by the World Medical Association* and the 1988 *Body of Principles for the Protection of All Persons under any Form of Detention or Imprisonment* lend substantive further support to this imperative.

Figure 8.1. The Romanian Air Force, working in conjunction with the Romanian Land Forces Academy, provided the University of Denver team two helicopters as part of its civil-military cooperation training program. Students practiced triage and transport of mock refugee victims.

The world order is shifting. The United States no longer represents the dominant force for progressive change. The increasingly militaristic stance demonstrated in the post-9/11 era through actions in Afghanistan and Iraq reflect a unilateral approach to international relations. As Judt (2005) notes, while most observers who believe in the general principle of humanitarian intervention believe that an Iraq free of Saddam Hussein is beneficial, the preemptive incursion into the Mesopotamian heartland by the United States was not. Humanitarian intervention based on "preemptive and preventive notions" is not appropriate. The concept of "American exceptionalism," based on a premise that the United States can and must do things differently for the greater good, is faulty (Forsythe 2002).

A Bosnian Perspective

To understand the military perspective, painted on a grand canvas, is to understand the soldier's perspective, painted on a tiny corner of that canvas. The possibilities for humanitarian assistance by the military are seen in simple acts of kindness by individual combatants.

My appreciation for what it means to be a soldier, and what it means to help others, has been enhanced by interviews with former enlisted men in Bosnia. (To respect their wishes, only the first name of one is used here.) Ismet, a Muslim, served for four years with the Bosnian army, his service spanning most of the 1992–1995 civil war. He found himself assigned to a single duty station, covering the Vareš area in the central portion of the country, for two of those years. It will be recalled that this is one of the areas discussed in chapter 4. Despite early Serb attacks, followed by counterattacks by Bosnian (BH) and Croat (HDZ) armies, over the course of several months the combat scenario evolved into one between the BH and HDZ forces. Both sides set up semi-permanent encampments in the same set of hills, near the polluted stream that flows through the valley where the town of Vareš sits. Both sides therefore found themselves to be dependent on an alternate source for fresh water, provided by a single nearby spring.

Ismet reported that during one three-month winter stint, it was bitterly cold. Neither side had much stomach for fighting. Much of each day, and all of each night, was spent at established campsites. He spent most of his time "in a cold tent on the bare ground." Yet humane events occurred between otherwise belligerent soldiers. Being dependent on the same spring, soldiers from one side and then the other took turns dashing to get water. Those on the opposing side would take aim at them, but rarely fire. When they did, they always missed. Sharpshooters of the BH and HDZ armies became "remarkably inept" as their fellow Bosnians sought this essential resource.

Such humane events are not unusual. They suggest that humanitarian activities can become part of military operations. These are bottom-up, not top-down, perspectives.

The Role of the United Nations

The United Nations does not have the power to initiate international interventions without the unanimous approval of the Security Council. Its five permanent members all hold veto power. In past years "resolutions" therefore often were the UN's most visible accomplishments. Yet in the post–Cold War environment, and with the increase in civil wars of the type seen in Kosovo, the agency and its affiliates increasingly have been called upon to serve as "the world's peacemakers, peacebuilders, and peacekeepers" (Judt 2005: 15). Many observers in the developing world believe that the UN often serves as a de facto functionary of the United States (and to a lesser extent Europe), thus diminishing its value. An imbalance exists among the United States, the UN and its Security Council, and other key nations (e.g., China, Russia, Indonesia). Less powerful yet pivotal nations (e.g., Egypt,

Pakistan, Syria) often pursue tracks that are at odds with the others. Small developing nations (e.g., Sierra Leone, El Salvador, Laos) find themselves able to exert little political pressure and, to innovate little in ways that will influence the human-rights regime.

Ironically, a nonactive organizational stance can prove critical. Weiss states: "Avoiding involvement can be considered 'intervention' because those humanitarians who fail to engage themselves on behalf of the oppressed are effectively helping the oppressors. . . . The need to be clear about solidarity with victims has been gaining ground in the debate [as opposed to] the more traditional view about the potential for neutrality and impartiality espoused by the [Red Cross]" (2005: 36).

A THEORY OF OBLIGATION

"What can you do for me?" We had been working on a water reconnaissance survey outside the town of Zalingei, in Darfur, during November 1979. After having provided me with a great deal of useful information about local water resources, my informant confronted me with this statement as I was about to leave. His words are what caused me to begin wrestling with the notion of "obligation." This wrestling match, for me, has been going on ever since.

This particular fieldwork had brought me into contact with both mobile and sedentary peoples, as discussed in chapter 6. Some of those whom I had thought would have access to more resources (land, water, livestock, produce) had fewer, and some of those whom I had thought would have access to fewer resources had more. Some shared resources, some fought over them. Some were assisted by government agencies (one of which my team worked with), some were marginalized or left out all together. The situation in Darfur was complex and confusing. Where were the most pressing needs for those who were marginalized, dispossessed, or displaced? What resources were at their disposal? How did external agents of change assist without imposing? How did indigenous people contribute, and indeed become empowered as they helped one another? Did those with more resources have a moral obligation to help those with fewer resources? In particular, what was the relationship between "obligation" and "humanitarianism"?

A Moral Imperative

Following our fieldwork in Sudan, I was inspired to pursue what has become one version of a theory of obligation by the work in Africa of Barbara Harrell-Bond (1986), Robert Gorman (1987), John Prendergast (1996), and

George Shepherd (2002). While none of the four contended at the time of those writings of theirs cited here that they had "a theory of obligation," all presented compelling information that pointed in this direction. Over a subsequent ten-year period I had conversations with three of the four that helped me flesh out my thinking. I kept returning to information that I had gathered in Darfur. Most recently, the ideas of Regina Nockerts (2005) have proven to be significant, and also are represented substantially in the following sections.

Underlying a theory of obligation is a single foundational assumption: There exists a moral imperative to assist the structurally dispossessed and functionally abused. This assumption should not be controversial, as Nockerts (2005) stresses. Humankind benefits from the compassionate aid afforded one to another; a greater good can be achieved. Even if viewed strictly from an adaptive perspective, a society benefits long-term as resources are expended in assisting those in need. Through this process they become more fit members of that society.

This theory stresses far more than fitness. Just as a notion of justice in its simplest form might lead to "doing what is humane, to right a wrong," a moral imperative might lead to "doing what is ethically right, to aid vulnerable people in need." Moral imperatives are by no means abstractions, as a number of scholars have noted (e.g., Blau and Moncada 2005; Ishay 2004; Farer 1999). In its simplest form, our theory of obligation plays out in organizational action, in the field, and asks this three-part question: What *should* individuals and agencies do, from a moral perspective, to help those in need? What *would* individuals and agencies do, as options are weighed and preferences stated? What *could* individuals and agencies do, as available resources are considered? To paraphrase Amartya Sen (2003: xvii), what is required for a *determined encounter*?

The theory of obligation has two major components: A moral/ethical element that guides the decision-making process and allows activists to select those issues most appropriate for humanitarian assistance, and a pragmatic element that steers those activists in evaluating the most effective use of scarce resources. It can be said that, as the theory plays out in real-world actions, the morally possible intersects the materially possible.

The Morally Possible

Standard understandings of Western ethics incorporate the principles of justice, autonomy, benevolence, and nonmalevolence. Springing from these are eminently useful notions of what constitute appropriate assistance and intervention. From the perspective of vulnerable populations like refugees, justice emphasizes "doing what is right" for people at risk. Autonomy emphasizes respect for the sanctity of the individual as assistance is offered. Benevolence emphasizes compassionate assistance to those in severe need. Nonmalevolence emphasizes assistance that does not lead to secondary negative consequences, such as the violation of privacy.

My notion of deep justice encompasses all four of the above principles, and therefore provides a conceptual foundation for what follows. A belief in deep justice restrains those in power from exacting evil on the powerless. It calls

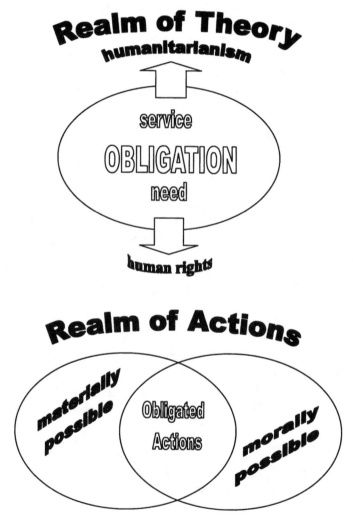

Figure 8.2.

for acts that demonstrate compassion and ameliorate suffering. It mandates aggressive efforts to overturn structural inequalities and structural violence. It mandates a determined encounter.

We have identified five factors we believe transcend cultural boundaries and constitute the morally possible. *Burden sharing* refers to the notion that burden of service to the dispossessed should be borne equitably among those activists who share in the moral obligation to give aid. Involved individuals and agencies should bear burdens not equally, but proportionally to the resources available to them, as the felt needs of, for example, IDPs are being addressed. In the case of El Salvador, which was covered in chapter 5, this was seen in the IDP camp known as El Transito, Numero Tres. Four primary agencies, two faith-based and two nonfaith-based, shared the burden of service. The UN affiliate covered the greatest proportion of the burden and the local Salvadoran service agency the smallest proportion. Effective interagency communication, that also included camp residents, allowed health and educational services to proceed successfully. One camp leader told me, "Our latrines work well because the agencies which installed them worked together."

Although often enacted through agency auspices, our theory of obligation is fundamentally concerned with the actions and needs of individuals, both service beneficiaries and service providers. The second factor is *personal responsibility*. This is the notion that responsibility for burden rests on the shoulders of individuals. Building upon the information presented in chapter 6 on the crisis in Darfur, the proposed multitiered peace negotiations must encourage personal responsibility on the part of government and local officials. This admittedly is difficult in the political sphere. Sometimes the exemplary efforts of others, such as the late John Garang, can inspire such responsibility. In its simplest form, the term means that one can (and must) accept credit for what goes wrong on one's watch, as well as for what goes right. A "devolution of responsibility onto others" in fact is not responsibility in the moral sense. However, there can be what we term "aggregate responsibility," as representatives of organizations like UNICEF and Doctors Without Borders carry out their duties. One UN aid worker from western Darfur recently told me, "It's my responsibility to correctly make the assessment [of women's health-care needs in IDP camps]. If I misdiagnose, a woman could suffer."

Complementing personal responsibility, at the organizational level, is the notion of *institutional accountability*. Accountability refers to the proper referencing of preestablished organizational objectives, as well as to their actual attainment, as services are delivered. "Accountability" and "outcome" go hand in hand. As exemplified by Bosnia (covered in chapter 4), we contend that aid organizations—from the large (e.g., UNHCR) to the medium (e.g., Mercy Corps) to the small (e.g., Limbs Unlimited)—primarily are accountable to their boards and to the aid recipients themselves. This concept mandates regular interaction among board members and beneficiaries, so that felt needs can be assessed and services adjusted accordingly. Using mental health care as the example, IGO, NGO, and PVO accountability in Bosnia has been achieved in a number of instances. That delivered through World Vision to traumatized IDP children during the late 1990s followed the institution's plan, utilized data derived from client-centered needs assessments, and employed locally available resources (including medications and counselors trained in play therapy). As a counselor told me, "We think this program works because our organization is accountable to the kids." Barbara Harrell-Bond (1986) suggested early on, based on her work in Africa, that beneficiaries should be the ultimate arbiters of accountability.

The fourth factor is in no way an abstraction. Obligation must be grounded in the actual experiences of *sympathy and compassion*. These sentiments, as emphasized in chapter 1, require us to become engaged on a very personal, emotional level. It is not recommended that we "wear our heart on our sleeve," but it is recommended that we "walk a mile in the other person's shoes." The refugees who fled Ethiopia's Red Terror were discussed in chapter 3. More than a dozen eventually made it to the Rocky Mountain Survivors Center in Denver, Colorado. After intake, it was clinically appropriate that counselors initiate mental-health interventions and physical rehabilitation only after detailed, emically attuned narratives of their preflight, flight, and postflight experiences had been collected. Episodes of human-rights abuse were recorded if the clients chose to share them. As compassionate care of this sort continues to be offered, suffering can be reduced. The center's nurse, Sarah Combs, begins by asking these simple questions: "What can I do for you? How can I help?"

Consideration of compassion leads directly, even intuitively, to consideration of the fifth factor. *Non-neutrality* is the notion that recognizes that, as humanitarian aid and service are rendered, impartial objectivity realistically cannot be achieved. Of equal importance, it recognizes that impartial objectivity should not be attempted. Sympathetic response to human suffering should trigger emotions and subjective actions disproportionately weighted toward the dispossessed, the disenfranchised, the marginalized. John Prendergast (1996) emphasizes the value of a nonneutral stance more powerfully than any other contemporary activist. He reminds that political considerations also necessitate this. The importance of this principle becomes clear when considering the assistance afforded indigenous tribesmen by the Catholic Crosier missionaries working in Papua. As suggested in chapter 2, the successful interventions they undertook to reduce the beatings being inflicted on villagers neither predisposed the missionaries to modify their Christian precepts nor caused them to cease criticizing the brutality of the Indonesian government. My on-site observations among the Asmat people convinced me that the Crosiers' nonneutral stance was, in part, what allowed them to be more effective in identifying human-rights abuse and in intervening humanely than any of the other agencies or individuals then present. Fr. Dave Gallus said this: "I'm called to serve. I've got to speak out."

The Materially Possible

Consideration of the morally possible is complemented (and necessitated) by consideration of the materially possible. From logistics to supplies to training to administrative oversight, humanitarian assistance depends on what can be procured and what can be delivered. In the context of a theory of obligation there are three main elements that need to be considered: Felt needs, networks of service providers and associated infrastructure, and pragmatism.

Recognition of the *felt needs* of intended beneficiaries is central to the theory. Felt needs are those needs emically derived, which from the beneficiaries' viewpoint are deemed essential to their welfare, and have not been modified by "experts." "Key to this is the assumption that the interests of the beneficiaries are of greater importance than those of the humanitarian organization, its workers, or its donors" (Nockerts 2005: 17). Once given voice, it is these needs that should determine the hierarchy of problems to be addressed and the assistance protocol to be implemented, not the (often independently) expressed needs of service personnel, agencies, donors, or policy makers "on behalf of the beneficiaries." Drawing from my experience in Palestine, which is covered in chapter 7, the comments of several Palestinian men I met who were living in the West Bank stand out. Their primary felt need was to move from a position of underemployment to a position of employment that tapped the skills they had learned in college. The prospect of improved Israeli-Palestinian relations was viewed with enthusiasm. Furthermore, for them the impacts of the Intifada were negative, not positive, because the flow of tourists—and thus tourist dollars—had been severely reduced.

The *network of service providers and associated infrastructure* obviously must be considered. In many complex humanitarian emergencies, and especially in refugee-producing situations, there often are a multiplicity of aid organizations, governmental agencies, and individual activists. Together they form what Nockerts (2005: 21) calls "a complex web of service providers and service obstructers." To render assistance the web must be untangled. This was nowhere more apparent than in Bosnia during the immediate postwar period. As noted in chapter 4, a plethora of NGOs, IGOs, and PVOs came into operation. During an eight-year period, my students worked with over twenty of them through summer service-learning assignments. At one point over a dozen NGOs were offering mental health and related psychological services alone to displaced persons, including children. World Vision was among the largest, and to its credit, it networked well with other organizations. It employed a triage-like process to decipher needs, rank them in terms of service priority, and communicate with other like-minded agencies. By contrast, Flower of Youth was among the smallest organizations, did not employ such a process, and did not network well with other organizations.

While associated infrastructure includes everything from roadways to radio communications, of particular concern here—since most assistance is provided to those in developing countries—are local medical clinics, potable water supplies, and sanitation systems (read: ventilated latrines). Humanitarian efforts in El Transito, Numero Tres, the IDP camp in El Salvador discussed previously, in part were succeeding because these three systems were relatively well funded and well organized.

Pragmatism refers to praxis, to the real-world practicalities that enhance and constrain operations. Our theory of obligation couples this with acceptance of the simple idea that the value of actions is realized in their on-the-ground consequences. Realistic goals must be set. Of particular importance, as Prendergast (1996) states, the humanitarian initiative itself must be programmatically sustainable without inadvertently sustaining the conflict that might be engulfing it. Operation Lifeline Sudan ran into this problem as it attempted to deliver food and supplies in the 1980s during the first phase of its activities in southern Sudan. A number of its convoys were taken over by rebel groups; food came to be used as a weapon (Van Voorhis 1989). When options are thoroughly evaluated a priori, when the assistance is issue driven and not donor driven, and when access to the vulnerable has been negotiated, such problems are less likely to occur.

"Pragmatism is the art of finding the overlap between the materially and morally possible, of recognizing which actions we therefore have an obligation to engage in" (Nockerts 2005: 16). The later work of Harrell-Bond (2002) has been inspirational as the theory has evolved. She recognizes, as do we, the vital importance of human dignity. However, we differ from her in one key way. Whereas she contends that the notion of fairness (read: equity) should be overridden by the notion of dignity, we contend precisely the opposite. Fairness is manifested in resource allocation and resource distribution for those being served, and is the ultimate pragmatic consideration. Dignity is essential, as stressed in chapter 1, but becomes more nebulous as actual interventions are initiated.

Pragmatic Humanitarianism

Pragmatic humanitarianism is the actualization of our theory of obligation. It focuses on what works, on the ground, as change agents engage those in need. It rests on the perhaps controversial real-world assumption that change and change agents must be nonneutral. It encompasses the notion of deep justice (i.e., the requirement that the ethical principles of justice, autonomy, benevolence, and nonmalevolence be kept at the forefront as assistance is delivered). Encompassing the morally and materially possible, the key elements of the approach can be summarized as follows:

- Moral imperative: a belief that change that addresses the felt needs of beneficiaries is "the right thing to do." The underlying values of beneficiaries, change agents, and other stakeholders must be articulated as the intervention is undertaken.
- Benign intervention: a belief that intervention conducted in concert with beneficiaries can be both effective and nondamaging to their socio-cultural and natural environments.
- Liberal tradition: a belief in the power of the individual to effect change, particularly in the context of well-organized NGO, IGO, and PVO initiatives. (This is to be distinguished from "liberalism.")
- Integrated solutions: multiple agents working in concert to effect change. These agents usually represent different disciplines, working with local counterparts.
- Incremental change: successful change occurs bit by bit, over time. It is rarely dramatic, usually cumulative.
- Learning environment: interventions that work are regularly used as learning devices by those involved. These learnings are regularly shared with other change agents, interactively.
- Facilitative empowerment: change agents must work to create environments wherein beneficiaries not only can assume leadership positions, but can thrive. This was covered in depth in my 1993 edited book, *Refugee Empowerment and Organizational Change*.

Pragmatic humanitarianism recognizes that notions of human rights are evolving. It recognizes that needs and rights are complementary categories, by no means mutually exclusive yet by no means similar in definition. Recent proclamations of "land rights as human rights" in Venezuela, "food rights as human rights" in Zambia, "health rights as human rights" in Haiti, and "water rights as human rights" in Sudan, while noble and well intended, serve to conflate needs and rights.

Emergent Civil Society

Pragmatic humanitarianism, at the broadest level, has the chance to help shape civil society. A theory of obligation suggests that pragmatic humanitarianism be engaged in any context, within any state, where vulnerable populations are in need. Many such states do not encompass civil societies. As obligations are carried out, improvements in the social condition occur. As conditions improve, it becomes more likely that structural inequalities will diminish. As conditions improve, it also becomes more likely that a civil society will emerge.

In a civil society, potentially oppressive and restrictive systems (e.g., as might be found with state police forces) are not present. Civil servants are not "grandfathered" into their posts, nor appointed through nepotistic practices. Elections are not rigged. Politicians do not serve life terms. A viable civil society has minimal bureaucratic entanglements and is relatively free of corruption.

Emergent civil society is a corollary, although by no means a foregone result, of obligation-in-practice. Briefly put, civil society is characterized by "rule of law," mechanisms for open debate, processes for effective dispute resolution, a viable election system, methods for the effective utilization of social capital, and support for progressive human-rights regimes. A civil society is one that nurtures its citizens, without oppression. The society comes to operate politically in both efficient and effective fashion, both pluralistically and peacefully. Pragmatic humanitarianism can contribute to this.

EXPECTED AND UNEXPECTED HEROES

Ultimately it is brave, selfless, competent people who make the difference. No successful humanitarian mission to benefit vulnerable people ever began without the inspiration and leadership of what I call "expected and unexpected heroes." All of those mentioned here engaged in actions that benefited refugees, IDPs, and/or immigrants.

• Gen. Romeo Dallaire of Canada was stationed with UN peacekeepers in Rwanda during the mid-1990s. He was among the first outsiders to realize that a genocide was in the offing. He made repeated attempts to engage a humanitarian intervention, through his primary line of communications:

The UN's department of peacekeeping operations in New York City. He also confronted *genocidaires* directly. He later blasted those in power who could have done more, including President Bill Clinton, but who did not. While he believes that he ultimately failed in the execution of his duties, and indeed was subsequently diagnosed with post-traumatic stress disorder, others believe his extraordinary efforts merit the label "hero." His character is featured in the film *Hotel Rwanda*.

- Fred Cuny worked on an even broader front. From Africa to Europe to Asia, he brought a maverick style to solving tough logistics problems confronting IDPs and war victims. Known as "Mr. Emergency," he was a brash Texan who taught his colleagues "that there is no reason to accept cowardice, unresponsiveness, and incompetence" in the world's governments and IGOs charged in assisting with tragedies (Weiss 2005: xxiii). His work in Sarajevo with infrastructural rehabilitation during the Bosnian civil war was particularly renown, as noted in chapter 4. He was murdered by unknown parties while on a humanitarian mission to Chechnya in 1995.
- John Prendergast is one of the most out-spoken advocates of what herein is termed pragmatic humanitarianism. His work in Africa with the International Crisis Group has taken him to a number of conflictive areas, including Darfur in 2004. His efforts are noted in chapter 6. To paraphrase his comments to me, he unequivocally believes that shorter-term aid and longer-term redevelopment processes should not be supplies-driven but justice-driven. "The tool" (as exemplified by a palate loaded with clothing bound for refugees) should never take precedence over "the mission" (as exemplified by an agency's long-term strategy for cohesive action). His prescriptions for how NGOs can best work together during complex humanitarian emergencies have been adopted widely.
- Renowned trumpeter Hugh Masekela has played his unusual renditions of South African music at concerts benefiting oppressed people in a number of countries. Considered the father of African jazz, one of his most well-known albums is *Grazing in the Grass*. He has touched so many lives that he was invited to serve as keynote speaker at the annual Comparative Human Rights Conference at the University of Connecticut in 2003.
- Helen Mack did what few thought was possible. Spurred to action following her sister Myrna's stabbing death by a Guatemalan army sergeant in 1990, during the fractious civil war, she finally succeeded in holding high-ranking army officials accountable for this act, and for their roles in directing that country's death squads. Aided by Human Rights First, her case finally reached the Inter-American Court for Human Rights. The conviction of Col. Juan Valencia Osorio in 2002 was followed by a $600,000 monetary award in 2003.

- A different tactic has been used by Otoniel de la Roca Mendoza. He is a Guatemalan citizen who was tortured during the protracted civil war in that country. Now living in Colorado, he speaks out about the abuses he and his family endured. He recently was featured as a guest lecturer at the University of Denver where he riveted an audience of faculty, students, and community members with stories of abuse and bravery. As he told me, he sees lecturing of this sort as a privilege and an obligation.
- Dr. Svetlana Broz is the granddaughter of former Yugoslav president Josip Broz Tito. A cardiologist, Broz went to Bosnia in 1992 when the war began to offer her medical services. As she began to hear remarkable testimonies of survival, she came to serve more as an ethnographer and less as a doctor. She is author of the book *Good People in an Evil Time* and founder of Sarajevo's Garden of the Righteous. It is modeled on Jerusalem's Yad Vashem Memorial. A likely candidate for the garden's symbolism in trees, planted one per person, is Asija, the "Queen of Sarajevo," whose story of quiet heroism was presented at the beginning of chapter 1. She survived and has gone on to help others, especially students visiting from the United States.

Some of the heroes live on, some have died. Some are adults, some are children. A poem authored by University of Denver student Leslie Olson, while on assignment in Bosnia in 2003, captures this best.

The Tragedy of a Hero's Burial

The living inflict so much
upon the easy lives of the dead:
order
segregation
permanence

1986–1992 says one stone
in a line of thousands
fenced in a cemetery

in '91 his mother had felt compelled
to hold his hand
lest he wander as he was prone

such injustice: he is buried in file
the style of a soldier
the boy whose laces drug through
mud, who ignored the lessons of his teachers,
who fidgeted in mass
preferring the brief lives clouds lived in wind

his sixth year began
obeying no order, ended
mistaken as a soldier.

REFERENCES

Aral, Berdal. "The Idea of Human Rights as Perceived in the Ottoman Empire." *Human Rights Quarterly* 26, no. 2 (May 2004): 454–82.

Blau, Judith, and Alberto Moncada. *Human Rights: Beyond the Liberal Vision.* Lanham, Md.: Rowman & Littlefield, 2005.

Coll, Steve. *Ghost Wars: The Secret History of the CIA, Afghanistan, and bin Laden, from the Soviet Invasion to September 10, 2001.* New York: Penguin, 2004.

Cutts, Mark, ed. *The State of the World's Refugees: Fifty Years of Humanitarian Action.* Oxford: United Nations High Commissioner for Refugees/Oxford University Press, 2000.

Dickson-Gómez, Julia. "'One Who Doesn't Know War, Doesn't Know Anything': The Problem of Comprehending Suffering in Postwar El Salvador." *Anthropology and Humanism* 29, no. 2 (December 2004): 145–58.

Donnelly, Jack. *Universal Human Rights in Theory and Practice.* 2d ed. Ithaca, N.Y.: Cornell University Press, 2003.

Dyson, Freeman. "The Bitter End." *New York Review of Books* 52, no. 7 (April 28, 2005): 4–6.

Farer, Tom. *Shaping Agendas in Civil Wars: Can International Criminal Law Help?* ISF Info/Bulletin 3, Institutt for Forsvarsstudier, Oslo, Norway, 1999.

——. "The Rise of the Inter-American Human Rights Regime: No Longer a Unicorn, Not Yet an Ox." *Human Rights Quarterly* 19, no. 3 (August 1997): 510–46.

Forsythe, David. "U.S. Foreign Policy and Human Rights." Keynote lecture presented at the annual spring symposium of the Center On Rights Development, Graduate School of International Studies, University of Denver, Colorado, April 2002.

Gorman, Robert F. *Coping with Africa's Refugee Burden: A Time for Solutions.* New York: Martinus Nijhoff, 1987.

Harrell-Bond, Barbara. "Can Humanitarian Work with Refugees be Humane?" *Human Rights Quarterly* 24, no. 1 (February 2002): 51–85.

——. *Imposing Aid: Emergency Assistance to Refugees.* Oxford: Oxford University Press, 1986.

Horne, Alistair. *The Price of Glory: Verdun 1916.* London: Penguin, 1993.

Ishay, Micheline R. *The History of Human Rights: From Ancient Times to the Globalization Era.* Berkeley: University of California Press, 2004.

Judt, Tony. "The New World Order." *New York Review of Books* 52, no. 12 (July 14, 2005): 14–18.

Kellberg, Love. "Torture: International Rules and Procedures." In *An End to Torture: Strategies for Its Eradication,* edited by Bertil Dunér. London: Zed, 1998.

Kelso, Nathaniel Vaughn, and Nancie Majkowski, researchers. "A Nation Trans-formed by Civil War." *National Geographic* [map supplement], April 2005.

Loescher, Gil. "UNHCR at Fifty: Refugee Protection and World Politics." In *Problems of Protection: The UNHCR, Refugees, and Human Rights*, edited by Niklaus Steiner, Mark Gibney, and Gil Loescher. New York: Routledge, 2003.

Lyttelton, Adrian. "What Was Fascism?" *New York Review of Books* 51, no. 16 (October 21, 2004): 33–36.

Mertus, Julie A. *Bait and Switch: Human Rights and U.S. Foreign Policy*. New York: Routledge, 2004.

Muggeridge, Malcolm. "The Great Liberal Death Wish." *Imprimis* 31, no. 12 (December 2002): 3.

Nanda, Ved P. "From Nuremberg to Baghdad: Nazi Trials Set Stage for Global Law." *Denver Post*, December 4, 2005, pp. 1E, 4E.

Nockerts, Regina. "A Theory of Obligation." Unpublished manuscript, Graduate School of International Studies, University of Denver, Colorado, 2005.

Prendergast, John. *Frontline Diplomacy: Humanitarian Aid and Conflict in Africa*. Boulder, Colo.: Lynne Rienner, 1996.

Rodley, Nigel S. Interview with former UN Special Rapporteur for Torture. Denver, Colo. November 20, 2004.

———. Foreword to *An End to Torture: Strategies for Its Eradication*, edited by Bertil Dunér. London: Zed, 1998.

Seifert, Ruth. "The Second Front: The Logic of Sexual Violence in Wars." In *Violence and Its Alternatives: An Interdisciplinary Reader*, edited by Nancy S. Lind and Manfred B. Steger. New York: St. Martin's Press, 1999.

Sen, Amartya. "Foreword insert in *Pathologies of Power: Health, Human Rights, and the New War on the Poor*, by Paul Farmer. Berkeley: University of California Press, 2003.

Shepherd, George W., Jr. *They Are Us: Fifty Years of Human Rights Advocacy*. Philadelphia: Xlibris, 2002.

Tomaševski, Katarina. "Foreign Policy and Torture." In *An End to Torture: Strategies for Its Eradication*, edited by Bertil Dunér. London: Zed, 1998.

Van Arsdale, Peter W. "The Deconstruction of Refugees and the Reconstruction of History: A Review of *States and Strangers*, by Nevzat Soguk." *Human Rights & Human Welfare* 1, no. 1 (January 2001): 17–21. accessible online at www.du.edu/gsis/hrhw

———. "Reconstructing Bosnia." *Anthropology News* 40, no. 6 (September, 1999): 80.

———. *Refugee Empowerment and Organizational Change: A Systems Perspective*. Arlington, Va.: American Anthropological Association, 1993.

Van Voorhis, Bruce. "Food as a Weapon for Peace: Operation Lifeline Sudan." *Africa Today* 36, no. 3/4 (Fall/Winter 1989): 29–42.

Weiss, Thomas G. *Military-Civilian Interactions: Humanitarian Crises and the Responsibility to Protect*. 2nd ed. Lanham, Md.: Rowman & Littlefield, 2005.

Bibliography

ABC News. "While America Watched: The Bosnia Tragedy." Peter Jennings Reporting. March 30, 1994 at www.markdanner.com/interviews (accessed February 10, 2005).

Agha, Hussein, and Robert Malley. "The Lost Palestinians." *New York Review of Books* 52, no. 10 (June 9, 2005): 20–24.

Ahmed, Abdel Ghaffar M. "The Question of Pastoral Nomadism in the Sudan." In *Some Aspects of Pastoral Nomadism in the Sudan,* edited by Abdel Ghaffar M. Ahmed. Khartoum: Khartoum University Press, 1976.

Alzaroo, Salah. "Palestinian Refugee Children and Caregivers in the West Bank." In *Children of Palestine: Experiencing Forced Migration in the Middle East,* edited by Dawn Chatty and Gillian Lewando Hundt. New York: Berghahn, 2005.

American Psychiatric Association. *DSM-IV: Diagnostic and Statistical Manual of Mental Disorders.* 4th ed. Washington, D.C.: American Psychiatric Association, 1994.

Andrić, Ivo. *The Bridge on the Drina.* Chicago: University of Chicago Press, 1977 (orig. 1945).

Anonymous. "A Reasonably Good Year in a Troublesome World." *Refugees* 4, no. 137 (2004): 6–15, 18–21.

Anonymous. "Palestinian Archaeologists Uncover Canaanite Dwellings." *Biblical Archaeology Review* 24, no. 6 (November/December 1998): 25.

Applebaum, Anne. *Gulag: A History.* New York: Doubleday, 2003.

Applied Social Science and Health Consultants. *Evaluación del Proyecto No. 519–0184, USAID/El Salvador, Oficina de Pequeñas Obras de Riego.* San Salvador/Denver, Colo.: ASSHC, 1984.

Aral, Berdal. "The Idea of Human Rights as Perceived in the Ottoman Empire." *Human Rights Quarterly* 26, no. 2 (May 2004): 454–82.

Arkun, Perin H. *Bosnia: Civil Society, Sovereignty and Peace.* Unpublished Ph.D. dissertation, Graduate School of International Studies, University of Denver, Colorado, 2004.

Armstrong, Karen. "Compassion's Fruit." *AARP Magazine* (February 2005): 62–64.

Arrighi, Giovanni. "Labor Supplies in Historical Perspective: A Study of the Proletarianization of the African Peasantry in Rhodesia." In *Essays on the Political Economy of Africa*, by Giovanni Arrighi and John S. Saul. New York: Monthly Review Press, 1973.

Bari Ts., Abdul. "Potensi Hutan Irian Jaya dan Prospeknya." *Irian: Bulletin of Irian Jaya Development* 3, no. 3 (October 1974): 1–50.

Bascom, Johnathan B. *Losing Place: Refugee Populations and Rural Transformations in East Africa*. New York: Berghahn, 1998.

Bell, Martin. *In Harm's Way*. London: Penguin, 1996.

Bennett, John W. *The Ecological Transition: Cultural Anthropology and Human Adaptation*. New York: Pergamon, 1976.

Ben-Yehuda, Nachman. "Where Masada's Defenders Fell." *Biblical Archaeology Review* 24, no. 6 (November/December 1998): 32–39.

———. *The Masada Myth: Collective Memory and Mythmaking in Israel*. Madison: University of Wisconsin Press, 1996.

Bernal, Victoria. "Eritrea Goes Global: Reflections on Nationalism in a Transnational Era." *Cultural Anthropology* 19, no. 1 (February 2004): 3–25.

Blau, Judith, and Alberto Moncada. *Human Rights: Beyond the Liberal Vision*. Lanham, Md.: Rowman & Littlefield, 2005.

Borg, Marcus J. "The Heart of Christianity." Lecture series presented at St. Andrew United Methodist Church, Highlands Ranch, Colo., March 2005.

———. *The Heart of Christianity: Rediscovering a Life of Faith*. San Francisco: Harper Collins, 2003.

Browman, David L. Review of *The Archaeology of Drylands: Living at the Margin*, edited by Graeme Barker and David Gilbertson. *American Anthropologist* 105, no. 1 (March 2003): 179–80.

Bulcha, Mekuria. *Flight and Integration: Causes of Mass Exodus from Ethiopia and Problems of Integration in the Sudan*. Uppsala, Sweden: Scandinavian Institute of African Studies, 1988.

Butt, Leslie. "'Lipstick Girls' and 'Fallen Women': AIDS and Conspiratorial Thinking in Papua, Indonesia." *Cultural Anthropology* 20, no. 3 (August 2005): 412–42.

Buur, Lars. "Truth and Reconciliation: A Briefing." *Aid Policy & Practice Series*. Copenhagen: Centre for Development Research, 2001.

Chatty, Dawn, and Gillian Lewando Hundt, eds. *Children of Palestine: Experiencing Forced Migration in the Middle East*. New York: Berghahn, 2005.

Chehade, Carol. "Darfur: The Color of Genocide." *Sudan Tribune*, March 31, 2005 at www.sudantribune.com/article.php3?id_article=8786 (accessed June 30, 2005).

Chowning, Ann. *An Introduction to the Peoples and Cultures of Melanesia*. 2nd ed. Menlo Park, Calif.: Cummings, 1977.

Clay, Jason W., and Bonnie K. Holcomb. *Politics and the Ethiopian Famine, 1984–85*. Cambridge, Mass.: Cultural Survival, 1986.

Cohen, Roger. *Hearts Grown Brutal: Sagas of Sarajevo*. New York: Random House, 1998.

Cole, B. Keith. *The Myth of Successful Humanitarian Intervention? Development, International NGO Management, Intercultural Communication, Continuous Quality Improvement and Post-Communist Legacies in the Former Yugoslavia: An Attempt at a Synthesis.* Unpublished master of arts thesis, Graduate School of International Studies, University of Denver, Colorado, 1999.

Coll, Steve. *Ghost Wars: The Secret History of the CIA, Afghanistan, and bin Laden, from the Soviet Invasion to September 10, 2001.* New York: Penguin, 2004.

Cuny, Frederick C. (with Richard B. Hill). *Famine, Conflict and Response: A Basic Guide.* West Hartford, Conn.: Kumarian, 1999.

Cutts, Mark, ed. *The State of the World's Refugees 2000: Fifty Years of Humanitarian Action.* Geneva: UNHCR/Oxford University Press, 2000.

Danner, Mark. "America and the Bosnia Genocide." *New York Review of Books* 44, no. 19 (December 4, 1997): 55–65.

———. *The Massacre at El Mozote: A Parable of the Cold War.* New York: Vintage/Random House, 1993.

de Waal, Alex. *Famine That Kills: Darfur, Sudan.* rev ed. Oxford: Oxford University Press, 2005.

Dejene, Alemneh. *Environment, Famine, and Politics in Ethiopia: A View from the Village.* Boulder, Colo.: Lynne Rienner, 1990.

Dickson-Gómez, Julia. "'One Who Doesn't Know War, Doesn't Know Anything': The Problem of Comprehending Suffering in Postwar El Salvador." *Anthropology and Humanism* 29, no. 2 (December 2004): 145–58.

———. "The Sound of Barking Dogs: Violence and Terror among Salvadoran Families in the Postwar." *Medical Anthropology Quarterly* 16, no. 4 (December, 2002): 415–38.

Dillinger, Johannes. "Terrorists and Witches: Popular Ideas of Evil in the Early Modern Period." *History of European Ideas* 30, no. 2 (June 2004): 167–82.

Donaldson, Jennifer. "The Power of Coalitions." *The Advocacy Institute Newsletter*, April 2005 at www.advocacy.org (accessed May 14, 2005).

Donnelly, Jack. *Universal Human Rights in Theory and Practice.* 2d ed. Ithaca, N.Y.: Cornell University Press, 2003.

Dubinsky, Zach. "The Lessons of Genocide." *Essex Human Rights Review* 2, no. 1 (Spring 2005): 112–17.

Dyson, Freeman. "The Bitter End." *New York Review of Books* 52, no. 7 (April 28, 2005): 4–6.

Farer, Tom. *Shaping Agendas in Civil Wars: Can International Criminal Law Help?* ISF Info/Bulletin 3, Institutt for Forsvarsstudier, Oslo, Norway, 1999.

———. "The Rise of the Inter-American Human Rights Regime: No Longer a Unicorn, Not Yet an Ox." *Human Rights Quarterly* 19, no. 3 (August 1997): 510–46.

Farmer, Paul. *Pathologies of Power: Health, Human Rights, and the New War on the Poor.* Berkeley: University of California Press, 2003.

Finley, Bruce. "Mission for God." *Denver Post*, October 27, 1996, pp. 1A, 10A–11A.

Fischman, Josh. "Family Ties." *National Geographic* 207, no. 4 (April 2005): 16–27.

Fleischhacker, Marcus. "Reflections and Dreams Inspire." *Crosier Drums* 3, no. 4 (November 1988): 5.

Forsythe, David. "U.S. Foreign Policy and Human Rights." Keynote lecture presented at the annual spring symposium of the Center On Rights Development, Graduate School of International Studies, University of Denver, Colorado, April 2002.

French, Kristine L. researcher. "Africa: A Storied Landscape." *National Geographic* 208, no. 3 (September 2005): map supplement.

Gebre, Yntiso. "Resettlement and the Unnoticed Losers: Impoverishment Disasters among the Gumz in Ethiopia." *Human Organization* 62, no. 1 (Spring 2003): 50–61.

Geertz, Clifford. "Very Bad News." *New York Review of Books* 52, no. 5 (March 24, 2005): 4–6.

——. Review of *Violence and Vengeance: Discontent and Conflict in New Order Indonesia*, edited by Frans Hüsken and Huub de Jonge. *American Anthropologist* 106, no. 3 (September 2004): 622–23.

Genocide Intervention Fund. "Creating a Genocide Intervention Fund to Support African Troops in Darfur." *Media Release*, February 5, 2005 at www.genocideinterventionfund.org/about/proposal (accessed July 6, 2005).

Gill, Lesley. "Book Review of *The El Mozote Massacre: Anthropology and Human Rights*, by Leigh Binford and *We Wish to Inform You that Tomorrow We Will Be Killed with Our Families: Stories from Rwanda*, by Philip Gourevitch. *American Anthropologist* 101, no. 4 (December 1999): 874–76.

Giraudoux, Jean. "Notes on 'The Madwoman of Chaillot.'" *Inside Out*, Denver Center Theatre Company, Colorado, March 2005.

Gitin, Seymour. "Excavating Ekron." *Biblical Archaeology Review* 31, no. 6 (November/December 2005): 40–56.

Glazebrook, Diana. "Dwelling in Exile, Perceiving Return: West Papuan Refugees from Irian Jaya Living at East Awin in Western Province, Papua New Guinea." Unpublished Ph.D. dissertation abstract, Department of Anthropology, Australian National University, Canberra at www.papuaweb.org (accessed June 6, 2005).

Glenny, Misha. *The Balkans: Nationalism, War, and the Great Powers, 1804–1999.* New York: Penguin Books, 1999.

Global Witness. *Paying for Protection: The Freeport Mine and the Indonesian Security Forces.* Washington, D.C.: Global Witness Publishing, 2005.

Gonen, Rivka. Review of *Across the Sabbath River: In Search of a Lost Tribe of Israel*, by Hillel Halkin. *Biblical Archaeology Review* 29, no. 5 (September/October 2003): 78–80.

Gorman, Robert F. *Coping with Africa's Refugee Burden: A Time for Solutions.* New York: Martinus Nijhoff, 1987.

Gorski, Eric. "Proselytizing During Relief Efforts Divides Christian Groups." *Denver Post*, January 17, 2005, pp. 1A, 12A.

Greenpeace. "East Awin Decision Could Spark a Humanitarian Crisis." *Greenpeace/Australia Pacific: Media Release*, November 17, 2003 at www.greenpeace.org.au/media/press (accessed June28, 2005).

Griffin, Greg. "Indonesia Charges Newmont, Mine Boss." *Denver Post*, July 12, 2005, pp. 1C, 8C.

Gutman, Roy. "A Daily Ritual of Sex Abuse." *Newsday*, April 19, 1993 at www .haverford.edu/relg/sells/rape (accessed May 15, 2005).

———. "Mass Rape: Muslims Recall Serb Attacks." *Newsday*, August 23, 1992 at www.haverford.edu/relg/sells/rape (accessed May 15, 2005).

Gutmann, Amy, ed. *Michael Ignatieff: Human Rights as Politics and Idolatry*. Princeton, N.J.: Princeton University Press, 2001.

Hagmann, Tobias. "Beyond Clannishness and Colonialism: Understanding Political Disorder in Ethiopia's Somali Region, 1991–2004." *Journal of Modern African Studies* 43, no. 4 (December 2005): 509–36.

Hailu, Tsegaye, Tsegay Wolde-Georgis, and Peter W. Van Arsdale. "Resource Depletion, Famine and Refugees in Tigray." In *African Refugees: Development Aid and Repatriation*, edited by Howard Adelman and John Sorenson. Boulder, Colo.: Westview, 1994.

Hammond, Laura C. *This Place Will Become Home: Refugee Repatriation to Ethiopia*. Ithaca, N.Y.: Cornell University Press, 2004.

Hamzeh, Muna. *Refugees in Our Own Land: Chronicles from a Palestinian Refugee Camp in Bethlehem*. London: Pluto, 2001.

Harrell-Bond, Barbara. "Can Humanitarian Work with Refugees be Humane?" *Human Rights Quarterly* 24, no. 1 (February 2002): 51–85.

———. *Imposing Aid: Emergency Assistance to Refugees*. Oxford: Oxford University Press, 1986.

Harris, Marvin. *Cannibals and Kings: The Origins of Cultures*. New York: Random House, 1977.

Hassan, Bassem. *The Palestinian Refugees Problem: The Past, the Present and the Future*. Unpublished master of arts thesis, Graduate School of International Studies, University of Denver, Colorado, 1998.

Hayner, Priscilla B. "The Contribution of Truth Commissions." In *An End to Torture: Strategies for Its Eradication*, edited by Bertil Dunér. London: Zed, 1998.

Henkin, Louis. "The Human Rights Idea." In *Human Rights*, by Louis Henkin, Gerald L. Neuman, Diane F. Orentlicher, and David W. Leebron. New York: Foundation Press, 1999.

Higgins, Annie C. "Clamoring with Portraits: Memorial Posters in Palestinian Refugee Camps." Paper presented at the annual meeting of the American Anthropological Association, Washington, D.C., December 2005.

Holbrooke, Richard. *To End a War*. Rev. ed. New York: Modern Library, 1998.

Horne, Alistair. *The Price of Glory: Verdun 1916*. London: Penguin, 1993.

Howard, Bradley Reed. "Mind-Forged Manacles: Resistance, Rebellion, and the Twilight of the Idols (or How to Anthropologize with a Hammer)." *PoLAR: Political and Legal Anthropology Review* 18, no. 2 (November 1995): 35–44.

Howells, W. W. "The Sources of Human Variation in Melanesia and Australia." In *Sunda and Sahul: Prehistoric Studies in Southeast Asia, Melanesia and Australia*, edited by Jim Allen, Jack Golson, and Rhys Jones. London: Academic Press, 1977.

Hukanović, Rezak. *The Tenth Circle of Hell: A Memoir of Life in the Death Camps of Bosnia*. New York: Basic Books, 1996 (orig. 1993).

Human Rights Watch. "Targeting the Anuak: Human Rights Violations and Crimes Against Humanity in Ethiopia's Gambella Region." *HRW On-Line Report* 17, no. 3A (March 2005): 1–67 at www.hrw.org/reports/2005/ethiopia0305 (accessed September 22, 2005).

Hutchinson, Charles F. "Will Climate Change Complicate African Famine?" *Resources* (Resources for the Future) 95 (Spring 1989): 5–7.

ICVA. *The ICVA Directory of Humanitarian and Development Agencies Operating in Bosnia and Herzegovina.* International Council of Voluntary Agencies, Sarajevo, 1998.

Ignatieff, Michael. "Human Rights as Idolatry." In *Michael Ignatieff: Human Rights as Politics and Idolatry*, edited by Amy Gutmann. Princeton, N.J.: Princeton University Press, 2001.

Igrić, Gordana. "Kosovo Rape Victims Suffer Twice." *Mother Jones, On-Line* (June 18, 1999) at www.motherjones.com/news/special_reports/total_coverage/kosovo/victims .html (accessed December 5, 2005).

International Crisis Group. "The Khartoum-SPLM Agreement: Sudan's Uncertain Peace." *ICG Africa Report*, No. 96, July 25, 2005a.

———. "Darfur Needs Bolder International Intervention." *ICG Media Release*, May 25, 2005b at notification@crisisgroup (accessed July 21, 2005).

———. "Sudan (monthly update)." *ICG Crisis Watch*, May 2, 2005c at www.crisis group.org/home/index.cfm (accessed July 21, 2005).

Ishay, Micheline R. *The History of Human Rights: From Ancient Times to the Globalization Era.* Berkeley: University of California Press, 2004.

Jacobson, David. "When Palestine Meant Israel." *Biblical Archaeology Review* 27, no. 3 (May/June 2001): 42–47.

Jaffe, Carolyn, and Carol H. Ehrlich. *All Kinds of Love: Experiencing Hospice.* Amityville, N.Y.: Baywood, 1997.

Jaleta, Assefa. "Oromo Nationalism and Ethiopian Ethnocratic Politics." *Horn of Africa* 20 (2002): 11–58.

Judt, Tony. "The New World Order." *New York Review of Books* 52, no. 12 (July 14, 2005): 14–18.

Kaplan, Martha. Review of *The Ambiguity of Rapproachement: Reflections of Anthropologists on Their Controversial Relationship with Missionaries*, edited by Roland Bonsen, Hans Marks, and Jelle Miedema. *American Anthropologist* 93, no. 3 (September 1991): 716–17.

Kellberg, Love. "Torture: International Rules and Procedures." In *An End to Torture: Strategies for Its Eradication*, edited by Bertil Dunér. London: Zed, 1998.

Kelly, Tobias. "Returning Home? Law, Violence, and Displacement among West Bank Palestinians." *PoLAR: Political and Legal Anthropology Review* 27, no. 2 (November 2004): 95–112.

Kelso, Nathaniel Vaughn, and Nancie Majkowski, researchers. "A Nation Transformed by Civil War." *National Geographic* 207, no. 4 (April 2005): map supplement.

Kennedy, Kerry, and Eddie Adams (photographs). *Speak Truth to Power: Human Rights Defenders Who Are Changing Our World.* New York: Crown, 2004.

King, Laura. "Israeli Missiles Kill 2 Top Militants." *Denver Post*, November 2, 2005, p. 2A.

Knauft, Bruce M. "Foucault Meets South New Guinea: Knowledge, Power, Sexuality. *Ethos* 22, no. 4 (December 1994): 391–438.

———. "Reconsidering Violence in Simple Human Societies" (with commentaries and rebuttal). *Current Anthropology* 28, no. 4 (August–October 1987): 457–500.

Koerner, Brendan I. "Who are the Janjaweed?" *Slate Explainer*, July 19, 2005 at www.slate.com/id/2104210 (accessed July 21, 2005).

Koff, Clea. *The Bone Woman*. New York: Random House, 2004.

Kotch, Nick. "African Oil: Whose Bonanza?" *National Geographic* 208, no. 3 (September 2005): 50–65.

Kreisberg-Voss, Debra, Dennis Kennedy, Peter Van Arsdale, and Karl Ferguson. "Clinical Considerations Concerning Refugees in the Denver Region." *Torture* 8, no. 3 (Fall 1998): 90–97.

Lang, Gottfried O. "Conditions for Development in Asmat." *Irian: Bulletin of Irian Jaya Development* 2, no. 1 (February 1973): 38–61.

Langewiesche, William. "The Accuser." *Atlantic Monthly* 295, no. 2 (March 2005): 54–81.

Laqueur, Thomas W. "The Moral Imagination and Human Rights." In *Michael Ignatieff: Human Rights as Politics and Idolatry*, edited by Amy Gutmann. Princeton, N.J.: Princeton University Press, 2001.

Lewis, Herbert J. Review of *Ghosts and Shadows: Construction of Identity and Community in an African Diaspora*, by Atsuko Matsuoka and John Sorenson. *American Anthropologist* 105, no 2 (June 2003): 443–44.

Li, Tania Murray. "Beyond 'the State' and Failed Schemes." *American Anthropologist* 107, no. 3 (September 2005): 383–94.

Limbach, Ian. "Special Report: The Axum Obelisk Returns, but Some Still Grumble." *Archaeology* 58, no. 4 (July/August 2005) at www.archaeology.org/0507/etc/specialreport.html (accessed August 30, 2005).

Loescher, Gil. "UNHCR at Fifty: Refugee Protection and World Politics." In *Problems of Protection: The UNHCR, Refugees, and Human Rights*, edited by Niklaus Steiner, Mark Gibney, and Gil Loescher. New York: Routledge, 2003.

Lyttelton, Adrian. "What Was Fascism?" *New York Review of Books* 51, no. 16 (October 21, 2004): 33–36.

Malcolm, Noel. *Bosnia: A Short History*. Rev. ed. New York: New York University Press, 1996.

Malley, Robert. "Israel and the Arafat Question." *New York Review of Books* 51, no. 15 (October 7, 2004): 19–23.

Margalit, Avishai. "The Suicide Bombers." *New York Review of Books* 50, no. 1 (January 16, 2003): 36–39.

Markowitz, Fran, and Natan Uriely. "Shopping in the Negev: Global Flows and Local Contingencies." *City & Society* 14, no. 2 (Fall 2002): 211–36.

Martin, Claire. "Bosnian Horror is Hard to Comprehend." *Denver Post*, January 28, 1996, pp. E8–E9.

Martín-Baró, Ignacio, and Rodolfo Cardenal. "Fifteen Years Later: Peace at Last." Introduction to the *Revolution in El Salvador: From Civil Strife to Civil Peace*, by Tommie Sue Montgomery. 2nd ed. Boulder, Colo.: Westview, 1995.

Maskovsky, Jeff. Review of *Pathologies of Power: Health, Human Rights, and the New War on the Poor*, by Paul Farmer. *American Anthropologist* 107, no. 2 (June 2005): 283–84.

McCann, James C. *People of the Plow: An Agricultural History of Ethiopia, 1800–1990*. Madison: University of Wisconsin Press, 1995.

———. "A Great Agrarian Cycle? Productivity in Highland Ethiopia 1900–1987." *Journal of Interdisciplinary History* 20, no. 3 (Winter 1990): 389–416.

McReynolds, Samuel A., Thomas Johnston, and Charles Geisler. "The Relationship of Land Tenure to Agricultural Practices and the Environment in El Salvador." *Culture & Agriculture* 22, no. 1 (new series, Spring 2000): 9–28.

McSpadden, Lucia Ann. "Resettlement for Status Quo or Status Mobility: Ethiopian and Eritrean Refugees in the Western United States." In *Refugee Empowerment and Organizational Change: A Systems Perspective*, edited by Peter W. Van Arsdale. Arlington, Va.: American Anthropological Association, 1993.

Mertus, Julie A. *Bait and Switch: Human Rights and U.S. Foreign Policy*. New York: Routledge, 2004.

Mitchell, William E. "The Ethnography of Change in New Guinea." *American Anthropologist* 98, no. 3 (September 1996): 641–44.

Mitton, Robert. *The Lost World of Irian Jaya*. Melbourne: Oxford University Press, 1983.

Montgomery, Tommie Sue. "Democracy in El Salvador." Unpublished circular, American Anthropological Association, Arlington, Va., 1997.

———. *Revolution in El Salvador: From Civil Strife to Civil Peace*. 2nd ed. Boulder, Colo.: Westview, 1995.

Moore, Lorna G., Peter W. Van Arsdale, JoAnn E. Glittenberg, and Robert A. Aldrich. *The Biocultural Basis of Health: Expanding Views of Medical Anthropology*. Prospect Heights, Ill.: Waveland, 1987 (orig. 1980).

Moorehead, Caroline. "Letter from Darfur." *New York Review of Books* 52, no. 13 (August 11, 2005): 55–57.

Moyers, Bill. "Welcome to Doomsday." *New York Review of Books* 52, no. 5 (March 24, 2005): 8–10.

Muggeridge, Malcolm. "The Great Liberal Death Wish." *Imprimis* 31, no. 12 (December 2002): 3.

Munro-Hay, Stuart. *Ethiopia, the Unknown Land: A Cultural and Historical Guide*. London: I.B. Tauris, 2002.

Murphy, T. Craig. "Cyclical Linkages between War and Hunger in Africa." Unpublished manuscript, Graduate School of International Studies, University of Denver, Colorado, 2003.

Nagengast, Carole, and Carlos G. Vélez-Ibáñez. Introduction: The Scholar as Activist." In *Human Rights: The Scholar as Activist*, edited by Carole Nagengast and Carlos G. Vélez-Ibáñez. Oklahoma City: Society for Applied Anthropology, 2004.

Nakashima, Ellen, and Alan Sipress. "Indonesian Police Chief Visits Site of Ambush." *Washington Post*, September 5, 2005, p. A22 at www.washingtonpost.com/ac2/wp-dyn?pagename=article&contentId=A38032-2002Sept4 (accessed October 4, 2002).

Namaliu, Amanda. "Refugees and PNG's Timber Industry." *PLN [Pacific Legal Network] News*, Summer 2005, p. 2 at www.pln.com.au (accessed July 5, 2005).

Nanda, Ved P. "From Nuremberg to Baghdad: Nazi Trials Set Stage for Global Law." *Denver Post*, December 4. 2005, pp. 1E, 4E.

Navarrete, Marco Pérez. "Un Reencuentro: Es Volver a Nacer y a Vivir." Asociación Pro-Búsqueda de Niñas y Niños Desaparecidos at www.probusqueda.org.sv/modules (accessed December 8, 2005).

Needles, Colleen. producer. "A World Away: Crosier Fathers and Brothers." Twenty-five minute video, WCCO-Television, Minneapolis, Minn., 1993.

Nockerts, Regina. "A Theory of Obligation." Unpublished manuscript, Graduate School of International Studies, University of Denver, Colorado, 2005.

Nordstrom, Carolyn. *Shadows of War: Violence, Power, and International Profiteering in the Twenty-First Century*. Berkeley: University of California Press, 2004.

Nussbaum, Debra. "Israel Ethiopia-Policy Debate: Hardship Cases? 40 Million More?" *Intermountain Jewish News,* July 3, 1998, p. 5.

Nuti, Paul. "Perspectives on the Crisis in Darfur." *Anthropology News* 45, no. 9 (December 2004): 12–13.

O'Neill, Thomas. "Irian Jaya: Indonesia's Wild Side." *National Geographic* 189, no. 2 (February 1996): 2–33.

Omberep, Joseph B. "Penindjavan Asmat Tahun 1963 dan Keadaan Sekarang Tahun 1972." *Irian: Bulletin of Irian Jaya Development* 2, no. 1 (February 1973): 19–23.

Orizio, Riccardo. *Talk of the Devil: Encounters with Seven Dictators*. Translated by Avril Bardoni. New York: Walker, 2003.

Pankhurst, Richard. "Ethiopia as Depicted in Foreign Creative Literature: An Historical Analysis." *Africa Quarterly* 44, no. 3 (November 2004): 57–78.

Pelton, Robert Young. "Into the Land of Bin Laden." *National Geographic Adventure* 6, no. 3 (April 2004): 74–78, 82–88.

Petermeier, Virgil. "Crosiers Embrace a Pastoral Plan for the Papuans." *Crossview* 11, no. 2 (Summer 2000): 10.

———. "Peace Comes to Asmat." *Crosier Drums* 1, no. 4 (November 1986a): 3.

———. "Exchanging Children Brings Peace." *Crosier Drums* 1, no. 4 (November 1986b): 1–2.

Porath, Yosef. "Vegas on the Med." *Biblical Archaeology Review* 30, no. 5 (September/October 2004): 24–35.

Power, Samantha. "Dying in Darfur: Can the Ethnic Cleansing in Sudan be Stopped?" *New Yorker* (August 30, 2004): 56–73.

PRC Engineering Consultants. *Western Sudan Water Supply Project: Phase I Report*. Denver, Colo.: PRC Engineering Consultants Inc., 1979.

Prendergast, John. *Frontline Diplomacy: Humanitarian Aid and Conflict in Africa*. Boulder, Colo.: Lynne Rienner, 1996.

Prunier, Gérard. *Darfur: The Ambiguous Genocide*. Ithaca, N.Y.: Cornell University Press, 2005.

Raffaele, Paul. "The People that Time Forgot." *Reader's Digest* (August 1996), pp. 100–107.

Reeves, Edward B., and Timothy Frankenberger. *Socio-Economic Constraints to the Production, Distribution, and Consumption of Millet, Sorghum, and Cash Crops in North Kordofan, Sudan.* Report No. 1, Department of Sociology/College of Agriculture, University of Kentucky, Lexington, 1981.

Reuters News Service. "Ten Years after the War, 14,000 Bosnians Still Missing" at www.alertnet.org/thenews/newsdesk/index.htm? (accessed December 6, 2005).

Ricklefs, M. C. *A History of Modern Indonesia since c. 1200.* 3rd ed. Stanford, Calif.: Stanford University Press, 2001.

Rodley, Nigel S. Foreword. In *An End to Torture: Strategies for Its Eradication*, edited by Bertil Dunér. London: Zed, 1998.

Roy, Ananya, and Nezar Al Sayyad. "Medieval Modernity: Citizenship in Contemporary Urbanism." *Applied Anthropologist* 25, no. 2 (Fall 2005): 147–65.

Sa'oudi, Mohammed Abdel-Ghani. "An Overview of the Egyptian–Sudanese Jonglei Canal Project." *The International Politics Journal: Al-Siyassa, Al-Dawliya.* January 2001 at www.siyassa.org.eg (accessed July 15, 2005).

Salisbury, Richard F. "Early Stages of Economic Development in New Guinea." In *Peoples and Cultures of the Pacific: An Anthropological Reader,* edited by Andrew P. Vayda. Garden City, N.Y.: Natural History Press, 1968.

Schirmer, Jennifer. Review of *The El Mozote Massacre: Anthropology and Human Rights*, by Leigh Binford, and *Power, Ethics and Human Rights: Anthropological Studies of Refugee Research and Action*, edited by Ruth M. Krulfeld and Jeffery L. MacDonald. *American Ethnologist* 20, no. 4 (November 2000): 980–82.

Schoorl, J. W. "Salvation Movements among the Muyu of Irian Jaya." *Irian: Bulletin of Irian Jaya Develoment* 7, no. 1 (February 1978): 3–35.

———. "Shell Capitalism among the Muyu People." *Irian: Bulletin of Irian Jaya Development* 5, no. 3 (October 1976): 4–78.

Schulz, William. *Tainted Legacy: 9/11 and the Ruin of Human Rights.* New York: Thunder's Mouth, 2003.

Schwarz, Benjamin. Review of *The Birth of the Palestinian Refugee Problem Revisited*, by Bennie Morris. *Atlantic Monthly* 293, no. 3 (April 2004): 109–11.

Seifert, Ruth. "The Second Front: The Logic of Sexual Violence in Wars." In *Violence and Its Alternatives: An Interdisciplinary Reader.* Manfred B. Steger and Nancy S. Lind, eds. New York: St. Martin's Press, 1999.

Sells, Michael A. *The Bridge Betrayed: Religion and Genocide in Bosnia.* Berkeley: University of California Press, 1996.

Sen, Amartya. Foreword. In *Pathologies of Power: Health, Human Rights, and the New War on the Poor*, by Paul Farmer. Berkeley: University of California Press, 2003.

Shabtay, Malka. Review of *The Hyena People: Ethiopian Jews in Christian Ethiopia*, by Hagar Salamon. *American Ethnologist* 27, no. 4 (November 2000): 982–84.

Shanks, Hershel. *Jerusalem: An Archaeological Biography.* New York: Random House, 1995.

Shepherd, George W., Jr. *They Are Us: Fifty Years of Human Rights Advocacy.* Philadelphia: Xlibris, 2002.

Smith, Keith. "Among the Peoples of the Agreste of Pernambuco: Thinking She was the Mother of the Murderer." *American Anthropologist* 99, no. 3 (September 1997): 513.

Sorenson, John. *Imagining Ethiopia: Struggles for History and Identity in the Horn of Africa.* New Brunswick, N.J.: Rutgers University Press, 1993.

Sottas, Eric. "Perpetrators of Torture." In *An End to Torture: Strategies for Its Eradication*, edited by Bertil Dunér. London: Zed, 1998.

Stephen, Lynn. "Women's Rights are Human Rights: The Merging of Feminine and Feminist Interests among El Salvador's Mothers of the Disappeared (Co-Madres)." *American Ethnologist* 22, no. 4 (Winter 1995): 807–27.

Stern, Ephraim. *Archaeology of the Land of the Bible, Volume II: The Assyrian, Babylonian, and Persian Periods 732–332 B.C.E.* New York: Doubleday, 2001.

Suarez-Orozco, Marcelo M. "Speaking of the Unspeakable: Toward a Psychosocial Understanding of Responses to Terror." *Ethos* 18, no. 3 (September 1990): 353–383.

Sudilovsky, Judith, and Miriam Feinberg Vamosh. "New Finds in Ein Gedi." *Biblical Archaeology Review* 29, no. 2 (March/April 2003): 18–20.

Teibel, Amy. "Palestinian Economy Growing." *Denver Post*, December 15, 2005, p. 16A.

Thomas-Slayter, Barbara P. *Southern Exposure: International Development and the Global South in the Twenty-First Century.* Bloomfield, Conn.: Kumarian, 2003.

Tiel, Jeffrey. "Rights Argument Invalid When It Comes to Matters of Evil Conduct." *Science & Theology News* 4, no. 11 (July/August 2004): 1–2.

Tomaševski, Katarina. "Foreign Policy and Torture." In *An End to Torture: Strategies for Its Eradication*, edited by Bertil Dunér. London: Zed, 1998.

Turnbull, Colin M. *The Mountain People.* New York: Simon and Schuster, 1972.

U.S. Committee for Refugees. "Country Reports: Africa." *World Refugee Survey: 1985 in Review.* New York: American Council for Nationalities Service, 1986.

UNHCR. "2004 Global Refugee Trends: Overview of Refugee Populations, New Arrivals, Durable Solutions, Asylum-Seekers, Stateless and Other Persons of Concern to UNHCR." *Population and Geographical Data Section Report*, Division of Operational Support, United Nations High Commissioner for Refugees, Geneva, June 17, 2005 at www.unhcr.ch/statistics (accessed July 30, 2005).

——. "Cartagena: 20 Years Later." *Refugees* 4, no. 137 (Fall 2004): 22–31.

——. "In PNG, Refugees from Indonesia's Papua Province Start Complex Journey to New Home." *UNHCR News*, October 1, 2004 at www.unhcr.ch/cgi-bin/texis/vtx/news (accessed July 30, 2005).

——. *The State of the World's Refugees 2000: Fifty Years of Humanitarian Action.* Oxford: Oxford University Press/United Nations High Commissioner for Refugees, 2000.

——. *The State of the World's Refugees: In Search of Solutions.* Oxford: Oxford University Press/United Nations High Commissioner for Refugees, 1995.

United States Holocaust Memorial Museum. "Extermination Camps." Unpublished manuscript, Wexner Learning Center, Washington, D.C., 2000.

Van Amelsvoort, V.F.P.M. *Early Introduction of Integrated Rural Health into a Primitive Society: A New Guinea Case Study in Medical Anthropology.* Assen, the Netherlands: Van Gorcum, 1964.

Van Arsdale, Peter W. Book Note on *This Place Will Become Home: Refugee Repatriation to Ethiopia*, by Laura C. Hammond. *Human Rights & Human Welfare* 5 (July 2005): 1–2. accessible online at www.du.edu/gsis/hrhw

———. "Rehabilitation, Resistance, and Return: Service Learning and the Quest for Civil Society in Bosnia." In *Passages: The Ethnographic Field School and First Fieldwork Experiences* edited by Madelyn Iris. NAPA Bulletin 22. Berkeley: American Anthropological Association/University of California Press, 2004.

———. "The Deconstruction of Refugees and the Reconstruction of History: A Review of *States and Strangers*, by Nevzat Soguk." *Human Rights & Human Welfare* 1, no. 1 (January 2001): 17–21. accessible online at www.du.edu/gsis/hrhw

———. "Reconstructing Bosnia." *Anthropology News* 40, no. 6 (September, 1999): 80.

———. *The Asmat: An Ethnography and Film Guide*. Denver, Colo.: Center for Cultural Dynamics, 1993.

———. "Cultural Persistence Despite Instability in El Salvador: An Anthropological Perspective." *High Plains Applied Anthropologist* 11/12 (1991/1992): 40–66.

———. "The Ecology of Survival in Sudan's Periphery: Short-Term Tactics and Long-Term Strategies." *Africa Today* 36, no. 3/4 (Fall/Winter 1989): 65–78.

———. "Resource Scarcity in Western Sudan: The Impacts of Nomads and Refugees." Paper presented at the conference *Ending Hunger in Africa*, University of Denver, Colorado, February 1988.

———. *Perspectives on Development in Asmat: An Asmat Sketch Book, No. 5*. Hastings, Neb.: Crosier Press, 1975.

Van Arsdale, Peter W., ed. *Refugee Empowerment and Organizational Change: A Systems Perspective*. Arlington, Va.: American Anthropological Association, 1993.

Van Arsdale, Peter W., and David E. Gallus. "The 'Lord of the Earth' Cult among the Asmat: Prestige, Power, and Politics in a Transitional Society." *Irian: Bulletin of Irian Jaya Development* 3, no. 2 (June 1974): 1–31.

Van Arsdale, Peter W., and Dennis F. Kennedy. "Treating Refugee Victims of Torture: Creation of the Rocky Mountain Survivors Center." *Journal of Immigrant Health* 1, no. 3 (Fall 1999): 155–64.

Van Arsdale, Peter W., and M. Wray Witten. "Effective Collective Action: A Consultative Approach to Enhancing Ecologically Responsible Development in Tigray, Ethiopia." *Applied Anthropologist* 26, no. 1 (Spring 2006): 65–80.

van der Veur, Paul. "West Irian's Refugees: What is 'Permissive Residence'?" *New Guinea and Australia, the Pacific and South-East Asia* 1, no. 4 (1966): 13–19.

van Enk, Gerrit J. and de Vries, Lourens. *The Korowai of Irian Jaya: Their Language in Its Cultural Context*. New York: Oxford University Press, 1997.

Van Voorhis, Bruce. "Food as a Weapon for Peace: Operation Lifeline Sudan." *Africa Today* 36, no. 3/4 (Fall/Winter 1989): 29–42.

Visser, Leontine E. "On the Meanings of Headhunting in Eastern Indonesia." *Anthropology and Humanism* 22, no. 2 (December 1997): 208–10.

Voutira, Eftihia, and Barbara Harrell-Bond. "'Successful' Refugee Settlement: Are Past Experiences Relevant?" In *Risks and Reconstruction: Experiences of Resettlers and Refugees*, edited by Michael M. Cernea and Christopher McDowell. Washington, D.C.: World Bank, 2000.

Weiss, Thomas G. *Military-Civilian Interactions: Humanitarian Crises and the Responsibility to Protect*. 2nd ed. Lanham, Md.: Rowman & Littlefield, 2005.

Weschler, Lawrence. "Life and Death of a Hero." *New York Review of Books* 46, no. 19 (December 2, 1999): 33–36.

Widzer, Martin. "Palestinian Political Fragmentation: Determining the Barriers to a Synthesized Government." Unpublished manuscript, Graduate School of International Studies, University of Denver, Colorado, 2005.

Wiesel, Elie. *And the Sea is Never Full: Memoirs, 1969–*. Translated by Marion Wiesel. New York: Schocken, 1999.

Williams, Robert L. *Savoring Life: Wisdom that Inspires, Challenges, Comforts and Provokes*. Golden, Colo.: Great Undertakings, 2004.

Yoman, Socratez Sofyan. "If you love our natural resources. . . ." [Letter to Lord Browne, Group Chief Executive, BP Indonesia.]" Copy received November 2, 2005.

Younger, K. Lawson, Jr. "Israelites in Exile." *Biblical Archaeology Review* 29, no. 6 (November/December, 2003): 36–45, 65–66.

Zegwaard, Gerard A. "Headhunting Practices of the Asmat of Netherlands New Guinea." *American Anthropologist* 61, no. 6 (December 1959): 1020–41.

Zimmerman, Bennett, and Yoram Ettinger. "Overestimating the Palestinians." *Atlantic Monthly* 295, no. 3 (April 2005): 44, 46.

Index

About the Author

Peter W. Van Arsdale, Ph.D., is an applied cultural and medical anthropologist. He serves as senior lecturer in the Graduate School of International Studies at the University of Denver, where he also serves as faculty advisor to the Center On Rights Development.

Photo of the author: Peter Van Arsdale stands on a hillside overlooking the town of Sarajevo. From this and other nearby locations, Serb forces bombarded the city during a siege lasting more than two years during the 1992–1995 civil war.